LOL ;-)

Living Out Loud

Through divorce, cyber-dating, blended families, and restraining orders, one woman's struggle to finally be true to herself.

Veronica Tanzen

AuthorHouse™
1663 Liberty Drive
Bloomington, IN 47403
www.authorhouse.com
Phone: 1-800-839-8640

Edited by Julia Fabian & Maja Petrovska
Cover design by Danny Carson

Published by AuthorHouse 04/21/2015

ISBN: 978-1-4969-0480-5 (sc)
ISBN: 978-1-4969-0479-9 (e)

Print information available on the last page.

This book is a work of nonfiction based on actual experiences. Names and identifying characteristics have been changed to protect the privacy of individuals. The conversations have been re-created and come from clear recollections of how they occurred; they are not written to represent word-for-word documentations. The sections of written correspondence, however, are true reproductions of the actual conversations and have not been altered in any way.

This book is printed on acid-free paper.

DEDICATION

To my amazing husband and beautiful daughter. The two people on this earth who have allowed me to be me and truly understand what unconditional love is. You make me excited for each day and I am continually in awe of both of you. Thank you for blessing my life.

CONTENTS

Dedication v
Acknowledgments ix

1 Hitting Rock Bottom 1
2 Matt and Rodolfo 8
3 Miguel—a.k.a. HV 1.0 17
4 Andrew—a.k.a HV 2.0 31
5 Dad 38
6 Andrew and Dean, Continued 43
7 Let the Games Begin 50
8 Ruth 56
9 Samantha… Samantha?!?!? 60
10 My Big Palooka 63
11 My Favorites List 70
12 Meeting Mick 77
13 Managing the Buts 83
14 Time to Get Picky 91
15 The Free Toaster Offer 94
16 Life Changes 100
17 Branden 104
18 The Move 108
19 Doe-Eyed Girl—Honesty Above All Else 117
20 Juggling 127
21 Time to Perch Safely on the Fence 139
22 Dear John 26 146
23 Meeting Greg 167
24 Clarity 174
25 Cloud 10? 181
26 Colors 189
27 Honoring A Prince 195
28 Meeting the Friends 201
29 Baggage 209

30 Stupid Is as Stupid Does..215
31 Three Hundred Sixty-Five Days..223
32 The Long Arm of the Law..227
33 Lies… Lies… Lies..231
34 Birthday Golf..241
35 My Muse..251
36 The Final Stretch..256
37 Wedding Plans..264
38 A Trip to Paradise..268
39 My Hero Past..273
40 Everyone Has a Greg..279

ACKNOWLEDGMENTS

To the many people who encouraged me to finally spread my literary wings. Special thanks to: My best half—my husband—for his love and patience during this process (and for doing all the dishes and laundry during this seemingly-endless project); Simone House, for her friendship and honesty which gave me the strength to bring this book full circle; Julia Fabian and Maja Petrovska, for their passion and enthusiasm towards ensuring that my heart came through clearly in my words; and John Bryant, for his fatherly guidance and encouragement to step out of my comfort zone and dig deep into my soul with everything I do.

CHAPTER 1
HITTING ROCK BOTTOM

"I want a divorce."

I know I wanted him out of my life for *many* years, but answering my phone and hearing those words hit me like a ton of bricks. Only a week before, we had agreed to go to counselling.

We had been separated for almost a month, and I took the day off from work with a terrible head cold—so you can imagine that I was not feeling my best to begin with. As I sat on the kitchen floor unpacking and organizing cupboards in my new apartment, I remembered his cutting words again and dissolved into a mess of hysterical tears.

Why am I reacting this way? Why am I so shattered?

What bothered me the most was not my involuntary and sudden reaction, but that my daughter had to witness her mother having a level 5 nuclear meltdown. I had always worked so hard to avoid subjecting her to the extremes of my emotions, and this was humiliating.

Once I finally composed myself, my phone rang again. It was him—Andrew, my soon-to-be-ex-husband.

"Where do I get one of those divorce kits? Can I get it from the bookstore?"

"I don't know, Andrew," I replied. "You're on your own for this one."

Half an hour later, he called me a third time. He was at the bookstore now and wanted help deciding which divorce kit to buy.

True to his lazy and immature self, he had the audacity to ask me for advice on how to get a divorce. Now he was on a mission to divorce me as quickly as possible. So, contrary to what my strong skills as a researchologist would prompt me to do, this time I had no desire to share my knowledge or opinion with him.

I spent the next few days reeling under waves of emotion. It was completely perplexing and illogical to me why I felt such an extreme mourning sensation after living so many years in misery with my husband. My only explanation was that, no matter how bad a relationship is, a couple will still cling to one another for any sense of comfort and security, however twisted that may seem. My incoherent sobbing on the phone with him at two a.m. a few days later was probably my lowest point.

Gawd. What is wrong with me?

I remember the first time I found out about his lies. It was a month before our wedding and I tried to call the whole thing off because of it.

It stemmed back to a few short weeks into our relationship—on my birthday actually. I drove excitedly to meet Andrew at his father's house (where he was living temporarily after separating from his wife) to see what spoils awaited me. My stomach was doing flip-flops, and my palms were sweating. Andrew had already proven to be so sweet and romantic, that I couldn't wait to see what was in store for me. Gone were the days of "Oh, is it your birthday today?" attitudes from previous partners. I was finally with a romantic. A true romantic.

I pulled up and was greeted with the most passionate kiss hello, but rather than being pampered and spoiled because it was *my* day, I ended up being ushered down to Andrew's bedroom and informed that he couldn't go out until he cleaned his room. *What? Are you kidding me?* Being the spineless jelly-fish that I was, I wholeheartedly dove in to cleaning Andrew's bedroom while he gave my van an oil change. (I guess *that* was my gift.) During my cleaning frenzy, I found a long string of condoms in an empty suitcase. Considering his life before I came along to be his business, I only advised that he find a better place for them before his religious and controlling father found them. He laughed nervously at that, and said they were a gag gift from his friends. Although I assured him that I didn't need to know details about his past relationships, he insisted he was telling me the truth.

As the months passed, there were never any other indications that he was being anything but honest with me, so I slept well at night with him by my side. Or so I thought…

Fast forward—one month before our wedding, I discovered that he had lied to me at the very beginning of our relationship. The condoms I found during my birthday cleanup actually came from a woman who had shown up unannounced at Andrew's father's house one night (on his birthday, no less) and begged Andrew for sex. Normally this wouldn't be any of my business, but that woman had since been quite involved in our life through Andrew's business, and repeatedly contacted him after hours asking for the same business advice each time.

Although I didn't know what had happened between the two of them, it was obvious to me that she was in love with him. During the few short months we'd been together, I asked him multiple times if they had been in a relationship. He swore up and down that he had never been involved with her and even seemed to physically recoil at the mention of it.

The day I found out about his indiscretion was on the heels of defending him to his two closest friends. Although I didn't care much for this couple—they were young, immature, and not the type of people that I would normally associate with—I was forced to accept them into our wedding party because Andrew had been the best man at their wedding. Every time we were with them, they made sure to tell me all the tales of dating and cavorting from Andrew's life before and after his separation and subsequent divorce. They constantly referred to him as a "ladies' man" or a "player". I would have never spoken to someone's girlfriend like that, so my assumption was that they were just bullies trying to make me feel bad about myself. Finally, I got so fed up with having Andrew's past pushed in my face that I defensively blurted out that he hadn't been intimate with a woman since he left his ex-wife, and continued to naively sing his praises. Little did I know that his friends were very close to the "Happy Birthday Mr. President" condom woman in question and knew the truth—as did four other couples that we dealt with regularly, both through business and social events.

One evening, when they were over helping with the bombonieres for the wedding, it started again. I took Andrew into another room and lost my cool. I told him I was sick and tired of all the things they were saying about him and the lies they were telling about his past. He finally broke down and told me about his indiscretion with his business associate.

I was devastated. I dropped to my knees and sobbed. Everyone knew except me! I had defended him in one way or another to each and every one of those people over the past few months and, in the end, felt completely humiliated and betrayed by all of them. More importantly, betrayed by him.

But then, the anger set in. I told him that the wedding was off and I wanted him out of my house immediately. I couldn't stand the thought of spending the rest of my life with someone who could look me in the face every day and lie to me. I also didn't think I could stand the humiliation of what everyone knew, and what a fool I had been over the past few months.

He begged me to stay with him and promised he would never lie again. His justification for lying so far? He wanted to "protect" me because he felt the truth would be more hurtful. As devastated and betrayed as I felt, I was so deeply in love with him that I truly didn't want to call off the wedding. His promise seemed so sincere that I pushed aside my feelings of doubt, humiliation, and anger and agreed to become his wife as planned.

The lies continued for almost a decade. I got to a point where I could no longer look at him or stand to be in the same room with him. Each time I uncovered a new lie, I would die a little more inside.

Why do I hate myself so much that I continue to live this way?

I loathed who I had become. I spent every day miserable and distrusting, with a hard knot in my stomach. Daniella (my daughter from my first marriage, but legally adopted by Andrew) couldn't stand him anymore either, but for different reasons. She was tired of being barked at, of being treated like she was both his mother and his slave when I wasn't around. His tirades of verbal abuse towards her were epic. One day he saw her eating the last piece of leftover pizza from the fridge, which he wanted as well, and he blurted out, "I hope you choke on it and die." Even though he may have said it as a childish joke, his message stung my poor eight-year-old. He berated or criticized her in some way every single day. Each word beat her down deeper and deeper.

When she told me about the incidents and I confronted Andrew, things only got worse for her. She, in turn, stopped confiding in me. One morning, when Daniella was about nine, as I was getting ready for work (ironically on Mother's Day), she became hysterical and said she wished she was dead or had never been born. I left the house devastated and sick to my stomach that I had to leave her.

How could a nine-year-old be feeling that way? What the hell have I done to her?

When I arrived at my job at the local steakhouse, I was hit from every angle with the whining and complaining of my coworkers, that *they* were "pissed" that they had to work on Mother's Day. I did my very best to hold my head up high and be the bigger person, but after the eight millionth complaint from a twenty-something-year-old, I finally lost my shit all over them.

"Are you all for real? Look around you! Have you noticed that I am the *only* one NOT complaining? Yet, I'm the *only* one working who IS a mother! Did any of YOU have to leave your child—your reason for BEING a mother—at home while you pander to the likes of a bunch of ungrateful customers all night? I didn't think so. So can we give the whining bullshit a rest and just go back to work please?"

Needless to say, the staff began to work rather diligently that night.

For four more years, Daniella and I remained his emotional hostages.

Andrew's childish and irresponsible behavior continued to mount and he made it clear that *he* was the victim—the third wheel—in this family. There was one situation that sticks out in my memory that summarizes his behavior marvelously:

We were at his father's having lunch with some visiting relatives. There were about ten of us there that day, and his stepmother made her delicious lentil soup. As she served everyone, Andrew turned to Daniella and said, "You have my permission not to eat that." The reason he was offering his "permission" was because Daniella was forced to eat everything he served her, even if he knew that she didn't like it.

"But I like this soup", she said to him meekly.

"Well, it's disgusting. So you have my permission *not* to eat it."

I replied to him incredulously, "Andrew. She *likes* this soup." And everyone else at the table chimed in as well.

Andrew shoved his chair back and, like a five-year-old, blurted, "Well fine! Be that way!" and literally stormed out of the room. We all sat in shocked silence.

A few minutes later, he came back and said, "Where's the pizza. I want my pizza now."

His stepmother, bless her heart, calmly replied, "Well, if you're not going to eat the soup, then there is no pizza for you." You could hear a pin drop as he stared at her in disbelief. He then, stomped his foot (no, I'm not exaggerating), spun on his heel and stormed down into their basement to watch TV. Again, the room fell silent, until his younger brother began to giggle. The giggle broke the tension and then one of his relatives turned to his stepmom and said, "Bravo. Bravo."

His sister turned to me and said, "I don't know how you live with that." I just shook my head. Another epic Andrew moment.

On other occasions, similar comments were made by his family to me. His slovenly behavior was usually one of the common discussions.

Andrew refused to put his dirty laundry into the hamper, and I stuck by my rule of, "If it's not in the hamper, it doesn't get washed." I learned the hard way with him because I was the one to iron his work clothes. He would bring his wrinkled clothes to me all the time and, like a dutiful wife, I ironed them to his exact specifications. After the umpteenth time of passing the iron over the armpit of a shirt and smelling musky sweat and deodorant, I realized that I was ironing a dirty shirt—again. I stopped ironing his clothes altogether. You can imagine the pouting and foot stomping that occurred whenever he was running late in his usual Dagwood Bumstead fashion and realized that he had not clean work clothes… or underwear, for that matter.

The childish behavior was not the worst part of it all, it was the emotional tirade against Daniella. It was a text-book school-yard-bully situation. Andrew was so insecure, that he had to prey on the weaker of the pack in order to feel like King Shit. He wasn't the dominant lion king that he thought he was, he was the pathetic hyena with the bulgy eyes and tongue hanging out. (Sorry, I think I've watched *Lion King* way too many times over the years.)

Andrew was a very scholastically-intelligent person, so I did lean on him considerably when it came to Daniella's homework. His way of teaching though, left so much to be desired. He spoke to her like she was an idiot, and expected her to understand everything when he used complex formulas and explanations. When she didn't understand, he wouldn't take the time to explain it to her in a more-simplified manner; he'd just bark it at her and ask her if she was "stupid or something". It was because of that behavior, Daniella would immediately put up defensive walls whenever I asked him to help. Her grades began to slip and her self-esteem began to fall through the floor.

What I once thought was a beautiful blending of souls ended up being the culmination of Daniella's suicidal thoughts. He proved correct of my tongue-in-cheek saying, "Parents these days don't need to save for their kids' education—they need to save for their therapy fund."

Daniella's negative feelings were also fuelled by how cold I was towards Andrew as well. I couldn't hide it anymore. I used to be so good and putting on a good face when she was around, but no more. I couldn't hide my disgust anymore. Daniella and I both lived with the attitude of just trying to get through each day with him, but now, four years later, we had finally escaped that misery. Now Daniella and I were gathering up the broken pieces of our hearts and embarking on our new future together—man-childless.

August 2006 (two weeks before school started up again), I found a place for us to live. Our new home was about fifteen minutes from where we had lived with Andrew. I could hop on a bus that would take me right downtown to my new job. I would be saving on car expenses and could get home quicker to spend time with my daughter. Because Andrew had left me in a huge amount of debt and didn't pay a dime in child support, cost effectiveness became my middle name.

The months that followed were filled with so much sadness and self-pity that I didn't think I'd ever be capable of moving forward. I found a well-paying job I didn't really care for, but it helped to validate me again as a person because I had stopped believing I had what it took to be successful in a professional career.

The hours were long and the responsibilities numerous, but I was starting to feel a little better about myself as a businessperson. Unfortunately though, the long hours caused an imbalance in my life with my thirteen-year-old daughter. Despite my goals to get home faster and spend more time with her, I barely saw her; yet she was always so gracious about my absence—she knew I was doing it for our betterment. What an angel. But still, I was very aware that thirteen was a crucial age and that I needed to be there for her as much as possible.

After about six months of separation, friends started talking about dating. Dating? Oh, my gawd! I couldn't even imagine it. I was in four relationships during my life: a long-term high school boyfriend, a fiancé, a husband, and a husband. I knew them all before becoming involved with them, so there was no dating per se. I never had self-confidence, so when a man showed interest, had ten fingers, ten toes, and no sign of a serious nervous tick, I figured he was good enough for me.

Am I even ready for this? This idea of dating?

The thought of it overwhelmed me and I pushed the idea out of my head. I was definitely not ready to put myself out there so soon. So you can fully grasp why I was so gun-shy about dating again, I will offer you a window into my past love life.

This is the part where I stare pensively at the ceiling as soft harp music fades us into the memories of my past…

CHAPTER 2
MATT AND RODOLFO

As I closed in on my twenty-first birthday in 1990, my high-school boyfriend of four and a half years said in passing, "I'll probably be a bachelor for the rest of my life."

What?

We weren't fighting, we didn't hate each other… it was just a comment while we were out for a drive one day. Matt was my first love and my best friend and he knew I wanted the white picket fence and 2.4 kids package deal.

I had to make a decision about my future and our relationship. I loved Matt's mom, and she adored me, and he and my parents felt the same way about each other too; I think that's why we stayed together as long as we did. Our relationship was comfortable and we settled into the routine of an old married couple.

I met Matt in 1986, when we were both in eleventh grade. His friend had just moved in at the end of my street. I remember what a scandal it was when his friend moved in. Here we were, a neighborhood of average nuclear families and a—duhn-d-dun-dun-duuuhn—*divorced* single dad moved in with his two teenage boys (who were, by the way, both from different mothers). I had lived on that street since I was two and there had never been a divorce for as far as our bikes could travel. Wow. Whoddah thunk, that now, "uni-marrieds" (the term I use for people who have remained married to the same person), would be the oddity. How times have changed.

Anyhoo, back to Matt.

I met him just a year after a brief stint living in France. I hadn't really dated anyone since, but did have a teenage long distance love affair with a guy I'd met during my class' tenth grade French exchange to Quebec. What's my definition of a "teenage long distance love affair"? Holding hands, making out, contracting mono, and allowing some innocent touching of my young-lady parts. Ah Benoit. Great kisser but his "backne" (back acne) was so disturbing. The relationship felt serious at the time (and he was very much in love with me), and I wondered if a relationship with this boy (who was a year my junior), could survive the distance until we graduated. I was confident that the backne would clear up one day, and he was so sweet, that I really hoped it could have worked. I think I was just holding onto the false hope because I wanted to be loved. To have a love. It just wouldn't work though. His mother was dead-set against him seeing a cradle-robber like me. That's when Matt fell into my lap.

He and his friends were a good group of guys: a nerd, a dumb jock, a nerdy jock, the nerdy jock's brother who was just average in school but a good athlete, and Matt—the star center of their school's basketball team. Matt was intelligent, but not nerdy. Cute? Nope. I would call him dorky-looking. Even though they went to a different school (and most lived at a bit of a distance), we all became good friends and hung out a lot. We spent most of our time at their school, where we shot hoops and I honed my basketball skills. I'll never forget the look on their faces the day I sunk a three-pointer. I haven't sunk one since, but I'm completely fine living on the memory of my glory days.

I'd always felt more comfortable around guys, and these guys were like brothers. I don't remember when the shift occurred between me and Matt, but we suddenly became inseparable. I do remember the first kiss, though. It made me melt. Very quickly, I was wearing his letterman jacket and was the envy of all my female classmates as the guys at his school were the most sought-after boyfriend material in town.

I fell deeply in love with Matt and absolutely loved that he was my best friend. I could be me and I could tell him anything. He was also pretty damn smart, so he helped me with my homework, which was an added bonus. I knew we were going to be together forever and couldn't imagine my life without him. That's when I decided to give him my everything. Matt and I were both virgins, and even though I didn't believe in sex before marriage, I justified it knowing that he'd be my one and only.

Before Matt came into my life, a couple of other guys had shown interest in me, but I always went to my emotional bottom line: Do I want to spend the rest of my life with him? No?

"No thank you, I don't want to go to the movies with you."

I am logical that way. If I couldn't see our future together, I was not going to waste his time or mine. But Matt was different… I simply could not imagine life without him.

Then it happened. Veronica met her distrusting side.

I was at Matt's one day and came across a collection of dirty magazines. Okay, when I say that out loud, I sound like an old hen. Is there a more hip term for them? I dunno, I guess I'm just not that hip. Anyhoo, I found a large stack of these magazines and my hands started to shake. I was so insecure about myself, my body, my face—my everything—that I felt sick to my stomach. Was I not enough for him? Did I confront him about it? No. Of course not… cowards don't do that. Instead, I spread the magazines out over his mattress and covered them with his quilt. Needless to say, I got a call from him later that night. He was upset, but he never got mad at me. He explained that his mom sometimes went into his room to use his phone and could have found them. Even though I wasn't really sorry for what I did, I apologized, and shared my insecurities with him. Being the wonderful boyfriend that he was, Matt told me I was enough for him and said he would get rid of the magazines. But the damage was done.

I became increasingly paranoid and jealous, without provocation. Although I was conscious of how irrationally I was behaving, I couldn't stop myself. One shameful night I snuck up to the window of his friend's house to see if he was in there playing Dungeons and Dragons like he said. Yes… Dungeons and Dragons was how that group spent their Friday nights. Well, that and painting D&D figurines (which I secretly enjoyed doing with him).

My jealousy and paranoia led to a few breakups, but Matt always came back a few days later and forgave me. I did, however, find out that he had stored the dirty magazines at his friend's house so he could still have visitation rights. I was devastated and no longer trusted him at all. It was exactly during our relationship that I started having serious emotional issues.

This is probably the part where the shrink tells me to lay back on his leather couch and tell him about my childhood; and say things like "and how did that make you feeeel?" So I guess I should pause and tell you a little more about the awkward little freckle-faced redhead.

In 1970, I was born into a blended family. In those days, the term, "blended family" didn't exist; and I never thought of us as anything abnormal. My sister was three and a half years older than me and she was just that—my sister. My dad legally adopted her and was the only father she ever knew. My dad, as far as I could tell, loved her like his own; and I think she felt the same way too. She was an adorable brunette with big blue eyes and ginormous dimples. I thought she was perfect and idolized her. As I grew older though, I tried to keep my jealousy towards her buried. She was so cool, had a ton of friends, and she and our mom were thick as thieves. I really didn't feel close to my mother, and always felt like I could do nothing right in her eyes.

My sister was so outgoing, and I was the polar opposite. I was shy and embarrassed easily. I was constantly the butt of everyone's jokes because of my behavior or appearance. I felt like God's little joke: take the formula of everything wrong and wrap it all up in one child. That was me. That was how I felt in my skin. And even though everyone told me daily how "shy" I was, whenever I was one-on-one with someone, I'd gab uncontrollably. I was always mocked for how much I talked. I remember one business dinner that I got to attend with my parents. I felt like such a big girl and one of the men asked me if I wanted to ride back to our house in his car (no, nothing weird—he wasn't a perv). I was so excited to go, because he had a big luxury car. But just as I was about to get in, my mother made some mocking comment to him to be careful because I'd talk his face off. I was mortified and had to fight back my tears. I sat in the front seat of his car in absolute silence even though he did his best to engage me in conversation.

Humiliation like that was a regular occurrence in my life. It wasn't just my mother though, it was a lot of the people around me. I seemed to always be the whipping boy. It also didn't help that I was quite awkward and didn't fit in, even at the best of times. One of the worst though, was when I got my first period while at work at my parents company, and my mother announced to everyone that I had officially "become a woman." I stored things like that in my mental inventory of "Things NOT to do when raising a child." It was only after my daughter was born that a friendship between us began to grow.

When I was eleven, I began suffering from undiagnosed knee problems, and the years of constant pain was taking its toll on me. My mom took me to a new doctor or specialist every year, but no one knew what was wrong. I've had so many x-rays, that I always say that my glow is not from a sparkling personality, but from being nuked so many times. By the time I went to France for ninth grade, I had been suffering with the pain for four years.

France? Oh, yeah. I lived in France for a school year. It was interesting how that came about.

My parents owned a thriving company, and the bank decided to go back on their promise and demanded their money back. Okay, so that's the simplified story they told us kids. Anyhoo, when my stepgrandfather died, my parents didn't want the bank to get a hold of the inheritance, so they decided to spend it. They bought my sister a car and me... Well, my parents came home from work one day with groceries and handed me some bags to put away. As I began unpacking the bag, I pulled out four airline tickets. Yes, that portion of the inheritance was going to be used to ship me off for ten months. Not meaning to sound melodramatic, but I didn't recall any conversations between us that contained anything that sounded remotely like "and so we're shipping you off to boarding school."

So at the age of fourteen, I was left standing on the doorstep of a school sobbing as I watched my family leave in a taxi. My dad was crying so hard that he couldn't speak. They called me from their hotel that night, and my father could still barely speak to me, I just kept listening to him blow his big Jewish schnozz in the background. That day in September of 1984 (over the phone), was the first time in my life that I ever recollect my mother telling me she loved me.

I felt like an outcast there. Not only was I my usually awkward and shy self, but now I was in a country where, even though I spoke the language, I was mocked because I couldn't speak it with a French accent. I sounded like a typical North American tourist. Although I'd been in French Immersion for three years, our teachers never forced us to hone our accents. We all sounded like tourists. My classmates mocked me on my very first day of school, and so I didn't utter a word in French again for the entire school year. What I did do though, was sit in my room every single night and read French books out loud exaggerating my throaty r's until they flowed naturally. Thankfully, I was befriended by a Dutch girl who wanted to improve her English—our deal was that she could only speak English to me, and I could only speak French to her. By the end of those ten months, I was completely fluent in French and had the most beautiful accent.

During that same year, I started a very committed drinking and smoking habit. I got and stayed drunk as much as I could to numb the pain of my loneliness and mystery knee problems. It was easy to buy booze in France; families sent their seven-year-olds to the market, so it was easy as pie for me to fuel my newfound habit. As for the smoking. I really don't know why that happened. I hated the smell of cigarettes. But one day though, I was with some friends and one of the boys pulled out a pack of cigarettes. I snatched them away from him and told him that smoking would kill him and I ran back to the dorm so he couldn't get them back. I hid them under a pillow at the top of my closet and forgot completely about them. One day though, a couple months later, I pulled the pillow down and the full pack of cigarettes fell to the floor. I don't know what possessed me, but I lit and smoked one—right down to the filter. It was stale and disgusting. What did I do then? I smoked the rest of the pack and officially began my two-pack-a-day habit.

Most kids that age smoke and drink to fit in; but that wasn't me. I was a closet smoker and drinker. No one knew that I did it. No one would ever believe that such a "goody-goody" like me smoked. I guess it was the first solid indicator that I was host to an emotional chasm. By eleventh grade I think I had a full-fledged problem; I drank more than I ate and was miserable all the time. Through all the alcohol combinations, I discovered that Long Island Iced Tea was the drink that numbed my pain the most effectively. I had found my escape.

I thought about ending my life—not because of the knee pain, but because not being alive was all I could think about. So when Matt came into my life, I was already battling these demons. I didn't know what was wrong with me, nor did I have the skills to even try to understand. The only thing that stopped me from killing myself was that I couldn't bear the thought of hurting my father, who meant the world to me. Unfortunately for Matt, he met me when I was right smack-dab in the middle of a teenage meltdown.

On at least two occasions, Matt stopped me from taking a handful of pills, and I vividly remember him wrestling a knife out of my hands and throwing me across my kitchen floor. Living in my body was like watching a movie on fast forward. I'd see it going by, but just couldn't compute everything I saw. To this day I feel sick to my stomach thinking about all the things I put poor, sweet Matt through.

After almost five years with him, I decided that if I didn't physically leave, I would find myself in the same situation in another five years; and if we broke up then, I would have wasted almost a decade of my life. As cold as that may sound, I've always been a little heavy-handed on the bottom lines in my life. Many have commented that I think too much with my brain and not enough with my heart. I'm not insensitive (the sight of a beautiful socket wrench set in a Home Depot ad can bring a tear to my eye, and don't get me started on the Christmas Coke commercials), but it just seems logical to avoid unnecessary heartache later by facing hard facts now.

On December 31, 1990, I kissed Matt goodbye and boarded a plane to Florida to start a new life in the cruise ship industry. Within a month, I had a job as an assistant purser (the bottom of the totem pole of officers on a ship, responsible for the administrative side of onboard operations—things like customs, immigration, and cashing traveller's cheques for passengers).

I tried to come out of my shell and enjoy myself for once instead of being a cookie-cutter workaholic.

When I was ten years old, my parents started a company and left me and my sister to be latch-key kids (that's what you called kids who went home to an empty house after school—nowadays, we call them kids of "dual income families"). Monday to Friday, I was responsible for cleaning the house and taking care of the five cats. My sister was a teenager at that point and was rarely ever home and barely ever helped out (or at least, that's how it felt to me during that time—I'm sure I suffered from a bit of childhood "pity me" syndrome). On Saturdays, I'd go with my parents to work and spent my mornings cleaning the warehouse bathrooms and lunch room, and then work my way into cleaning the office bathrooms and general areas. I wasn't the fastest, but I did my best. I took pride in how I could make the faucets sparkle. Then, in the afternoons (when I wasn't pushing myself up and down the halls in one of the wheelie executive chairs), I'd help in the office typing envelopes or doing filing. My fondest memory of all this? We'd get to have McDonald's for breakfast and then I'd snack on Wasa crackers covered in mayonnaise and cheddar cheese.

As the psychiatrist pauses to have his "ah-ha" moment over my, now obvious, addiction and comfort food issues.

I continued that working schedule until I went to France and, upon my return, spent my teen years working in various retail and restaurant jobs until I landed a job at an accounting firm.

So, because I'd always had one or more jobs since childhood, I knew how to focus on work, work, work. It was my way of hiding from the social situations of life that I just, plain and simple, didn't belong at. I only ever attended one school dance and had no idea how to act in those kinds of social settings. I remember attending a couple victory parties for Matt's basketball team and I just *knew* that I didn't belong. Everyone was laughing and chatting and drinking, and I just clung to him and couldn't even strike up a conversation with anyone. It was then I realized that I was really good and blending into the background. No one ever remembered me. No one ever even cared that I was there. I was invisible. Needless to say, enjoying myself on the ship was definitely going to be easier said than done—work was my protective shelter.

I met a man soon after I joined my first ship. Rodolfo, the chief sommelier, was a Spaniard and terribly dashing. His French was better than his English, so we mostly spoke in French. One thing about him bothered me, though—his lisp.

It was a strange lisp that I really couldn't wrap my head around. When he spoke to me in French, he didn't have a lisp. When he spoke in broken English—no lisp. He only lisped when he spoke Spanish. During a conversation with one of my multilingual co-workers a few weeks later, I expressed my annoyance at Rodolfo's perplexing speech impediment. After my co-worker picked herself up off the floor and dried her eyes, she gently explained to me that he spoke Castilian Spanish in which the soft "c" is pronounced "th." Good ole naive Veronica strikes again. Insert red face.

He was shorter than me, but was sweet and romantic; and despite feeling like a big fat ogre around such a diminutive man, I fell in love. We would sit after our shifts and talk for hours, and I loved every minute with him. Honestly, it felt like I'd known him for years and we never ran out of things to talk about. He was five years older than me, and had a maturity about him that was so refreshing. He was well-educated and well-traveled.

Since relationships with "crew" were taboo, we had to hide it from the masses. If the ship's officers found out, he'd be fired or transferred without hesitation. We spent much of our time on the rope deck which was sheltered from prying eyes, but allowed us to sit outside once in a while to enjoy the sea air. Because of our opposing shifts, we were very rarely able to spend time together ashore, so our main time together was spent in my cabin. Not only was a good portion of it spent horizontally, but we enjoyed drinking wine and smoking cigarettes together while we got to know one another more.

After a very brief time together, he asked me to marry him and I excitedly said yes.

Wow! This is what true love feels like.

Soon after the proposal, a jealous co-worker (who I thought was my best friend) decided she wanted to further her career and her horizontal relationship with my boss, and framed Rodolfo for stealing open bottles of wine left over from the main dining room. He was quickly fired and sent back to Spain. I was devastated, but it didn't matter because we decided that I would go back to Canada for a friend's wedding, finish my contract with the ship, and join him in Spain to be married. I was also going to become an insta-mom to his seven-year-old daughter. I was so excited for my new, exotic future.

During the first week of my two-week shore leave in Canada, Rodolfo and I spoke on the phone every day and stuck to our plan. During my second week at home, I called him at the time we arranged, but an elderly lady answered the phone. As I did not speak Spanish, all I could say was, "¿Rodolfo en casa?" The woman started rambling on in Spanish (complete with that annoying lisp I hated so much) and hung up. I tried a couple days later and no one answered. When I returned to the ship, I called him at each port we stopped in. I wrote him letters, but gave up after a month; his message was coming through loud and clear. Sure enough, I never heard from him again. I guess "out of sight, out of mind" really is a valid statement. I threw away his photos, stayed for a second contract on the ship, and focused on moving upwards in rank, but unlike some people, I wasn't going to lie down to do it.

I hated the company I worked for and patiently waited for one of the ships from a different company to come out of dry dock so I could—yes, I'm going to say it—jump ship. Fate intervened when some friends asked me to stay where I was a little longer because they were going to be cruising on my current ship. I stayed, and that delay led me down a new path. The path of meeting my future husband, Miguel.

CHAPTER 3
MIGUEL—A.K.A. HV 1.0

Miguel was the captain's steward and originally from El Salvador. He had milk chocolate skin and a thick Hispanic accent and was again an inch shorter than me (which still made me feel extremely self-conscious). I fell in love with him almost immediately—or so I thought.

The passion I felt for him was overwhelming. I hadn't felt this way about Matt past our first month together. I ached to be with Miguel. Our physical relationship was completely amazing, and every day we spent hours intertwined and pleasuring each other. Any spare moment we had we'd meet in my cabin for morning, afternoon, and evening delights; and all I could think about was when we could see each other again. Two thumbs up for my Latin lover!

It wasn't just physical, though—we had a great relationship and never argued (the polar opposite of how things were with Matt).

Now THIS really is love.

I remember my thoughts clearly the evening that Miguel proposed.

Well, he'll never be my best friend… but I'll find other friends.

I lay awake that night convincing myself that he was the man I wanted to spend the rest of my life with.

Seriously… this really, really is what love is supposed to feel like.

I accepted his proposal, but we couldn't get married right away—Miguel was still married.

He had met his wife Julia in university and they had become study buddies with perks. She suffered from female issues and was told she could never have children. Therefore, Miguel and his "buddy" didn't bother taking precautions, and about a year into their multifaceted relationship, they found out she was pregnant. Both sets of parents insisted that they marry, but Miguel secretly vowed to only stay married long enough for his child to be old enough to handle a divorce. Miguel's father forced him to join the ships so he could provide his new family with a good life and, because Miguel was three years shy of the joining age of twenty-one, had a fake birth certificate made for his son.

Miguel had left El Salvador before his son was born and did not see him until he was two years old. He would go home on shore leave, spend two months with Julia and Rodrigo, and then return to the ships for another two years. That pattern continued until the day I met him ten years later.

You'd think his attitude towards marriage would have been a red flag for me. But it wasn't. I was in love and I believed that he had finally met his true love and that we would be together forever. After all, I didn't believe in divorce. I was marrying for life. After what felt like years, his divorce was finalized, and on June 5, 1992—eight months after we met—Miguel and I wed at City Hall in St. Martin with a handful of our friends as witnesses.

If you're not familiar with ship life, the unwritten rule is, "If you have nothing nice to say, make sure you tell as many people as you can." Ship living is a horribly negative way of life.

Working on a ship is a lifestyle that is difficult at the best of times. You're away from your family and friends, and forced to get along with people you wouldn't necessarily associate with. I know that we all have to deal with different personalities, but when you are also living, eating, and breathing with these people, the saying "familiarity breeds contempt," pretty much hits the nail on the head.

Some might be quick to say that, because the money is so good, it brings in the dredges of the earth. That's not true. Yes, the majority of the crew members come from impoverished countries or neighborhoods; but some of the truest and most genuine people come from humble backgrounds. These people spend years away from their families in order to give them a good life. Women leave their children to be raised by family in order to help them get ahead. It broke my heart to hear the stories of separated families; or the father who had yet to lay eyes on his two-year-old child. So I don't think a poor socioeconomic situation could be the blanket reason for people treating each other with so much disrespect. Wealthy or poor, the "cream of the crap" is everywhere. And no matter what rank, most people just wanted to do what they could to get ahead. Quite honestly though, the "officers" were the most lecherous of all. They wanted everyone to believe that they were superior, but they too, were mainly just a bunch of uneducated sailors. But again, I must remind you of my disclaimer—this is not a blanket statement. I worked with some really wonderful people.

Aside from hearing about how many men I apparently slept with (so, sad that I can't even remember all of them… sigh… I guess our imaginary sexcapades weren't memorable enough to me). One situation stands out in my memory though.

I woke up in terrible pain one night and assumed I had food poisoning from eating fast food in Puerto Rico the night before. As the computer programmer for the ship's cashless system, my shift began at two a.m. and I was all alone in there, with no one to pick up the slack for me. I lay on the floor writhing in pain as my reports printed. Every once in a while, I'd go up and lay in my bed with Miguel who put cold compresses on my forehead. By the time all my reports finished, it was six a.m. and everyone was still asleep. At Miguel's insistence, I left a note on my Chief Purser's desk telling her that I needed to see a doctor as soon as we docked that day.

Very long story short, the ship's doctor and the doctors ashore did not know what was wrong with me. Since they didn't know why I was in so much pain, they did not want to risk heli-lifting me back to Miami to go to the hospital, so they left me in St. Thomas. With still no insight as to my condition, they opted to perform exploratory surgery. When I awoke from the surgery, I was informed that I would be fine, and that it had been caused by my appendix. Luckily for me, it hadn't burst.

While I was away, one of the crew took it upon themselves to approach my soon-to-be-husband and informed him that he knew why I was in the hospital. In the middle of a crowded crew mess hall, he loudly informed Miguel, that it was "because of the way she screws." He further continued that he knows this because we'd "screwed". Miguel did not engage him (oh how I wished he had knocked his block off), but the story made me livid. This "gentleman" was actually Rodolfo's best friend and was told to protect me after he left. If that was his version of protection, I'd rather smear myself in pig's blood and dive into shark infested waters.

Thankfully, I didn't hear about this story until after my return and adequate healing time. True to Latino stereotypes, Miguel was an extremely jealous man; and he believed this rumor about me. I was humiliated and angry when I heard what happened and did my level-best to assure him that it wasn't true. He wasn't convinced. About a month later, I ran into Rodolfo's friend while collecting my mail shore side. He was with a group of his ignorant buddies and made a smarmy comment to me in Spanish. I handed my mail to the coworker I was with and walked over to him calmly.

"I heard what you announced about me to Miguel and the crew."

He just laughed and gloatingly looked at his buddies. As he looked back at me, everything went into slow motion, and I cold-cocked him across the jaw.

His buddies burst out laughing and, as he lunged at me, I inserted my boney knee forcefully into his groin. Doubled-over in pain, he shouted out, "You whore! You are going to pay for this."

I calmly stared him straight in the eyes and said, "So you haven't had enough of a beating? Bring it on, you pathetic little bitch." Little did he know that my hands and legs were shaking uncontrollably. It was that day though, that I realized I *could* be a force to be reckoned with. I didn't have to be the shy little redhead that I was as a child.

What I didn't realize was that Miguel's reactions to the rumors allowed me a glimpse of the violent person he could be. I ignored the signs because, remember, *this* truly was love. A month after we were married, our contracts ended and we moved to El Salvador to begin our life together. At the time, I didn't realize that I was about to embark on what would soon become my own personal hell.

Miguel rented a house for us and moved his mother in with us immediately. You can imagine that this seemed a little unusual to a typical North American woman—especially since we were newlyweds. I lost count of how many times she knocked at our bedroom door while we were in the throes of passion. Mood killer? I think yes.

I got to meet his ten-year-old son, Rodrigo, as well. He lived with his mother in a different city, but came for the occasional weekend visit. He was the spitting image of his father—two peas in a pod. They literally could have been twins—same eyebrows, teeth, hands, hair, face, everything. There were obviously some very strong genes on that side of the family. Rodrigo's lack of respect towards me was obvious, so I was not looking forward to the battle of being a stepmom. At the tender age of twenty-two, was I equipped to be the surrogate mother to a boy who was only twelve years younger than me? In a country where I didn't speak the language? In a family that was not my own? I was not optimistic about our future as a blended family.

Not only did I have to deal with how disrespectful or dismissive this young boy was towards me, but Miguel never stood up for me when any of his other family members were rude or disrespectful towards me. I felt like everyone's whipping boy.

Apparently though, respect was not overflowing in this family because Miguel was horrible to Rodrigo too. Impatient and insulting. I felt awful for Rodrigo, and wondered if I could find a way to give him the love and respect he obviously craved. I could tell that he idolized his father. But each time he tried to do anything, Miguel would cut him down. He called him stupid, lazy, fat (the child was in no way fat—he just had an average adolescent's body). I think what made the relationship between me and Rodrigo more strained was that Miguel humiliated him in front of me. He didn't have the parenting skills to know that you don't cut children down like that publicly. Was this the way Rodrigo was treated by his mother too? Were Miguel and his ex-wife resentful that the child even existed? I really didn't know. I was dumbfounded by the ignorant behavior I witnessed on a day-to-day basis.

Shortly after we arrived, Miguel decided to start a cheese-making business. He rented another house in town to use as a makeshift factory and left every morning at dawn with his mother to drive to a farm to collect the milk to take back to the rental house for processing. They worked every day until about six in the evening, while I stayed at home alone, sitting in that barren house listening to music and watching the neighbors peer in at the foreigner who never left the confines of the four walls.

About a month into my new life, I started getting very ill and threw up after each meal. *Could it be? Could I be pregnant?* I prayed that my dream of becoming a mother was coming true. The symptoms were bizarre, though—not the standard morning sickness we all hear about. I got weaker by the day.

One morning before Miguel and his mother left for the day, she asked me if I wanted to go to the doctor. Although I barely spoke Spanish, I could understand quite a bit and told her yes. She informed me that she would send Miguel back after they collected the morning milk. I was so weak that I had not bathed in days, so I dragged myself into the bathroom and tried to sponge bathe myself as best I could without passing out. I sat in the living room and waited for him. For hours I waited, and blacked out so many times I could barely stay conscious for more than a few minutes. We didn't have a phone, so I couldn't call anyone. I finally got up enough strength to walk out to the street and flag a taxi. I knew enough Spanish to say "left" and "right," and prayed that together with pointing, it would be enough for the taxi driver. I also prayed I would remember how to get to the cheese factory house. Just as the taxi pulled up outside the rental house, I saw Miguel getting into the truck to do the afternoon milk run. I had caught him just in the nick of time. But he was angry that I was there, because he had work to do; and his mother hadn't bothered to tell him that I needed to go to the doctor. Impatiently, he ushered me into the truck and took me to the doctor. Not just any doctor... an allergy doctor. *Really? What kind of a country is this?* The doctor, who was very kind, established that I had malaria and said we were very lucky we hadn't left it untreated any longer. So for the next three weeks I got to enjoy the daily ritual of Miguel's mother (who was a retired nurse) jabbing me in the ass with a needle.

The emotional and physical abuse began after I recovered from the malaria. One particular day, we were arguing in the bedroom and he pinned me down on the bed. I'm a fighter (and a stubborn Capricorn), so I tried to kick him and push him off me. It only made him angrier. He had to prove that he was the man of the house, so he pinned my arms down with his knees and began to choke me. I fought hard, so he squeezed harder. Just as I was about to black out, I stopped fighting and he released me, apparently satisfied that he'd won. After that episode (which was the worst to date), I decided that ending my life would be the most honorable way out of the situation. I had worked so hard to sell Miguel to my family and friends that I couldn't bear the humiliation of admitting I was wrong. While he slept one night, I locked myself out of the bedroom (so that I couldn't tuck tail and go back to him) and began my search for something I could use to kill myself. The house was pretty empty, so all I could come up with was a dull butter knife. I began to saw away at my wrist but just couldn't break through the skin. So I sat on the living room floor and cried my eyes out. Obviously, plan A hadn't worked, so the next day I convinced Miguel to let me go back to the ship to start earning and saving more money. His cheese venture had depleted the savings we'd arrived with two months prior, and he was quite possibly more concerned about money than about being with his new bride, so he agreed without hesitation. I returned to ship life with the promise that I would return to El Salvador in a year.

A few months later, the company brought Miguel back to the ship I was on, and we rekindled our incredible relationship. I realized that Miguel was incapable of functioning on land and needed the simplicity and lack of responsibilities that ship life provided. As he found his sea legs again, we found each other, and quickly conceived our daughter. My job on the ship was extremely stressful, so we decided it would be best for me to return to Canada for the pregnancy and birth. I was back at home within two months.

Things had been rocky in El Salvador, but when I left Miguel on the ship to return to Canada, our relationship was idyllic and we were both thrilled to be having a baby. I was confident that he would treat our child differently, this child who was wanted and conceived in love. This child would solidify our marriage. I was sure of it.

Although I was with my family, I felt so alone. It hurt that I couldn't share this experience with my husband. He didn't get to hear the heartbeat, talk to my belly, or look at the ultrasound. I even had to drive to the store to fulfill my own cravings. It wasn't fair.

During my time back in Canada, I got to meet and bond with my little niece, Emma. I fell in love with her and she became like a daughter to me. My mother looked after her Monday to Friday, and because I was living with them, I spent all my time with her. We were inseparable. She called me *tía*, Spanish for "aunt," because it was easier to say than Auntie Veronica. It made me feel special. Emma got to feel the baby kick, hear the heartbeat, and watch my belly grow. Even though she wasn't quite two years old, she understood that I had a baby growing inside me. She understood so much that whenever we were out and she saw a pregnant woman, she'd point and excitedly exclaim: "Baby, tía! Baby!" The sweetest moment of all occurred at a local shopping mall when she pointed and made her usual excited exclamation. When I looked over and saw she was pointing at a man with a very large beer belly, I couldn't help but laugh and embrace her innocent confusion. Initially, I had wanted to have a boy first, but being with Emma made me long to have my own little girl.

Miguel joined me a month before my due date and was to stay for the birth before we both returned to start our lives, again, in El Salvador. January 1993 changed my life forever. My angel, Daniella, was born. She was the spitting image of her father and brother—three peas in a pod. I was thrilled to see that she had his beautiful hands, but not thrilled that she had his bushy unibrow. I guess I'd be teaching her the masterful art of eyebrow sculpting one day.

Five days postpartum, there was a "scratch and save" sale at a local department store and I was extremely excited to use my gift cards to stock up on clothing for the baby before we returned to El Salvador. After nursing Daniella, I passed her to my husband to burp and change, so that I could go get ready. As I innocently went to pee, I felt a strange sensation and realized that I was haemorrhaging. Scared to stand up from the toilet for fear of ruining my mother's flooring, I waited for someone to come downstairs and check on me. After what seemed like an eternity, my mother finally came down to find me stranded on the toilet. She immediately called the doctor's after-hours number to seek advice. More than an hour later, a doctor finally returned her call and advised that we go directly to emergency. Since my husband did not have a driver's license in Canada, my mother rushed me to the hospital with my husband and baby in tow. Needless to say, I was rather upset that I missed the sale. Pout.

As I lay in the emergency room bleeding to death, my darling husband decided it was the perfect time to inform me that all of my savings in Miami were gone. He had withdrawn everything while I was away and built a house with it. My mother thought it was the most romantic thing she had ever heard, but what she didn't realize was that he had been lying to me for months by telling me that the money was there—and safe.

Although he had done things like this before, they were on a much smaller scale. I guess he felt he had nothing to lose by telling me this as I lay on my deathbed.

Twelve hours later, they wheeled me out of surgery. I had lost more than half my blood, but was going to live. Now I had to try to digest the news I had just heard.

The day we got home from the hospital, my mother took Daniella upstairs and I shakily went to the bedroom that Miguel and I shared in her basement. He put down the diaper bag, crawled into bed with his clothes on and said, "Go make me a sandwich." I stood stunned for a moment, then went upstairs to the kitchen and cried. *What have I gotten myself into?*

Miguel returned to El Salvador to prepare things for our arrival, and Daniella and I were to join him two and a half months later once all of her documents were complete. I was so torn about this next phase of my life—the thought of taking my child away from her grandparents was killing me, and I could see that they felt similarly about not being able to watch her grow up. On top of that, I feared that my relationship with Miguel would be just as violent and volatile as it had been when we first moved to El Salvador. But the unyielding optimist in me tried desperately to believe that he would change because of his beautiful little girl. She would soften him.

Rodrigo spent a bit more time with us now because he no longer lived with his mother. She had remarried and had another child (so much for the infertility theory), and was also a raging alcoholic. While Miguel and I were back on the ship, Julia had sent him away to live with his school's headmistress. Rodrigo was happy to have a little sister; he adored Daniella and never wanted to put her down.

Within two months of returning to El Salvador, I got sick with malaria again. My body fought so hard to stay alive that I could no longer breastfeed Daniella. I was devastated. I felt robbed of one of the greatest gifts of motherhood.

Both our marriage and my health continued to deteriorate, so we decided that Miguel would immigrate to Canada as our last-ditch effort to make the marriage work. Eight short months after our arrival in El Salvador, Daniella and I returned to Canada to wait for him.

Since Spanish was Daniella's first language, my mother and I hired a Colombian nanny to help keep it up. It wouldn't hurt for Emma to be exposed to a foreign language either. Very quickly we discovered that the nanny spent the day speaking broken English to both of them. Bye-bye nanny.

Since moving back to Canada was our last chance at this marriage, I started working on me. I feverishly began reading books on how to better myself as a wife. Every night I went through scenarios of how I would handle situations better than I had before. I wanted to escape the pattern of jealousy and anger we continued to find ourselves in.

Our time apart was taking its toll on me, and after almost a year without Miguel, I broke down while on the phone with him. I was always so careful to hide my meltdowns from Daniella, but this time I just couldn't hold back. After I hung up the phone, my little eighteen-month-old angel walked up to me, put her hands on my cheeks and said, "It's okay, Mommy… I'll take care of you." That is what *I* always did when she was scared or upset. I dissolved further into tears and held her tight.

As upsetting as the time apart was, I kept hoping that absence *would* make the heart grow fonder. I prayed that all those feelings would come flooding back the moment I laid eyes on him again. The moment that his lips touched mine again. Those weren't the only thoughts I was having, though. I also hoped that he'd cheat on me or die so that I could escape this marriage honorably by being the victim.

Immigration took fourteen months, and by the time Miguel arrived on our doorstep in January 1995, we had a lot of emotional healing to do—he had a new country and lifestyle to get used to, and Daniella—a new father figure.

Miguel refused to speak Spanish to Daniella. When I questioned him about it, he snapped back at me that she wouldn't understand. She was in her bedroom at that moment, so I called to her and asked what she was doing—in Spanish. Although she answered me in English, I thought I proved my point. But he still refused.

The emotional abuse towards Daniella and me began immediately, and the physical abuse towards me didn't take long to follow. Miguel got a kick out of shouting Daniella's name and startling her, and took no notice of me when I asked him to try to speak more softly to her. He also took to gently kicking her on her butt whenever she walked past him. When she started crying, which she did each time, he'd just laugh and mock her by pretending he was crying too.

Daniella became a very whiney child (which our doctor warned might happen due to our life change) and Miguel accused me of being a horrible mother for raising such a crybaby. He tormented her constantly and things got so bad that she started literally pulling her hair out. I begged him to stop tormenting her, but he found it amusing. I finally got us in to see a child psychologist and you'll never guess what her advice was to him—"stop tormenting her." He finally stopped, but his emotional reign of terror continued in different forms. She was afraid of him and didn't want to be alone with him.

The physical abuse against me began to escalate at a rapid pace. I lost count of how many times he pinned me down and choked me in order to get his point across. I still remember how it felt to have his hands around my neck. He would emphasize each abusive word by choking me harder and banging my head against the floor or bed. What made it worse was when I stayed strong—when I didn't cry. If I gave him a dead, cold stare while he did it, he just squeezed and throttled me harder. Because I was being choked, I could speak, so he would only release me when the tears started to flow from my eyes. He would then get a smug look on his face, release me from his grip but, before he stopped straddling me, he always made sure to tell me how pathetic I was—remind me that *he* was the *man*, and I was to treat him with respect. And then he would finish with a firm slap across my face.

One day, I got so sick of his lazy behavior that I couldn't hold it in anymore. He had been in the country for a short time, but refused to do anything about getting a job. In addition to working full-time, caring for Liliana and my niece, and cooking for my entire family almost every night at my mother's house, I had to look for a job for him too. I finally got him a job at a commercial greenhouse, which was perfect for him. Since he studied agriculture, this was right in his back pocket. Since he didn't have a driver's license in Canada, I was now also responsible for driving him to and from work each day, because his job was not in an area serviced by public transit.

A few short months later, the greenhouse shut its doors and everyone there lost their jobs. *Great. Here we go again.* Once again, the burden was on me.

After the umpteenth week of him just lying around the house all day, I finally confronted him. Looking back now, I probably could have dealt with the situation a little better. "Use your words, Veronica," is what my mother always taught me. Well, I became incensed as he lay in bed ignoring my "words," and without thought, I introduced him to my right hook. In my head, I thought I could "knock" some sense into him, since my words never had any effect. But in my emotional exasperation, I guess I didn't realize the ramifications of my actions.

To this day, I firmly believe that Daniella saved my life when she walked into our bedroom right after I delivered my punch. Miguel was about to lunge at me. I saw the look in his eyes. It was not just the usual proving-himself-as-a-man look—it was going to be the end.

Did I leave him? Of course not. We all hear about abused women and wonder why they are so stupid to stay in situations like that. I used to be one of those people who snubbed and judged the victims of abuse. Why did I stay? I wish I could explain it, but I can't. I just stayed.

Instead of leaving, I came up with one more brilliant idea. "Let's bring Rodrigo here to live with us." I was determined to make this family work. Miguel agreed and we began the tedious legal process. Rodrigo was so excited, and I was too. I envisioned that he and I would bond and I'd be the one to help him grow into a wonderful young man. I was ready to embrace him despite how he treated me back in El Salvador. I had even hand stitched him a Christmas stocking to match ours and purchased gifts for him for his first holiday with us.

Six months into his stay, Miguel achieved his driver's license and I could finally have a bit of pressure taken off of me. I didn't have to be the chauffeur anymore (although, he was still a terrible driver). Now that he had his license, I was able to get him a job as a general laborer with a general contractor my mother and I did bookkeeping for. Every weekday, he got up at six in the morning, was home by six at night, ate his dinner in silence (when he was not shouting at Daniella), then went and watched TV until two in the morning. This went on day after day after day.

Our once-healthy sex life also began to dwindle. He criticized me constantly and no longer seemed attracted to me. I exercised every day to ensure I stayed in peak physical form, but it was never enough. I made sure that my hair and makeup were always perfect, but he spent too much time primping and preening in front of the mirror himself to notice me.

I felt pathetic. Sex always seemed to make things better between us, and now I didn't even have that anymore. All of my insecurities came flooding back. The ogre reared its ugly head. Once again, it was clear that I was not attractive or appealing to any man. My body had bounced back completely after child birth, so it's not like that could have been the reason for his disgust towards me. I had about three stretch marks on my right hip (that were barely even visible), but was back to my flat stomach and general firm physical pre-pregger state. The only thing different was that I now had large breasts. Most men like that right? Then why did he look at me with disgust? The look of desire never came into eyes anymore.

I confided in a friend once about my insecurity of being taller than Miguel. She assured me that men liked that. It made them feel like they were with a model, she said. I tried to believe her, but I still felt like a fat, hideous beast next to his firm little soccer body.

One night we had a formal business dinner to attend (which actually fell on my birthday), so I took the opportunity to buy a sexy-yet-stylish dress and have my hair and makeup professionally done. He didn't say a word when he saw me. While we were at the dinner, two of my associates who knew it was my birthday approached our table to give me their best wishes. One of them was Andrew actually. He said, "You look absolutely beautiful." He turned to Miguel and said, "Did you tell your wife how amazing she looks tonight?" Miguel actually snorted and walked away. I couldn't hide how embarrassed and crushed I was by his reaction.

Oh wait, I stand corrected. There was one time that Miguel did comment on my appearance. I was lying on the sofa with a 104-degree fever and the flu and he said, "You look like shit. You really look disgusting." My prince charming. What did I ever do to deserve someone so wonderful?

Why had he changed so much? What had I possibly done to make our relationship change so much?

In retrospect, I think his move to Canada emasculated him. He wasn't the king anymore. He was so highly respected on the ships; and then his tall-tales in El Salvador always left the people fawning over him. He felt he was better than them because he had a partial university education. But he didn't have that fan-base here. He was just an immigrant. Just an average person. The times that he opted to be fully entrenched in his pity party, he also pretended that his English was a barrier. It wasn't. He was completely fluent, and no one ever mocked him if he made a mistake. Despite my strong Capricorn personality, I never tried to be the *Alpha* with him. I just wanted to be with a real man. A man who would stand up for, and protect, me and our children. Is that what it was? Was it his way of trying to cut me down to submission? That is my only assumption—he felt that my "manhood" was bigger than his.

Things exploded in December 1996 and I begged Miguel to seek counselling with me, but all he wanted to do was go back to El Salvador. My father, also an immigrant, gave him the "do your duties as a man" speech and browbeat him into staying. When I approached him about counselling again, he said we could work things out ourselves and didn't need assistance. Luckily, Rodrigo still hadn't arrived, so he didn't have to live on the constant emotional roller coaster as Daniella did every day.

The following year, I could see that absolutely nothing had changed, and I felt compelled to make the change on my own.

He came home from work one night and, as usual, silently sat down to eat his dinner. I sat across from him and calmly asked, "Counselling or airline ticket?"

He looked up at me with a look of putrid disgust, shook his head incredulously, and went back to his meal. He ate slowly and methodically and didn't acknowledge me. Every fifteen minutes I repeated, "Counselling or airline ticket?" After an hour and a half of silence from him, he finally said, "I will never go to counselling." So I asked, "Miami or El Salvador?" Another forty-five minutes of repeating myself went by before he replied, "El Salvador."

"I'll be back in an hour."

I went straight to the local mall to buy his ticket.

One week later, on June 23, 1997, I took him to the airport where he kissed me passionately goodbye, and, for the first time in the eighteen months he had lived in Canada, told me he loved me. As I drove away from the airport, the most incredible sense of peace and relief filled my heart and soul. Next to my daughter's birth, I can honestly say that it was the happiest day of my life.

After his departure, I was so grateful for the slow-turning wheels of immigration because, had Rodrigo moved here, Miguel probably would have left him with me. But at least then he might have had a better life with me and my family.

Speaking of immigration, since I had sponsored Miguel to come to Canada, I knew I was responsible for him for ten years and I worried about what that meant for me now. What if he got himself into legal trouble in another country? Would I have to pay for his mistakes elsewhere in addition to paying off the debt he left me in here in Canada? Miguel had also threatened that if something happened to me, he would come and take Daniella back to El Salvador to live with him. Although my mother's statement of "over my dead body" should have been comforting enough, I thought it would be best to call immigration. I explained to the officer that my husband had left Canada and would never return. I further explained that we were divorcing and asked what my legal responsibilities were during the ten-year commitment that I had made.

"So you're saying, your husband abandoned Canada?"

"Um... no... he left me and my daughter."

"So what you're saying is that he abandoned Canada."

"Um... nooo... he abandoned *me and my daughter*."

"So *what you're saying is* that he *abandoned* Canada."

"Um... n-ohhh... yeah. He totally abandoned Canada. He said that Canada was killing him and he'd never come back."

I could almost hear the giant red flag being placed on his file. I guess my mom's dead body had nothing to worry about anymore.

About two months after Miguel left, I experienced a debilitating panic attack as I drove across a bridge with a business associate in the passenger seat. So debilitating that she had to grab the steering wheel to pull us safely over to the other side of the bridge. I was crying, hyperventilating, and shaking like a leaf. From that day on, the panic attacks became a regular fixture in my life. Here I was, trying to move on and be strong, and yet, I would dissolve into tears walking into a public place or hyperventilate in the produce section of a grocery store. But more on that later. For the time being, I moved in with my sister and started to focus on my new path forward.

CHAPTER 4
ANDREW—A.K.A HV 2.0

In August of that same year, I planted a seed with Andrew. I had known him for a year and a half through business, and we had become good friends. Nothing more, I swear. I do remember, though, that on a few occasions while we chatted between meetings, I thought, "Why can't I be married to you?" He was so kind and well-spoken and seemed like a genuinely wonderful person. All the single women at work did their very best to get his attention. I used to make fun of him for being such a distraction and for making all those young women collapse into giggles whenever he walked into the room. Shortly after Miguel's departure, I started to see Andrew in a different light.

He was separated from his wife, with no chance of reconciliation. She had cheated on him with one of their friends and gotten pregnant with that man's child. She was completely out of the picture. Andrew dressed well, smelled good (although too strong at times, which is why my sister never liked him visiting), and was intelligent and extremely driven… or so I thought.

The seed I planted grew very quickly. One night, he showed up at my door with cheesecake for me and my sister and his heart just for me. We sat and talked for hours that night, and at about two in the morning, Daniella woke up and came out to the living room where we were sitting. The two of them giggled together and got along famously. You could tell that she was completely taken with him and he with her. I sat back, beaming and excited that I may have found the perfect father for my beautiful little girl.

The first time Andrew kissed me was like fireworks. I knew right away that I was completely in love with him. The best part of that feeling was knowing that it wasn't attached to sex. We had not been intimate, so I knew that my feelings were true. As much as I craved being intimate with him, premarital sex was against his religious beliefs. I was okay with that because I knew it would give us time to really get to know each other without lust clouding our judgement… my judgement actually.

One night after a late meeting, he asked if he could come over to see me. I literally had to sneak him into the house so my sister wouldn't know. Had she woken up, she would have smelled the cologne a mile away. We lay in my bed talking and kissing and innocently touching until it was no longer innocent. He could not control himself and proved that he was not completely bound to the beliefs of his faith. Despite that sinful feeling in the back of my head, I enjoyed every second of the most mind-blowing sex I'd ever had. His stamina was like nothing I'd ever experienced and he only required a few minutes' rest between each session. I knew I'd met my sexual match. No man had ever been able to satisfy me to that degree before; no man could ever keep up.

At seven o'clock that morning, he snuck out to go to work. The sound of the door closing woke Daniella and she came to my room and snuggled in bed with me. I fell fast asleep, completely satisfied. I was woken abruptly by the phone ringing. It was Andrew. He had just gotten into a car accident and needed me to come get him. I was so delirious that I wasn't even sure I understood where he said he was, so I drove praying I'd be able to find him. I was shaking like a leaf and having selfish thoughts like, "If he dies, I'll never be allowed to mourn him because no one knows about us." As I neared the accident scene, my stomach lurched. There was his car, completely underneath a flatbed truck. *How the hell did he survive that?* He stood at the side of the road without a scratch. I thanked God and knew that He had bigger plans for him. Plans for him to be in my and Daniella's lives.

A month later Andrew asked me to marry him and I couldn't think of anything I wanted more. Watching him, Daniella and Emma together made me positive that he truly was the man of my dreams.

We didn't marry right away because we both needed to finalize our respective divorces, and during that time there were signs of bad things to come. As I mentioned before, one would think that spending my birthday cleaning a grown man's bedroom would be an indication that maybe he wasn't as put together as he made himself out to be. I ignored those things because of how happy he made Daniella and me feel. Daniella was happy again and I thought I had found the father she was meant to have. But, despite everything, I still had nagging feelings in the back of my head.

One of the main reasons we both felt our marriage would be successful was because of the people we associated with. Our business associates were, for the most part, Christians with strong family values and ethics. We felt bulletproof and believed the experiences we had been through in our first marriages would only help us improve on ourselves and become better spouses. We looked forward to an incredible future together, and once again, I said to myself:

Now THIS really is love.

With the love I felt for Andrew, I realized that I had confused love with lust when I met Miguel. Miguel and I had a very healthy and passionate physical relationship and I, like so many women, confused it with love. I guess maybe, subconsciously, I had used Miguel to get what I wanted—a baby. Now I had my child and was about to marry the most amazing man I had ever met. Have I said this yet?—*or so I thought.*

Andrew turned out to be a disgusting slob and there is no nicer way to put it. I've never seen anything like it. I accepted it because I was no longer being emotionally or physically abused, but after a while, it really started to wear me down—especially as I watched Daniella follow suit.

As I mentioned earlier, I uncovered Andrew's first lie a month before the wedding and tried to call it all off. Despite the lie and the slovenly behavior, on June 24, 1998, we were wed (365 days after Miguel left the country).

I need to backtrack to Miguel again. When I came back to Canada during my pregnancy, he called me every other Sunday when the ship was in its homeport. That continued after Daniella and I moved back to Canada permanently, and also after he left us to return to El Salvador. He would call every other Sunday to talk to Daniella. In August 1998, I was the one to call him on one of his usual Sundays to give him the phone number and address of our new home. I also asked him permission for Andrew to legally adopt Daniella. Needless to say, his answer was no, but my lawyer had told me that I was obliged to ask him before proceeding with the adoption application. During the rest of that phone call, Miguel told me he was going to be a better father to Daniella and send her gifts on her birthday and special holidays (which he'd never once done). I told him that his sentiment was very sweet but was not necessary, and assured him I would never do anything to keep him and Daniella from knowing each other. I did ask one thing of him though, that he let me know if he goes back to the ship, in case of emergency. He assured me that he would. In truth, I needed to know what country he was in to serve him with the adoption order. Our conversation ended without conflict, but he didn't even bother to ask to speak to Daniella. That was the last time we ever heard from him.

When it was time to serve him with the adoption order, I found out he had actually returned to a ship six months before. His cousin gave me that news and didn't have a clue that we were no longer married—never mind the fact that I had a new husband. Miguel never told his family the truth. For years, I continued to send his family photos of Daniella, but never once received a reply. To this day, I have no idea why he abandoned her that way, and I wonder about Rodrigo and if Daniella has other siblings. So very sad.

Andrew was unemployed when we got married, but had already secured a consulting position to start a week after our wedding, so I saw things going up and up and up with us. As the years passed, though, I watched him systematically sabotage all of his jobs and either get fired or have his consulting contracts go un-renewed. Andrew informed me that he "just wasn't meant to be someone's employee" and decided to start his own consulting business.

During the year and a half of job gains and losses, Andrew started driving us deep into debt. He spent uncontrollably and justified it to me. I've heard it all.

"You deserve it, honey."

"Don't worry, honey; it will all be fine once our business takes off."

"You worry too much. By this time next year, we'll be millionaires!"

Although he tried to pacify me with comments like that, it still didn't change the fact that, in addition to raising my daughter, I had to hold down two jobs.

I was still optimistic, for two reasons. Firstly, the people we associated with were successful and wonderful business mentors. I was confident that Andrew would learn from their tutelage and his business would soon take off. Secondly, he had two successful businesses during his first marriage—his consulting business and the restaurant that he started for his then-wife. She still had that restaurant (and it was thriving), but he sold his successful consulting business to take a sabbatical prior to meeting me. How could I not be optimistic? He just needed time.

Don't get me wrong: Andrew was talented at what he did, but in order for him to be a success, he needed someone to do all of the scheduling and purchasing (in addition to finding the clients) and then say, "Okay, go here and do this." By himself, he just spent money on equipment he never used.

Our finances were a mess. Our finances were always a mess. That was reason number one for the misery, but I always believed him when he promised he would do something to pull us out. I always waited for him to go around that proverbial corner, find himself, and realize it was time to step up.

I wanted so much for him to be the man of the house. Despite the fact that I'm a red-headed Capricorn, I never wanted to wear the pants; I just wanted to be a strong support to my spouse in a loving partnership. Why couldn't I have that? How was it that, no matter how much I worked or how many jobs I had at once, I could never keep up with his spending?

I felt defeated. I felt like a failure in my daughter's and family's eyes. One of the most ridiculous reasons that I hadn't left him years earlier was that I didn't think I could make it on my own financially.

Oh my gawd. What was I thinking?

If I had been on my own all that time, I wouldn't have had to work so hard and watch someone spend my money so carelessly. Oh boy. We humans sure have an interesting way of thinking "logically."

The debt crept higher and the creditors began to call. I sunk into a deep depression and could barely look at Andrew. To top it all off, he spent the entire day and night in his home office and came to bed in the wee hours of the morning, just like Miguel used to. Our physical relationship no longer existed. When I would stand naked in the doorway of his office and ask him to come to bed with me for once, his response would always be, "I'll be there in ten minutes." Night after night, I fell asleep with a book on my face, waiting for him. Up to that point, our sex life had continued to be amazing. We couldn't keep our hands off each other and had at least two or three complete sessions a day. What had happened? Why did it change? During the misery of our financial situation, sex was still something of an escape for me. I craved him. I ached for him. I couldn't understand why he didn't want to be with me anymore.

From the moment we got married, we began trying to conceive a child, but our wish was never granted throughout the eight years we were together. Once we separated, I viewed this as a blessing, but at the time, it was a horribly emotional roller coaster that took a toll on our marriage. During the many years of trying to have a baby with Andrew, I sunk into a deeper depression caused by my already depressed state, the fertility medication I was on, and the forty pounds I had gained. As women, we are so much *in our bodies* that it is hard to break out of depression when we are disgusted and ashamed by our appearance.

I was grateful for having been given my beautiful daughter, and I felt bad for putting my faith for the future in doctors instead of in God when it was He who had given me my daughter. It didn't help that Andrew felt like the third wheel and constantly played the victim. No matter how much I tried to bond us as a family, he always chose to walk around with a big "V" on his forehead. It was exhausting to deal with.

Throughout the infertility challenges and Andrew's unemployment, he continued to spend. One night I came home from work at three in the morning to find that he had, once again, bought fast food for him and Daniella and rented a stack of DVDs. Another night, when I came home and he proudly showed me the thousand dollars' worth of new equipment he'd bought, my knees buckled and I began sobbing as soon as I hit the floor. I didn't know what to do anymore. I had tried begging, pleading, shouting, and threatening, but nothing worked. I was officially defeated.

Three years into our marriage, I stopped working at my mom's bookkeeping company and went back into the restaurant industry. The school in our neighborhood was so bad that even teachers warned me not to send my daughter there. So I made the decision to homeschool Daniella by day and work at a restaurant at night. Although I never wanted to go back into that industry (I'd bussed, served, and managed in restaurants before and hated it), I swallowed my pride and got a job at a steakhouse within walking distance from our home. I'd get up every day at seven to have my day with Daniella and be done by three in the afternoon in time to open the restaurant. My shift would be finished by three in the morning and then I'd start all over again. I worked as many shifts as possible to keep us afloat financially, but I couldn't keep up.

To add a thick layer of icing to the cake, Andrew started a business with someone behind my back. Now you may find this a very melodramatic statement considering that I wanted him to get a job and help us get out of debt, but wait for the details.

Andrew met a man named Dean through a mutual business associate and started to do little consulting jobs for him free of charge. I assured him that I didn't mind him helping people out, but from nine to five each day, he needed to either be looking for work or working for income. What he did in the evenings was his choice. He agreed to my conditions.

I noticed that he was not trying to find work or get new clients, and asked him outright if he was doing business with Dean. He assured me he wasn't. I then asked him to promise that he wouldn't sign anything without talking to me first, to which he also agreed.

It's not like I knew everything about business, but I could at least have pointed him in the right direction, towards people who could ensure that he made the right decisions. In addition, I didn't trust his secret partner as far as I could throw him. I'd heard bits and pieces from others that really left me feeling unsettled.

One day he proudly presented me with a trade magazine featuring him and Dean and the success of their innovative seedling company (complete with photo). I acted supportive and took the magazine to bed (since we all know I had nothing better to do while in bed). I noticed something odd in the caption under the photo, though. It listed Dean as president of the company, and Andrew as vice-president. I went to his office and asked him why it said that. Was it just their way of establishing credibility? His response made me weak in the knees. "No, that's the title I was given when we started the company."

I just about fainted. I literally felt my blood drain to my feet.

Understand that because Andrew was unemployed, I always knew his whereabouts. He would tell me if he was going to a breakfast meeting with Dean, or over to his house. Not once did he say, "I'm going downtown to Dean's lawyer's to sign the legal documents for starting a new company with him." Trust me, I would have remembered that and *never* agreed to it. Andrew told me that their agreement was as follows: because he had no money to invest, he would invest *sweat equity* instead. In layman's terms, "You ain't getting paid a dime, chump."

He produced the document to me and it was true. We were officially screwed.

I cried. It was all I could do. I had heard of Dean's unethical behavior in the past, so I was fairly certain we were doomed.

CHAPTER 5
DAD

In the middle of all this chaos, my father was hospitalized for a kidney operation. I had been oblivious to his health challenges… maybe because I was too self-absorbed with my own life, or maybe I was just being protected because I was the baby of the family.

Dad was in the hospital for about three weeks, and was to be released on Father's Day 2003. Since I was working in the restaurant industry at the time, days like that were days we were never given off, so I went and visited him the day before and brought him homemade brownies.

My father came to Canada in the sixties from Brazil. Although he and his four siblings were born in Egypt, they were forced to leave in 1956 because they were Jewish. Eventually, my father and three of his siblings left Brazil and came to Canada to start their new lives. My father met my mother and, not-so-long story short, they welcomed me into the world just after his 49th birthday.

My dad was everything to me. I idolized him. He was kind and generous, and something inexplicable surrounded him, some energy that drew people in. He was a salesman and travelled a considerable amount. I never expected him to bring gifts from his trips, only waited for his phone call from each new hotel when he would report the color of the sheets to me. It was our thing; no one else shared that with him but me. I feel sorry for the children of travelling businessmen today… the sheets are only ever white in hotels now.

When Dad was home, he was the designated shopper. Every Sunday he embarked on his routine—two supermarkets and the health food store. Sometimes, we'd even go on Saturday to the Lebanese grocer for olives and feta cheese or to the butcher where I'd be gifted with a freshly made wiener. Yes, in the seventies, we could say "wiener" without people snickering.

I held those shopping days close to my heart. When I was with my dad, I felt ten feet tall; I walked beside him with immense pride and felt as if everyone could see he belonged to me. Just me.

I lived my life in a way that would live up to his example. He had never treated me with anything but love and kindness, and I couldn't stand the thought of upsetting him or seeing disappointment in his eyes; I held him on such a high pedestal that I never wanted him to ever be anything but proud of me.

Since my father was the same age (or older) than my friends' grandparents, I grew increasingly worried he'd die before I could give him a grandchild. I cringed whenever one of my friend's grandparents or a celebrity his age passed away, especially if I was travelling or living abroad at the time. I truly believe that is why my first marriage happened—I wanted him to experience the joys of being a grandfather.

When Daniella was born, it was a dream come true for me. I named her after my father. My own name was supposed to have been Daniella Amanda, after my father and grandmother, but neither of them wanted me to have their name, so I was named Veronica Josephine (Veronica after the actress Veronica Lake, and Josephine? I don't know). Because I'd worked with an Amanda who was the most hateful person I'd ever met, I couldn't imagine giving my daughter that middle name. So I chose Daniella Angelina (after all, she was my little angel). My dad adored Daniella and their bond was undeniable.

My mom told me that he was never comfortable holding me when I was a baby because he was afraid he might drop or hurt me. So I constantly gave Daniella to him to hold and he would just sit and stare at her with the biggest grin on his face.

On Saturday, August 9, two days after my dad retired, my sister called to tell me he was back in the hospital, but in emergency this time. I raced to the hospital in a panic and was told that he was retaining fluid and that they were waiting to transfer him to another hospital so they could put a shunt in to drain it off.

I remember sitting at his bedside in emergency and my mother hovering around to make sure we didn't get emotional. She'd come scurrying over and say something like "None of that! None of that!" It angered me that she couldn't just leave us to have time alone together, but I was not the type to stand up for myself.

The next day, I found out that he hadn't been transferred but was staying in that hospital and going into the palliative care unit. Color me naive, but I'd never heard that term before, so the gravity of it didn't register. Daniella and I were visiting my dad while my mom was out plugging the parking meter.

While she was out of the room, a woman came in to introduce herself. "Hello, Mr. Daniel." (Everyone always called him Mr. Daniel, and never referred to him by his last name.) "My name is Olga. I will be here for you if you need anything. If you want me to come and sing or dance for you, you just have to ask. I'm here for you." My dad was always such a sweet and cordial man and he thanked her graciously before she went on her way.

He turned to me with a big grin on his face and said, "She wants to *dance* for me?"

"Leave it to you, Dad. You're the only man I know who can get a lap dance offer in the hospital. You might not want to tell Mom about this." We had a good laugh about it and I was still, at that point, unaware of what "palliative" meant.

The next day I was informed that my dad had cancer. I don't remember the technical name of it, but it was cancer of the connective tissue and he was riddled with it. I was beyond shocked and now completely livid that it had been kept from me.

Dad was told he could live another ten years if he started aggressive chemotherapy and radiation treatments. Being the type who never wants to be a burden to anyone, he refused and asked how long he would live without any treatment. They estimated six months to a year. My father said, "Nope. I'm done." Stubborn immigrant to the end, he was going to do this on his own terms.

I was working a Monday-night closing shift at the restaurant when a wave of emotion came over me. I started exhibiting flu-like symptoms so one of my co-workers told me to go home and she'd finish up. I wasn't sick, but I was overcome with a feeling that something had happened to my dad. I didn't want to call and get the news over the phone so, at eleven o'clock at night, I drove to the hospital.

My father's room was directly in front of the nurse's station and as I walked down the hall towards it, everything went into slow motion when I saw a piece of yellow tape over his name plate. My knees got weak and I stared in silence at the door. The nurses' incessant chatter stopped when they noticed me standing there. "May I help you?" one of them asked.

"Uh… um… I'm Daniel's daughter. I just wanted to know if he was okay." Even my words felt slurred. I was in shock and trying to keep myself composed.

"Oh, Mr. Daniel. Yes, he's fine. I was just in there. Do you want to go see him? He's awake."

As I approached his door, I was able to read what the glaring yellow tape said: "Do not feed by mouth." I slowly felt the blood return to my face.

Needless to say, my dad was surprised to see me, and we had our first moment alone. I was trying my best to keep it together, and not doing a very good job.

"Dad. Are you at peace with your decision to go?"

He assured me that he was and, with that, I told him everything he meant to me and how much I loved him. Unbeknownst to my mother, Dad and I cried in each other's arms. I know my actions were selfish, but I couldn't stand the thought of him leaving without saying goodbye.

On Thursday, August 14, 2003, at the age of 82, my father went to join his brothers for a long-overdue game of backgammon. I could just picture them up there with their cigars and scotch, telling jokes in Arabic. The day he left, the power went out in northeastern North America. I always knew he was a great man, but the fact that he knocked the power out when he left just proved it to me.

When my mother called to tell me the news, I did cry, but I proceeded with my day: tae kwon do and then my shift at the restaurant. I was rather disgusted with myself because I always thought I'd be a mess when my dad passed away, but I felt almost emotionless.

At work that night, one of my managers was acting very strangely towards me so I confronted her. Apparently, Andrew had taken it upon himself to call her and tell her about Dad. I was livid. I had never been one to cry on someone's shoulder, so the fact that he did that felt like a betrayal. I was a professional and always lived by my motto "There are twenty-four hours in a day. You don't need to mourn for all of them." My father was the same way. We weren't insensitive, we were logical.

The next day I received a bouquet of flowers from Andrew's partner Dean. Again, I was livid. "What the hell is this?" I asked venomously. I hated Dean and he hated me, so why did Andrew tell him? I knew exactly why—because Andrew always had to be the center of attention.

"Why the hell did you tell Dean?"

"Why shouldn't I? He was *my* father-in-law!"

"My father *hated* you, Andrew. Give me a break! Everything isn't always about you!"

One of the reasons I was not planning on sharing this with anyone at work was that I knew some of my colleagues were going through their own set of problems: one of our bartender's boyfriends had been beaten into a coma a few days earlier, and one of our servers had miscarried at five months. Was I supposed to go in there and try to trump what they were going through? Everyone has their own challenges, and I was not going to burden anyone with mine.

It wasn't until four days later that I cried myself to sleep. It was the night before my first day off. I sobbed uncontrollably and realized that I hadn't been dead inside, it was just my mind's way of keeping me together so I could get through my shifts in one piece. After all, I was the only stable breadwinner in the house. I had to keep going, no matter what.

A week to the day after my dad's passing, Andrew's aunt died. He couldn't stand that particular aunt so I really didn't think much of it until I heard him on the phone. He was talking to one of the guys who worked with him and Dean and said, "I'll be here today, but my aunt just died. So if I don't answer right away, just leave a message and I'll call you back." I could tell by Andrew's responses that the fellow was giving him his condolences, and Andrew was playing the martyr. I'm sure this sounds bitter, but I was so fed up with that man, it felt like my mouth was filled with battery acid.

Knowing that what I just heard was him doing his best to get attention, I decided to… well, be a bitch.

"Andrew, are you expecting some calls today about your aunt?" I asked innocently.

"No, why?"

"Well, I have a bunch of phone calls to make, and I heard what you just said, so I was concerned that I might cause you to miss some important calls."

"Nope," he said glibly, "I'm not expecting any calls."

"So then why did you tell him that your aunt died?"

"Well, she was my aunt."

"Sooooo… what bearing does that have on his day with you?"

Andrew started to squirm. "Well, nothing. But she was my aunt and she just died."

"You are so pathetic! You couldn't stand her! You haven't even shed a tear. Why the *hell* does *everything* have to be about you? Why do you always have to seek out attention for *everything*?"

He couldn't even answer and just stared at me with his mouth gaping open.

"You're pathetic." And with that, I got up and left him to wallow in whatever he was wallowing in.

CHAPTER 6
ANDREW AND DEAN, CONTINUED

To make a very long and painful story short, the business relationship between Andrew and Dean dissolved and we were driven to the brink of bankruptcy when Dean secretly overtook Andrew's position and locked him out of the company. Andrew was shocked and devastated that his "buddy" would do that to him. I had to bite off the end of my tongue not to say "I told you so."

This episode exacerbated the issues between us and we started going to counselling. For some bizarre reason, I was still optimistic that we could save our marriage. Before starting our sessions together, the counsellor wanted to spend time with each of us separately. She opened my eyes to a lot of things during that first session and I was able to understand some of Andrew's behaviors. One particularly frustrating example was how childish he always acted. She asked me if he had ever been subjected to any form of severe trauma. The only thing I could think of was his parents' separation.

He had originally lived with his mom, then decided to live with his dad full time. They lived two provinces away from each other, so he'd get to see the other parent only a few times a year. One summer, he spent full two months with his mother, and when he returned to his dad's house, he was told they were moving to the other side of the country. He was livid and hated his father for that. He soon became the stereotypical brooding stepchild when his father met his new wife.

The counsellor informed me that many people (especially men) experience emotional stunting at the time of a traumatic circumstance in their life. Andrew was twelve at the time it happened, which explained everything. Now the question was, how could we get him to start growing again?

During one of our sessions together, the counsellor asked me if I felt I was an argumentative person, and I said I was. Andrew whipped his head around and said, "I can't believe you just admitted to that!" I calmly replied,

"Andrew, we're paying her eighty dollars an hour… why would I lie to her?" It was obvious that only one of us really wanted to heal. Thousands of dollars later, we were back at square one. Actually, we were in the negatives.

After he and Dean parted ways, Andrew found work at a private investigator's firm and was now living his dream of being in that industry. Even though he had nothing to do with the investigation aspect of things, he was thrilled to be in and around the cloak-and-dagger life.

Whatever.

I also suspected mounting lies. So much so that I began a daily routine that would prove to be the demise of our marriage. Andrew came to bed every night between two and three in the morning, and I got up at four-thirty to exercise before going to work.

Before I started my exercises each morning, I used to spend twenty minutes saying prayers and devotions for Andrew. As time passed, I began to forego the prayers and go through his computer instead. I read all of his sent messages, instant messages, and blogs, and started to uncover the lies.

I found one blog where multiple people were talking at once (I think it was a blog… it just looked like some kind of multiple-people instant messaging session) and the conversation bounced back and forth on technical topics of his industry. Out of the blue Andrew made some comment about how wild he was when he was younger, and everyone ignored him and continued with their technical conversations. Then he said, "Okay… I'll tell you about it then." He proceeded to tell all of these strangers about a sexual conquest he'd had in his university dorm room shower. He went into extreme detail and I felt my entire body begin to shake. What were the responses he received from his boastful story? One person replied, "Umm… okay…" and then carried on with the industry talk.

During this same time period, I was using a rental car as my car was in the shop for a repair. Andrew told me one evening that he had to go back to work for a few hours after dinner, and left with the rental car. I immediately went down to his computer and found a conversation between him and his cousin. They were going to a movie. Why the *hell* did he feel the need to lie to me about that? I wished it was my car because I would have had my mom take me to the movie theatre and then I'd drive it away. Unfortunately, though, he had the one and only key with him, so I couldn't go through with my devious plan. Maybe I could report the car stolen and tell the police where it had been seen and have him become the next character on *Cops*. Maybe my imagination is sometimes just a little too wacko for the real world.

I pretended I was asleep when he came home and then snuck his clothes out of the room after he fell asleep. I removed the movie ticket from his pocket and returned his clothes to the bedroom. The next morning before I left for work I asked him if he wanted to go to that same movie with me and Daniella because I knew how much he wanted to see it. Then I said, "Unless you've already seen it?" He said that he'd love to go and that no, he hadn't seen it yet. I proceeded to throw the ticket at him and flip out. I was so fed up with the senseless lies. I wasn't even sure he knew how to tell the truth anymore.

I discovered that he was asking that same cousin to lie to me for him. I read one conversation where he lied to his cousin about me in order to make it sound as though he had a very sad life. Once he even told his cousin to tell me that it was *he* who had eaten two bags of cookies that Andrew had hidden in his office and eaten. Who does that? I was angry and humiliated, and every morning I started my day with a knot in my stomach. Every day, I spent every waking moment realizing what a disgusting human being I married.

I discovered The Big One on October 31, 2005.

An innocent search for a notebook I needed ended in me finding a box filled with the lingerie catalogue that I subscribed to. My self-confidence has always been very low, so whenever I received the catalogue, I buried it in the bottom of the recycling bag. Finding them in this box meant that Andrew had been regularly digging through the bag to retrieve them. I pulled one out and found the pages stuck together. Same with the next one, and the next one and the next one. All those nights that I went to bed alone, he was keeping busy with my magazines. I felt like vomiting. I confronted him with the lie and he begged and pleaded for my forgiveness and promised that he would change. He told me that he was always thinking of me when he did it, which he admitted was sometimes two to four times a day for the past FOUR years. Needless to say, I cancelled that subscription.

This discovery made me think back to a few years earlier when I was innocently (really… it was innocent) searching his computer system for some of our family photos. I didn't know where he stored them on his hard drive, so I just searched for *.jpg and came up with very shocking results. Hundreds upon hundreds of photos of naked women. When he came home that day, I sat him down at his computer and asked him to search the same thing that I did. When all of those photos came up, he began to shake uncontrollably and could barely speak. He finally said that he rented out parts of his server to people, so they must be photos that one of the users had put on there. He promised that he would contact that person and no longer allow them access, and I actually believed him. Now, years later, I think it was just the beginning of his new favorite pastime.

The months passed, and I kept spying on him. The lies were only getting worse. When he thought I was asleep one night, I was actually standing in the darkness of the basement, with binoculars, watching him in our home office (please don't judge me… desperate times call for desperate measures). There was a mirrored wall behind his desk, so I could see what was on all four of his computer screens. He was watching porn. When I stormed in there to confront him on that one, he quickly closed the movie and denied what he was watching. He was shaking like a leaf and finally said that he was watching it so he could learn things to do with me. Seeing as we did not have a physical relationship anymore, I wasn't sold on the manure he was shovelling.

As we were driving in the car one day, I said I wanted a divorce. His reaction was to put his foot down hard on the gas pedal and aim us in the direction of the concrete median. I grabbed the steering wheel and jerked it in the opposite direction, and screamed and begged for him to stop. I knew he was unstable but I didn't think he would purposely try to crash the car.

I promised that I wouldn't leave him.

The final straw fell when Andrew's brother was getting married at a resort in Barbados. We couldn't afford to go, but his father offered to pay all three of our flights. Andrew was livid that I didn't want to attend, but I tried to reason with him; we were both paid by the hour, so the free airline ticket wouldn't cover our loss of wages and hotel and food while we were there. He insisted that we go and promised he'd work extra hours to make up for it. I caved and agreed, but stressed that we could only afford to go for five days. A week later he came home with the airline tickets—seven days for me and Daniella and fourteen days for him. I didn't even know what to say anymore.

It was the most horrible trip ever. To top it off, Andrew informed me that his solo week was to join his father on a missionary trip of sorts. Daniella and I returned home and I discovered that he had not invoiced his company as he'd promised he would, so I was left without any money to pay our rent. Graciously, my sister loaned me the money. I was suffocating.

The day Andrew returned from the jungles of Barbados, he strut into the house like a proud peacock, but doing his best to keep one of his arms out of view.

"What did you do to yourself now?" I asked, as I pointed at the large white bandage on the inside of his bicep. My assumption was that the perpetual klutz had, once again, hurt himself. He's the only person I knew who could trip on air multiple times a day.

"Oh, this? It's a tattoo."

"Where did you get the money to pay for a tattoo? You didn't have any money left when we came home."

"My dad left a few days earlier than me, so he gave me cash to buy food. So I got a tattoo instead and bummed my meals off of my brother."

He made that ridiculous statement with so much pride, that I just wanted to slap him. The glib statement wasn't the best part of all this, though. He had a tribal gecko etched into his flesh and, when I asked him why he chose a gecko, he said, "It just came to me while I was there in the jungle. I realized that the gecko was just totally symbolic of the trip." What the idiot didn't know is that, while he was away, I was performing my usual audit of the secrets hidden on his computer and saw his internet history—he had been researching those effing geckos for two weeks before we left.

The next day, he removed the bandage and proudly showed off a tattoo that sincerely looked like the chalk outline of a dead body. I couldn't stand looking at it from that point on and Daniella did make private comment to me that she thought it was totally stupid looking.

I couldn't stand to be around him anymore and we decided to separate a couple months after his return from his life-changing jungle trip. He moved into his father's house but didn't realize that his father had actually approached me saying he preferred that Daniella and I came to live with them instead of Andrew. How sad that the man's own family didn't want him around.

I also decided that it was time for me to go back to my professional roots. I signed on with a temping agency so I could get back into administration roles and quit working in restaurants. Time for me to remember who I was. Very quickly, I accepted a four-month contract with a mining company while their office manager was on medical leave with some mysterious ailment. I was nervous but excited. I had allowed my marriage to beat my self-confidence so deep into the ground that I was no longer sure I had what it took to be a professional. I had to do something, though. I had to make a positive change for me and my beautiful daughter.

Daniella and I got ourselves a spacious basement suite and began our new life as two strong and liberated women. One night when we came home, she said, "You know what? It feels really good to come home and not have him here." I was so glad that she was happy, but it broke my heart because it reminded me of the torment she'd endured at the hands of the man-child she once loved and respected.

As we began to rebuild our lives, Daniella dove into her schoolwork, I immersed myself in my new job and we both began ramping up our training in tae kwon do. I loved that we did this together. I remember, as a teenager, always wanting to study martial arts, but I was too damn shy to get up the courage to do it. When Daniella was four, she came with me to drop off some friends' kids at class and she instantly wanted to start. As much as I wanted to join with her, my work commitments (i.e., working two jobs to keep our family afloat while my louse of a husband sat around doing nothing) did not allow it. It wasn't until she was seven that I finally got fed-up with the hamster wheel I was on and started training as well.

Andrew also joined about three months into my training. He pouted and whined, that he felt left out, so I signed him up too—thinking that the mentorship might straighten him out. He was ridiculous and clumsy. I could probably write about four chapters on this one topic, but I'll just summarize it with a visual. The men and boys in the classes were expected to wear a protective cup at all times, but Andrew would complain [read: whine] that it was uncomfortable and made him chafe. So, as the sensei approached the men with his bow staff to perform a "cup check," Andrew would run to his bag and put it on OVER his uniform and wear it that way for the rest of the class. I was humiliated. He was such an unbelievable effing child.

Breathe Veronica. Breathe. It's all in the past now…

Daniella and I both tested and received our black belts (2nd degree for her, 1st degree for me), just after her fourteenth birthday. I was so proud of her. I was so proud of me too. Although I wasn't anywhere near the top of the class, I loved how strong and in control I felt learning new skills. I also loved that my daughter could protect herself when she was at school too. She did actually use her skills on three separate occasions over the years (fourth, seventh and ninth grades); when words could not solve a bullying issue. My little Ninja!

After only a few short months in the basement suite, we were forced to move because the upstairs neighbors were smoking us out. It was so bad, that I came home one night to a foggy house and asked Daniella if she had burned something. Daniella's allergy to cigarette smoke became increasingly worse and when I found her doing her homework in my car, wrapped in a quilt, in the dead of winter, I had had it. I spoke to the owner numerous times and the tenants swore that they didn't smoke.

For close to a month, I passed by an apartment building every day after work and saw a rental sign in the window. When I called, it was available and they said they'd consider taking our three cats and us. That was the hardest part of finding a place to rent—the three cats we loved so dearly.

In January 2007, we moved one more time. The apartment was a much better location for my commute, but was unfortunately facing a four-lane main artery into the city. It was an acceptable sacrifice, and this is where my story begins.

CHAPTER 7
LET THE GAMES BEGIN

After Andrew's frenzied inquiry about divorcing me, he never mentioned it again. He must have realized that I wasn't going to swoop in and help him, and he'd actually have to do it all by his lonesome. Lazy, lazy, lazy Andrew. I didn't care, though. I had no intention of getting remarried, so it was the last thing on my mind.

Being technically married wasn't going to stop me from moving on with my life, so, although I didn't know if I was completely ready for the dating world, I finally let peer pressure win and promised my two dating mentors, Jessica and Brenda, that I would start to window shop.

Brenda was married (without kids) and was the original office manager at the company that I was contracting for. Shortly after she returned from her medical leave, she decided to take on a better position at a new company, and I was subsequently offered her role. As much as I hated what I did at that company, I accepted it so that I could keep moving forward professionally and financially. Brenda and I got along really well and I told her a lot about what I had been through. She even had the pleasure of meeting Andrew when he showed up at our office to borrow my camera wearing a wife-beater, flip-flops, and shorts. I was disgusted. What nerve to come sauntering into a professional, corporate office as if he were king shit. Brenda told me that he had crazy eyes and made me vow never to take him back. After that incident, she had my word.

Jessica, who joined our company shortly after Brenda left, was the main champion of hope for me. Jessica met her boyfriend Zack online. The story of how they found each other was so inspiring to me it gave me goose bumps, but her journey was not a positive one. Jessica got married at a young age and lived a life of materialism and parties. She was happy on the surface, but felt empty. One day, she decided to walk away from it all and start a new career and life path. She remained friends with her husband but turned to online dating after the traditional way of meeting men turned up nothing but duds.

She told me stories about some of the men she met online that made me cringe. The one that sticks out in my memory is when she went to one guy's house for some wine and a dip in his hot tub. They had gone on a few dates and it was her first time going to his place. While they sat outside chatting, flirting, and enjoying their wine, they heard a rustling coming from his hedges. There, in his bushes, was a woman that he'd also met online. They had gone on two dates and he made the mistake of giving her his address. Now, there she was, hiding in the bushes watching them. Jessica didn't pursue that relationship.

She went on about a hundred dates before being contacted by Zack. She was a few days shy of leaving for a two-week trip to Cambodia when their paths crossed. She told me she just *knew* he was the one even before meeting him. Upon her return, they met for coffee, and she said that the world stopped. Their coffee date lasted seven hours. The irony was that Zack was actually leaving on a three-week trip to Europe the very next day. The two of them communicated feverishly from every internet café he could find. Once he returned, they became inseparable, and she had feelings for him that she'd never had for her first husband or anyone else. She found her soul mate. She gave me hope.

At the eight-month mark in my separation, Jessica and Brenda were still nagging me about dating, so I started to look at a few dating sites. I soon realized that I still wasn't ready to be with another man. I had always jumped from one relationship to another, and I needed to make sure I was dating because I was ready for a relationship, not because I felt incapable of getting along without a man. I had many scars that needed to heal, and massive trust issues to boot, and it wouldn't have been fair to subject anyone to that.

Although I proved to be a horrible judge of character in the romance department, there is one thing I am good at, and that is being honest with myself. It was almost a full year after my separation that I actually posted my profile. And not even on purpose.

I was told about a very popular paid dating site, so I went for a little cyber-stroll along the path of *coupledom.* Unfortunately, though, I couldn't look at the profiles unless I created one of my own—luckily, this part was still free. I established my profile without text or photos—just the bare minimum information to start window-shopping for some guy-candy. I saw a few men who appeared quite intriguing, but there was one in particular who caught my eye. He was an average-looking man, and seemed so normal—that's what attracted me the most. He had many ideals that were the same as mine, and the clincher was his body type—average. I could see by his photos that he was fairly well insulated, and that was just fine by me. I was not feeling very good about myself because of the pity weight I had put on since my separation, so the thought of spending time with someone who also wanted to be more active was very appealing to me.

Being the curious yet frugal person that I am, I thought I'd see how far I could go in communications before having to pay.

Send email. Nope.

Wink. Nope.

Send postcard. Yup!

Choose your postcard style then click here to type your message.

I swear that's what it said.

I chose a simple "Hello" style and duly followed the prompt so that I could then enter my message.

Your message has been sent.

WHAT?

Wait a minute. Where's the part that says, "We're sorry, you must initiate your membership to proceed"?

Oh my gawd. Oh my gawd. Oh my gawd. This man is going to receive the equivalent of a Nicky Nicky Nine Doors message. What if I want to legitimately contact him later and he remembers my screen name as being the stalker that sends empty postcards? Oh my gawd. Oh my gawd. Oh my gawd.

I quickly paid for a one-month subscription, filled out my profile, scraped together a couple of photos, and then sent him a legitimate email introducing myself and apologizing for the blank postcard. Thinking back on it now, my desperate email probably completely ruined my chances of appearing normal to this man. Needless to say, I never heard from him.

Once my hands stopped shaking and the heart palpitations subsided, I started to look around a bit and found a few nice men. I added some to my "favorites" list and kept browsing for a couple more hours.

Time sure does fly when you're man-hunting. I have to admit, though, the majority of my time was spent looking at all the—how do I say this nicely?—*unique*-looking gentlemen. The ones that made me laugh the hardest were the guys who took flexing shots in the reflection of their bathroom mirrors (always the bathroom mirrors). Pamela Anderson's movie *Barb Wire* must have been a big hit with the men, because I lost count of how many of the vexing flexing fellows thought it was a great idea to get a tattooed armband like hers.

Okay *stop.* Don't point a judgmental finger at me. We're all human and you know darn well that everyone has enjoyed a good session of people-watching/bashing. These guys were such easy targets… do you blame me? Now the women. Oh my, the women.

I looked through profiles of women my age to get an idea of how to best present myself for my yet-to-be-found HV 3.0.

HV 3.0? I should probably explain.

Husband Version Three-Point-Oh was how I referred to my future life partner. You see, my view was that my first two husbands (HV 1.0 and HV 2.0) came from a software development company and were just beta versions, and were therefore not fully compatible with my own complex system. I've seen emails circulating that have a similar philosophy about men and women's compatibility, so I'm obviously not the only one who's experienced this. I just needed to be patient and wait for HV 3.0, who I was positive would have perfect compatibility with my system and would not require further upgrades.

Now that you understand my relationship philosophy, let us get back to the nuances of posting a profile on a dating site.

I discovered that the main requirement as a woman posting on the site was that I adorn myself with some type of animal print for my amateur photo shoot. Also, it was important to purse my lips and squeeze my voluptuous breasts together. And if I put my hands like this, my left knee there, my right knee there, arch my back, and point my hindquarters at the camera, I might just master the obviously popular doggie-style pose.

After my visual tutorial of these stunning cougars… umm, I mean *l-a-d-i-e-s*, I decided upon which photos to post. All head shots. Not one photo showed off my double-D-cup sisters. Maybe that would hurt my chances of finding Prince Charming, but I was willing to take the risk.

Now that I've mentioned the *sisters*, I'm sure some of you are wondering what I looked like upon embarking on my shopping spree for a soul mate.

I've never considered myself a beautiful woman, and that is in part due to how everyone in my life up to this point assisted me in realizing that I fell short by society's standards. Hell, society reminded me of that daily with the barrage of tight, bouncing, nubile goddesses trotting around everywhere the eye could see. It's not like I needed my loved ones to reiterate it as well.

Wait. Did that sound bitter?

Here are some examples of the ego-crushing comments I received from the people closest to me (with a smattering of school-kid fodder tossed in for fun): Daddy Longlegs, Freckle Juice, Pinocchio, Gap-Tooth Bertha, Casper,

Carrot Top, Mosquito-Bite Tits (my daughter later gifted me with the double-D-licious sisters), and my all-time favorite, "you have a gap between your teeth that a freight train could go through." *Thanks, Mom.*

Then, after living in France for a year and gaining a considerable amount of weight from the scrumptious cuisine, I learned the term *balaise.* Loosely translated, that's French slang for "you have a big gross ass" or "you have an ass like a tame bee" (another thing my mom used to say to me). Predominant butts may be acceptable (and even highly regarded) in this day and age because of the onset of bootyliciousness, but back then, the only descriptive adjective my big fat ass was qualified for was the ever-so-eloquent *balaise.*

Finally, there was the kicker. The one that spoke volumes. The one I never really recovered from.

I was nineteen years old and working in an accounting firm in a building attached to a shopping mall. I went down to get lunch one day and thought I was looking pretty damn great. At the time, I was a size three, with a 22" waist and great calves (they were always my best feature, especially when showcased in the four-inch heels I was wearing that day), and I was wearing my favorite green dress that made my breasts look bigger than the 34Bs they were at the time. Anyway, as I walked through the mall, I heard a shout and a wolf whistle. As human beings, we all turn around when we hear something like that. Well, when I turned, I saw that it had come from a group of about six or seven guys in their twenties, and they all, in unison, recoiled at the sight of my face. They literally recoiled. To a young woman, that overrides any "but *we* think you're beautiful" comments from your parents.

So with the past comments lingering in my psyche (and trust me, that wasn't even a quarter of the things I've been called in my lifetime), I did my best to pull myself together and just be respectable looking. But it was hard because in front of a mirror I have only ever seen the ugly, awkward girl.

Five foot seven, auburn hair, brown eyes, one hundred mumble-mumble pounds, fair skin, straight teeth (but a little too spaced apart for my liking), 36-31-36 (I told you I was carrying pity weight). I was 160 lbs, but no one would have ever guessed it because of my height and how I dressed and carried myself. I wouldn't say that I was overweight, but I was *fluffier* than I would have liked to be.

Although five foot seven is not Amazonian in any way, I've always felt like a big, awkward ogre around other women. They're all cute, petite little things and I sometimes feel like my knuckles drag on the ground. Awesome visual, I'm sure.

As a woman of height, I am also somewhat of a height discriminist. My high-school sweetheart, Matt, was 6'7"—loved it! My first husband, Miguel, was shorter than me and I absolutely HATED it! My second husband, Andrew, was three inches taller than me but, since I spent most of my time in three- to four-inch heels, I was taller than him. So, while man-shopping on the internet, I sought out the vertically gifted men in lieu of the ever-available compact models.

Apparently, though, I'm like crack cocaine for any man *under* five foot eight. Oh geez. I'm sure there are many lovely men of that stature that I was discriminating against, but my self-confidence was already in the basement; I knew that I couldn't handle towering over anyone ever again.

Messages started coming in and I established my first "chat" session with one gentleman. He was from California and thought I was "just gorgeous." We chatted for a while and he came across as being very nice, and I wasn't really intimidated because he was geographically out of the question. He initially contacted me asking if I attended a particular church in my area, as he claimed I was the spitting image of a woman he had met there on a business trip. Ahhh… a church-goer… good start, Veronica. A man of faith and 6'4". But there was the location issue and the fact that I hadn't even seen his photo.

He told me about his past visits to my city and that once he got a little turned around and found himself in the gay district. I *LOL*'d nervously, not knowing what else to write back. He described his misadventure in a little too much detail (including sights and smells) and it left me feeling completely awkward. Not the homosexual content, but the narrow-minded, homophobic comments he made. I was just about to end the conversation when he sent me a few photos of himself. He was not an unsightly man, but the story that had now burned a nasty image into my mind left me spent. He then became quite upset and rude when I wanted to end our conversation.

End scene.

Please, oh Lord…

END SCENE!!!!!

CHAPTER 8
RUTH

A few days later, I received a message with the subject line: *Hi... and... sigh...* The message said, *I read your profile and liked what you had to say, and I love how you write. You have a killer smile and incredible eyes. If I lived closer to your city, I'd kill to take you for a coffee. Good luck in your search. Phil*

Wow. Talk about making a girl smile. No one had ever said anything so sweet to me before. My smile is my least favorite feature, so I was shocked that someone actually found it attractive.

I went to Phil's profile and saw that he hadn't been exaggerating—he lived clear across the country. So he was actually giving me a sincere compliment, then, not just putting the moves on me. I've always felt it's important to give credit where credit is due, so I replied by saying, *Thank you so much for your message. You sincerely made my day.*

I went on to explain that it was my first time on a dating site and admitted that I found the whole process completely overwhelming.

The next day Phil messaged me again, saying that although he was not a serial dater, I could surely knock on his cyber-door if I had any questions. He ended by writing, *You have me at a bit of a disadvantage because I told you my name, but you did not tell me yours. Thusly, since I do not know your name, you shall be known as Beatrice.*

I laughed so hard. It was a feeling that I hadn't known in ages. Seriously, it had been *years* since I allowed myself to laugh.

As I had yet to learn the etiquette of cyber-dating, I was hesitant in giving Phil my name, but seeing as he was in another province and his profile said he was "unwilling to relocate," I figured I was safe from any potential stalking situations such as I'd heard about from my dating mentor, Jessica.

> *Oh Phil. I can honestly say I haven't laughed that hard in years. Thank you so much for that. My name is Veronica, but you may still call me*

Beatrice. Here's a question though. How do I know you're not actually a 250-lb woman named Ruth who is doing "five to ten" in the Arkansas state pen for physically harming the ice cream truck driver who denied you your fudgesicle?

I assure you that I do not have a fudgesicle addiction of any sort, and that my photos are of me. Veronica... I have only ever known of one Veronica in my lifetime...

Phil then proceeded to ramble on with a mini biography of Veronica Lake, the actress for whom I was named. I was impressed with his knowledge of her life and untimely passing and duly informed him that she was my namesake. Phil was slightly embarrassed for shamelessly trotting her out in an effort to impress me with his knowledge.

From that day on, "Ruth" and "Beatrice" were thick as thieves. We were the *Thelma and Louise* of the cyber-world.

Phil became the reason I looked forward to going home each evening. I'd come through the door and kick Daniella off the computer so I could check for messages from my new cyber-buddy. On one occasion, Daniella saw his photo and location and said, "He lives so far away. That's too bad." I asked if she was being sarcastic, but she said she was being sincere and that he looked like a really nice guy.

Phil's blond-and-blue looks were not my cup of tea, though. Growing up, I was in love with many blond men—Timothy Gibbs, Dirk Benedict, Ricky Schroder, the blond *Dukes of Hazzard* brother, Shaun Cassidy, and each member of the band Platinum Blonde—but as an adult, I had only been attracted to men with dark hair and skin. It's not that Phil wasn't a nice-looking man, he just wasn't my type. But then again, what did it matter? We lived on opposite sides of the country and he was nothing more than my very bestest and favorite cyber-buddy.

While we chatted every night, I looked at other profiles; at times, we'd even look at profiles together and mock them relentlessly. I told Phil about the overzealous guy that lived on the second floor of my building—RD 24B (Random Dude from Apartment 24B). RD 24B became obsessed with me and I would find him wandering about in the most random places, trying to get a chance to talk to me. I made damn sure he never found out which unit I lived in. One night while Phil and I were chatting, I got an instant message from someone whose profile photos were of a young man in full army fatigues (yes, even the helmet) standing in what looked like his mom's basement. Before answering him, I looked at his profile—he was twenty and lived in the city where I grew up. I couldn't resist. I answered his hello. He told me he was bored and asked how I was doing. I responded kindly and then he blurted out, I think older chicks are hot! You wanna meet?

I wrote back, *Well, seeing as you are pretty much the same age as my own child, I don't see anything happening between us.* He quickly ended the chat and Phil and I had a good laugh at his expense. The intricacies of online dating were becoming more and more brilliant with each click of my mouse.

I realized that I was also very popular with gorgeous, fit men in their twenties from all over the world (especially Australia); but Phil burst my bubble by informing me that they were scam artists trying to dupe unsuspecting, lonely women. Thanks, Phil. Couldn't he have said, "Of course they fancy you, you're gorgeous and a true catch." Leave it to Phil to smack me back into reality.

The pickins were slim on the site I met Phil on, so I began to investigate others. A Google search provided me with a comprehensive list—some sites I had heard of, others not. What options did I have to choose from to satisfy my dating needs? I'll list a few:

Hot women looking for a sugar daddy: Although the thought of being spoiled and lavished with monetary trinkets would appeal to most, I have never been referred to as "hot," so I'm probably not the arm-candy that the Daddy Warbucks of the cyber-world were looking for. In addition, the thought of doing the horizontal nasty with a rich and wrinkled man named Horace for the sake of a bauble made me throw up a little in my mouth.

Hot women and hot men looking to share their hotness: Again—average woman does not a *hot woman* make.

Computer-generated match-ups: These sites subject you to a litany of questions—they want to know everything from your food preferences to the level of elasticity left in your prettiest pair of panties. On one such site, I was about halfway through the inquisition when it asked for my marital status—*separated*—and I was informed I was not entitled to proceed and duly kicked off the site. I tried again (even using a different email address), but it had my computer's IP address and shook its cyber-finger at me, admonishing me for my perseverance. So much for a free one-month trial.

Free sites… conditionally: You could window-shop as much as you wanted, but the minute that you tried to contact someone—bam! "Credit card, please."

Average people looking for average farm animals: *What? Next!*

Average people looking for average people (paid sites): As I explained earlier, I am too cheap to join those, unless I accidentally send someone a blank postcard and pay for a month's subscription in order to save face.

Average people looking for average people (free sites): Now *there's* my domain! Although every Tom, Dick, Harry, Denise, Jane, and Barb were on these sites (some of whom I actually knew and prayed wouldn't see me), they had the best variety for shopping—the Walmarts of the online dating world, you could say. Sign me up!

CHAPTER 9
SAMANTHA... SAMANTHA?!?!?

I came home one day to a message waiting in my email inbox. Until I logged in to the dating site, I could only see the picture of the sender—it was a woman!

Oh my gawd. What wrong button did I click this time? What list have I gotten myself onto?

I nervously logged in and checked my profile settings to try to figure out what I had done to be of interest to women all of a sudden. When I didn't find anything, I finally read Samantha's message—and breathed a sigh of relief. As it turns out, she'd seen my profile and felt that our personalities were similar, and wanted to know how my search was going. Phew. No need to learn how to write a *Dear Jane* letter today.

Samantha and I quickly became great cyber-buddies and exchanged anecdotes almost daily. She was getting great responses to her profile, but was just as hesitant as I was about taking the plunge and actually meeting anyone in person. Ironically, she lived in the same province as Phil, about three hours from him.

Samantha was a beautiful and classy woman whose marriage had broken down when her husband decided that, even though he was hopelessly in love with her, he needed to "find" himself. She was devastated; she adored him and loved every second of their life together. They didn't have kids, so he was her whole world. He was so guilt-ridden that he gave her the most ridiculous divorce settlement in the hopes that she could live a full life without him. But she didn't want the money; she just wanted him. Then, after two years on her own, she decided that she deserved to be happy. To be with a man who adored her, a man she could also love and adore.

Samantha met a few nice guys and a few... others, and we laughed together about her experiences. One that stands out was her date with "Sebastian the Artist."

> *Oh gawd, Samantha. Let me guess... he forgot his wallet?*

Sebastian the artist didn't forget his wallet, but definitely wouldn't be needing it to take Samantha out again—she was done with him after he made a snubbing comment about her Mercedes. I guess his dreams of romantic nights sharing his bus pass were now dashed. Samantha met two more candidates and then Lawrence came along.

The connection between them was incredible, even before they met—I got goose bumps reading her anecdotes. They talked on the phone for hours every day, and it didn't seem to matter to either of them that he lived six hours away from her, in the United States.

I was so jealous. Happy for her, but so darn jealous. Why couldn't I find my "Lawrence?"

Their romance was so passionate that it made me ache inside. When they finally met, it was like a collision of two planets, and I could feel the shockwave from across the country. They didn't have sex that day, but got to know each other *very* well. She told me that she felt more passion with him than she ever had with anyone before—even her beloved husband. It was on their third meeting that they made love… in every corner of her house… on every piece of furniture… in the woods while walking her dogs… on the deserted beach. Oh gawd, did I ache when I read her stories. He drove to her house every single weekend, and they began to plan their future together.

Lawrence was about to have a major knee operation, so he and Samantha decided that he would live with her so she could help him with his recovery. Samantha didn't need to work because of the very comfortable settlement from her failed marriage, so she could dedicate all her time to being the best Florence Nightingale possible.

It wasn't all a fairy tale romance, though. Samantha admitted that when Lawrence pulled up to her house in a car chock-full of his personal belongings, she felt a sense of suffocation. Samantha dearly loved her privacy and space. But she sloughed off the feelings of doubt to welcome her Prince Charming with open arms.

They say that to truly know a man is to witness how he behaves in times of adversity. Lawrence soon started to show his true (or medication-induced) personality. The strong, optimistic, and driven man had quickly become a whiney, negative, and bitter twit. Samantha continued to write to me almost daily, distraught and at her wit's end about what to do.

Once he recovered enough, they decided (well, Samantha decided) that it was time for some long-overdue alone time, and back Lawrence went to his home across the border. During his recovery period, Samantha had realized that they had very different goals and that he really wasn't the man he sold himself as. So she got back on the dating horse once again. But she was disheartened and also haunted by continued feelings for her ex-husband.

Thankfully, I only experienced this turmoil through her and didn't have it in my own life. With my track record, I probably would have already been married by now.

Oh gawd.

CHAPTER 10
MY BIG PALOOKA

The bond between Phil and me grew daily and my heart started to ache more. I couldn't understand why I couldn't have a man like that in my life. Because he was so far away and not a romantic possibility, I allowed myself to open up to him and speak freely and honestly. He said the most wonderful things to me about how he feels a woman should be treated. His stories painted vivid, romantic images in my mind that left me shaken and in tears—wallowing in my own self-pity, essentially. This just wasn't fair. Where was my local "Phil?"

One day, we made plans to watch a baseball game "together." Unfortunately, I don't think my province has enough baseball fans to make the telecast worth it, so it wasn't broadcast and he had to watch it alone. We decided to meet back online after the game and have a twenty questions date. I went for my usual 7km run while he sat on his couch with a bowl of fatty treats. During my run, I came up with questions for our get-to-know-you session. As I approached the final hill of my trek, a song came on my MP3 player and I thought, *I wonder if I should admit to anyone that this thirty-seven-year-old woman likes The Pussycat Dolls' music?*

When I got back, Phil was already online waiting for me. Without much of a hello, he sent a music file transfer request (we'd never done this before). I stared at the file, stunned, because it was the song I had just been listening to. Then the next two songs were from my favorite artist, and I finally said, *Why did you just send me those?*

His reply was that he didn't mean anything by it and they were just songs he really loved.

Oh my gawd. How could this be? How could we be so much alike?

We began our question-and-answer session, and our similarities became very obvious. I hurt more and more with each one we discovered, with each new way we meshed perfectly together. I had always been cynical when I heard stories of how people "met" and fell in love online, but now I knew it was possible. This was ridiculous; how on earth could I be having these feelings for someone I had never met and could never be in a relationship with? Phil had a career that would not allow him to relocate, and I had a child who I wouldn't dare uproot to follow my heart.

During our chat, I finally had to say it. *I think I'm falling for you, Phil.*

Then we have a huge problem.

My stomach started to do flip-flops and I kicked myself for what was probably going to ruin a wonderful friendship. His response was, *Because I have a HUGE crush on you!* And then he said we needed to meet face to face.

My head was spinning out of control now, so a friend of mine took me out that night to help me drown my sorrows. She urged me to throw caution to the wind and go to him.

Ironically, my co-worker Jessica had asked me the day before if I would ever consider moving to Phil's province. I snorted and replied, "Hell no. I would die with their winters." My only experience with that province was spending one week there with HV 2.0 in the dead of winter. I remember being cold and miserable and an icicle falling on my head.

Phil and I continued to message each other and started to talk on the phone almost daily. We decided to meet. We thought we'd meet in at a neutral location and both fly somewhere new. After looking at all the deals for flights, we realized that it would be cheaper for both of us to meet in Scotland than in Canada. Needless to say, Scotland was a little far off the beaten path, so we decided that I would fly to him for a weekend. Although the fare was a little high, the savings would be the fact that I could stay at his house instead of a hotel. We agreed to share the expense and split the fare in half.

Cue Phil's first meltdown.

Phil's frequent not-so-subtle comments were making it very clear that he envisioned my trip as something that included me with a dozen suitcases, three teetering cat kennels, and my child in my carry-on luggage, all coming to rest in his safe little haven. I didn't want to go there if he was feeling guarded, so I kyboshed the trip. Although I told him that I wasn't going to come see him, our getting-to-know-you talks continued, as did our searches for our respective matches.

Once in a while Phil would turn on his webcam and make funny faces at me, or film the dog; but he said it wasn't fair that I could see him but he couldn't see me. So, after his umpteenth attempt to coerce me into buying a webcam, I finally caved and he saw me for the first time. The look on his face was pretty self-explanatory, and three days after his meltdown (and my subsequent trip cancellation) his first words upon seeing me were, *When are you coming here?*

I took the plunge (again) and decided to fly to meet him for the long weekend at the end of June. By that time, Phil and I would have been communicating for one day short of a month. It felt like we'd known each other for much longer, so visiting him didn't feel like a crazy thing to do.

The weeks before the trip were filled with one meltdown after another—on my part this time. I was exercising, tanning, exercising, exercising, exercising, and exercising. I was still carrying my pity weight, and although Phil was not a Greek Adonis himself, I felt extremely insecure about meeting him.

One night during a phone conversation, the topic of age came up. Phil admitted that the age listed on his profile was slightly off. He was two years older than that, which made him almost ten years older than me. For some reason, the age difference really bothered me; but the lie bothered me more. He explained that his profile was a couple of years old and he had never updated it. I accepted it at the time, but later gave my head a shake when I realized that you enter your year of birth in your profile, and the site updates it automatically. That meant he had lied twice.

Deception aside, I tried to convince myself that the age difference was acceptable. After all, my father was nineteen years older than my mom, and my first husband was eight years older than me. Regardless of how deeply it bothered me, the old Veronica reared her ugly head and started justifying the *buts* again. Might as well just go buy my wedding dress now. Sigh…

As the visit grew nearer, the expectation of intimacy became very clear. I started to melt down even more. I liked Phil a lot, but I didn't know if I was quite there yet. I had never been intimate with anyone I wasn't in love with. I had never been able to even consider kissing anyone I wasn't in love with. Women told me stories of their sexual escapades and I could never relate. I wasn't a prude, I just couldn't imagine sharing myself with someone who I wasn't already planning to marry.

My two cyber-dating coaches, Jessica and Brenda, told me to just do it and stop thinking of it as anything but simply having a good time. It still felt strange… but I remembered an episode of *Seinfeld* in which George decides to do the opposite of everything he would normally do. Being the anti-George proves to be the Midas touch for his life, and the results are amazing. Since they say that life imitates art, I figured I had nothing to lose by trying to be the anti-Veronica.

I kept reminding myself that the way I lived my life before didn't turn out so well, so I needed to put my all into the new and improved Veronica. Shall we call her Beatrice? I started to do a lot of self-talk, a.k.a. coaxing, to convince myself to be intimate with a stranger.

As I got off the plane and walked across the tarmac to the arrival area, my legs were shaking uncontrollably.

What the hell am I doing?

There was no turning back now.

I finally saw him and he wasn't what I had expected. At the beginning of our cyber-relationship, we gave each other many nicknames; my main nickname for Phil was my *Big Palooka*—or *Palook* for short. Although I knew he was 5'10" and almost ten years my senior, he looked so much smaller and older than I expected. *Palook* was larger than life to me, and I was shocked by this normal, average man standing in front of me.

Nonetheless, I fell into his arms, every part of me noticeably trembling. His response to my physical display of affection? "Oh my," and he held me tight. I was so nervous I could barely make eye contact with him for the first few hours.

When we got to his house, his nineteen-year-old son, Jake, was scurrying around getting dressed for a formal dance. He barely paid me any mind at all, as to him (and to all concerned), I was just an old friend coming for a visit.

After Jake left, we went out for a light dinner; when we got back, Phil drew a bath for me (in the infamous soaker tub I had heard about and longed to lounge in) and left me to relax. Afterwards, we spent the evening cuddling on the couch with the dog. Then the inevitable was about to occur as Phil asked if I wanted to "cuddle" upstairs.

To say that it was the most awkward event of my life thus far would be an understatement. I'm not sure if it was my nerves, the fact that this was a life first for me, or a combination of the two, but the encounter was completely "meh" for me. Thoroughly underwhelming. We slept in separate beds that night, which rather shocked me, but I knew that Phil wanted to keep up appearances for his son.

The next morning, we made breakfast together and sat at the kitchen table reading the newspaper. Those were also firsts. A lifelong dream of mine was to be with a man who I could sit and have a morning cup of coffee with;

not one of the men I had ever been with drank coffee. It may sound silly, but it was my dream.

I looked across at Phil and said, "You're just 'Phil,' aren't you?"

Phil didn't put on airs, he was just who he was. He then did the unthinkable… he gave me another dose of reality.

He knew that I was looking to buy a condominium back home and that I'd found one near my work that was soon to be completed. I'd driven past it every day waiting for contact information to be posted so that I could inquire. When I finally called, I was informed that the 1,200-square-foot unit that I was interested in was $500,000. I realized that, although I earned a very good income, I could never afford to buy something on my own.

Phil handed me the local real estate pages and pointed to the back page. They were profiling a one-and-a-half-acre property complete with an average-sized three-bedroom home. Selling price: $125,000. I dissolved into tears and Phil got a look of panic on his face.

"No, no, no! That wasn't the reaction I thought I'd get."

Yet another thing to make me ache to change my life.

Later that day, in the car on our way to go sightseeing, Phil suddenly grabbed my thigh and blurted out, "It's okay, Veronica! We'll be over it soon!" I jumped out of my skin and began to shake uncontrollably because of how he had startled me. Why did he do that? Because I had confided in him about my issue with crossing bridges. If only he'd known that I was feeling so relaxed around him that I hadn't even noticed we were crossing an overpass! Not a bridge. Not the Grand Canyon. Dude was driving on an *overpass* and thought I was going to have a panic attack. Therefore, when we did actually go over a bridge, I had a full-blown meltdown. Thanks Phil. Thanks a lot.

We had a great weekend together (in my eyes at least). It was so normal and so relaxed, although I cried a lot during those few days. Phil treated me like a queen. He didn't do anything over the top to try to impress me; he was just being himself and treating me the way he felt a woman should be treated. I had never experienced that before.

At the airport on the day of my departure, I got the feeling that I'd never see or hear from Phil again. It felt as though he was just being nice and cordial on the weekend, but couldn't wait to have his man-cave to himself again. The flight home was the longest of my life, and I did a lot of thinking about what I had just experienced and where I wanted to go from there.

When I was at his house, I felt an inexplicable peace come over me. At first, I thought it was because of how comfortable the bed was in his spare room, but it was more than that. Once I returned home, I felt as though I had hit an emotional wall.

When Phil sent me a message the day after my return, I was honest with him in stating that I didn't think I'd ever hear from him again. He was shocked at my admission and called me immediately. He explained that his standoffish behavior was the usual wall he kept around him, but claimed that he'd loved having me there. Having a woman in his home was a first for him, and he said that the house didn't feel the same without me in it now.

Phil and I continued to communicate with the same enthusiasm, but I became increasingly lonely, and also increasingly unsettled over whether his feelings towards me were truly sincere. He didn't know that I knew he was surfing the dating sites as we messaged each other at night.

I discussed relocation with Daniella, but she would hear nothing of it. I don't blame her, really. I mean, what thirteen-year-old would want to just up and move to another province? In Daniella's thirteen years, I had moved her twelve times between where we were living now, El Salvador, and neighboring cities once we returned permanently to Canada. She never really got a chance to make long-term friends because we normally lived outside of the community she went to school in.

Although being a mother was such a blessing for me, I really felt as though I dropped the ball and had not given Daniella the healthy, emotionally stable life she deserved.

One night, my situation got the best of me and I lost it completely. I began crying uncontrollably and proceeded to spend three hours locked in my room, sobbing into the phone to Phil. The poor man kept trying to tell me jokes to cheer me up, but I was inconsolable. I came to the realization that, because I made the commitment to be a mother, I had to put my happiness and dreams aside until Daniella grew up and moved out. I had never really allowed myself to live life before; I only ever just existed. So now, as I finally felt I was on the verge of change, I knew I would still have to wait—for the good of my daughter.

Daniella approached me later that night and said that she couldn't stand to see me so upset and that she'd move if that's what I wanted. I told her there was no way I could live with myself if we moved because I had thrown a tantrum. I couldn't do that to her, not after all the negative things she'd been through most of her life.

As for Phil's supposed feelings towards me, he still went on the dating site constantly. To the point where it started to really hurt me.

Although I did not renew my membership on the paid site that Phil was a member of, I could still see when he logged on. I became obsessed with it. I still didn't let on that I knew he was chatting with others on the site while chatting with me on instant messaging.

So I did what any normal and mildly passive-aggressive person would do: I started chatting with other people too. When Phil went away on his annual week-long trip with his buddies, I began my search for the local "Phil" I had always wanted.

CHAPTER 11
MY FAVORITES LIST

My dating mentors, Jessica and Brenda, became very active in pushing me forward to keep going and get back into the dating scene. Brenda knew of my past relationship choices and had made me promise not to marry the first guy I met. So even if I had feelings for Phil, or feelings that I might have feelings, the Brenda-enforced guideline forced me to move on. He was, after all, the first guy I had met.

I put an organized and methodical system into place. After my 4:30 a.m. exercises, I would eat my breakfast and go through the site, bookmarking profiles I wanted to read more closely when I got home that night. My efficiency gave me a rude awakening on one particular occasion, though.

While I was at work one day, I received an email notification saying I had a message from a man I'd bookmarked that very morning (what the site calls putting him on my "Favorites" list.

What are the odds of that? That the same guy I bookmarked this morning would actually take an interest in me.

Although I tried to keep my personal and professional lives separate, I was curious about this guy, so I logged on to take a gander at what he had to say.

"Astronaut" had gentle eyes and what looked like very kissable lips. Although his blond hair and blue eyes were not normally my type, I held strong with my new life approach after being very successful at failing in two marriages: do the opposite! I'd skimmed through his profile that morning, and a couple of things he said caught my eye—thus, the five a.m. bookmarking.

Good morning! I saw that you put me on your favorites list and I must say, I'm very flattered. You have such a great smile and beautiful big brown eyes. The things you wrote in your profile sound like we may have a lot in common. I'd love to chat with you some more if you'd like. Erick

What?

I ran to Jessica's office and started talking a mile a minute.

"Did you know that when you bookmark profiles by putting them on your favorites list, that they can see that you've done it?"

After Jessica picked herself up off the floor from laughing hysterically at my plight, she calmly explained how the site worked. I think I died a little that day. How humiliating.

Mortified, I replied to Erick, confessing what happened and expressing my absolute embarrassment at the situation. Our communications began from there.

We exchanged quite a few messages that day and it all flowed so easily, just like it had with Phil in the past. I'd begun communications with other men where there was just no communicatory "clicking" going on, so I stopped them there.

Communicatory.

Is that even a word?

I have made up many very eloquent words in my lifetime, but that would be a whole other book on *Veronicisms*. Anyhoo (you can blame my mom for *that* one), Erick and I really started to click that day.

A few hours after my first message from Erick, I received notification that a message from a new admirer had arrived.

What the heck? Don't you people work for a living?

What was I getting myself into, chatting with a bunch of men who were probably sitting at home watching soap operas and eating bonbons? The message from "Dublinie" read,

> Hi. I saw your profile and you have a really nice smile. My name is Mick. If you'd like to chat, I'd be honored to hear from you.

Again with the "nice smile" comment… I was sensing a common theme. Maybe I actually wasn't the snaggle-toothed walrus that I saw myself as. Anyhoo, very sweet, but totally not my type. "Dublinie" was not particularly handsome (but I ain't no goddess and his photos were also very poor quality), and his profile was pretty sparse, but I swear I didn't judge him on the fact that he was wearing a kilt in one of the pictures. On the contrary. The fact that he might be wearing a kilt because he's truly Scottish would be a point in his favour. Although Irish is the accent that makes me weak in the knees, Scottish comes in at a close second.

Jessica saw his profile and told me that if I didn't reply to him, she would do it for me. I agreed, but begrudgingly; as I said, his photo didn't appeal to me, and his message and profile were about as passionate and deep as: *Hi my name is Mick. I like toast.*

I duly replied:

> *Thank you so much for your message. How could I not reply to a man who would be "honored" to hear from me? Maybe you could tell me a little bit about Mick?*

I moved here from Ireland when I was fourteen. I have studied martial arts for twenty years. I am in law enforcement.

Hmm. A man of many words, apparently. But let me tell you what I actually read—*My name is Mick. I like toast.*

What the *heck* do you say to that? Ever since Erick's first message that morning, the banter between us was flowing wonderfully; but I couldn't form any words for the toast-eating cop. I tried three times to reply to him, then finally gave up and went home for the evening. Oops. Did I just admit that I was cyber-dating while at work? Um… yeah. When you work fifteen hours a day, you don't feel much guilt in spending a few minutes on yourself. Enough said.

When I got home I started to reply to Mick… for the fourth time. Just as I clicked "send," an instant message window popped up, and it was him. I told him that I had just answered his message and he might want to read it before we continued. Mick and I instant messaged for about four hours, and it definitely brought him up from his initial position of bottom-runner among the men I was communicating with.

I was a little concerned, though, because all he did was laugh. Every bloody thing I said was responded to with "LOL" or "ROTFLMAO." Either I was fricken' hilarious or this dude just did *not* get out much. He finally asked if we could speak live, and said I could call him if I felt uncomfortable about giving him my number.

Now? It was already midnight.

After much coercing (he's a cop, you know… they're trained at that), I finally agreed to call him, but my hands began to shake uncontrollably. Being the smart woman I am, I blocked my number before dialling for two reasons: 1) so that he could not have my number yet; and 2) in case I dialled the wrong number and woke someone up. I *never* call anyone after nine p.m., so this was intimidating to me.

A man answered the phone and I said, "Good evening, Officer Dublinie."

The man on the other end was very rude and proceeded to reprimand me for having the gall to call at such an hour. He went up one side of me and down the other and all I could do was apologize profusely. I could feel my face and ears on fire as I apologized one more time. Just as I was about to hang up, I heard him break in and say, "Veronica. Veronica. It's me, Mick."

I wanted to reach through the phone and throttle him. I was shaking even more now and couldn't believe that someone could do something like that. I couldn't quite recover from that, and it made our conversation a bit strained.

The next morning after finishing my exercises, instead of my usual window-shopping, I sent Mick a message reiterating that he had freaked me out by making me experience one of my biggest fears—calling the wrong number late at night—and that I would one day repay him for it. He replied later that day with an apology, but was still gloating at his trickery.

Mick and Erick and I continued to communicate throughout that entire day. Well… *they* never spoke with each other, but you get what I mean.

Erick and I quickly switched to corresponding via regular email, but then something strange happened. At the bottom of his email, there was a personal motto and the author was listed as E. Wellington. I remember when I first saw his name, I thought, *Wow. I've only ever known one other Erick who spelled his name that way.* Now seeing "E. Wellington," I recognized the last name too.

I promptly responded to his email and finished by asking, Erick, is your ex-wife's name Brianna and your stepdaughter's name Madison? You could almost sense the shock he would feel as he read it.

It turns out that Erick and I had met ten years earlier. HV 2.0 met him and his then-wife at a playground and proceeded to prospect them for the purpose of business, under the guise of becoming friends. We had a wonderful couples' dinner with them at their house and then we were supposed to reciprocate a few weeks later. Things were so bad in my marriage that I backed out at the last minute and we never spoke to them again.

I never liked it when HV 2.0 was nice to people just so that he could rope them into a business venture. Dishonesty is just not what I'm about.

Now the unfortunate thing is that I remember his ex-wife very well—she was lovely and I was looking forward to a true friendship with her—but I couldn't remember a thing about Erick except that he worked in telecommunications.

After four days of chatting online, Erick called and asked how I felt about going for brunch instead of the standard first-meeting coffee date. After all, we had met before and he recalled that we got along swimmingly back then too. I agreed, and we decided to meet for Sunday brunch. Ironically, while I was getting ready for my date with Erick, Mick called. I was pretty sure I knew why he was calling, and it had to do with something that happened the night before.

We had been on the phone for hours, as usual. Despite my initial dry-toast impressions, Mick was growing on me, and I felt safe enough talking to him that I didn't mind sharing my phobias. He, in turn, told me about the demise of his marriage.

After fifteen years of marriage, Mick's wife decided that she wanted to quit her career as a schoolteacher and become a police officer. He supported her completely in her decision and took on as many responsibilities around the house and with their daughter as he could, so that she could focus on her studies. With his support, she passed with flying colors and graduated at the top of her class. They were both so excited for her new career, and she devoted every waking moment to being the best at it. Mick pushed aside the unsettled feelings he was having about her change in personality and chalked it up to just being the learning curve of her new career. He soon discovered that he, too, craved change. Now that she was established in her career, he started following the same path as his beloved wife.

But she wasn't supportive of him like he had been of her. She became distant and he was left with the burden of running his general contracting business, studying, and caring for the house and their seven-year-old daughter. His wife's personality continued to change, but he once again dismissed it as the stresses of her job.

Until one night, when he picked up the phone not knowing she was on the line. She didn't hear him pick up and was in the middle of a very passionate conversation with her police partner… and her lover. Mick's heart fell into his stomach. He said, "How could you?" and slammed the phone. Afterwards, she tried to convince him that he hadn't heard what he heard, but he kicked her out. He later discovered that they had been having an affair for over a year. He was devastated. The two men had become good friends and Mick had welcomed him into his home on countless occasions.

I felt sick for him, but I also felt a strange sense of relief. Maybe because he had been cheated on, he'd never do the same to me. I was now even more excited to meet him.

At one point, he asked me a question that prompted quite a lengthy reply. After I finished my response, I was met with total silence.

"Mick? Mick? Mick? Helloooo? Mick?"

No answer. I hung up, figuring we had gotten disconnected (while I blathered on endlessly), and waited for my phone to ring again. After a few minutes passed, I called him and the line was busy. What the heck? I then deduced that he must have fallen asleep on me.

Great. You see? You talk way too much. I knew that you should have just shut up and listened. When are you ever going to learn?

I awoke the next morning to a message from him apologizing for being such a "goof" (yes, he had fallen asleep) and asking if he had totally ruined his chances with me. Seriously, he had such an adorable voice (especially when his Irish accent came out), how could I possibly be mad? Later, he called to say sorry again, and that's when I lied to him and told him I had a brunch date with a girlfriend (did I mention that I don't like dishonesty?). We agreed to talk later that afternoon when I got back.

As much as lying is a complete no-no in my books, I felt that my lie was justified. First of all, my mentor, Jessica, informed me that the name of the online dating game was that people communicate with multiple cyber-partners simultaneously; therefore, I owed Mick no explanation. Secondly... well, that's all I could come up with. I was too busy trying to convince myself that he was also talking to other people to come up with more excuses.

Back to sweet Erick. I was nervous about meeting him, but it was a good nervous. This was still so very new to me, and he would be my first face-to-face meeting since Phil. When I arrived at the restaurant, I thought he hadn't arrived yet, but one of the servers informed me that there was a gentleman in the restroom. Sure enough, out walked Erick.

Jessica told me it was acceptable to give a polite hug when you first meet someone, so I leaned in for the polite hug. It was like hugging a giant tongue depressor. I could tell he was not expecting the friendly gesture. *Awkward!*

We proceeded to break the cardinal rule of cyber-dating—we talked about our exes. But it didn't feel weird, maybe because of our past, albeit brief, connection.

Throughout the entire meal, I could not stop staring at him. I'd never had such a good-looking guy interested in me before. He had crystal-blue eyes and an obviously amazing physique, judging by the way his T-shirt fit him. I did my level best to ensure that he didn't catch my frequent glances at his pecs and biceps. But those amazing lips, those were the biggest challenge for me. I kept thinking about getting all up in there and kissing the hell out of them. So much so, that I had many moments of not hearing a word he said. Jessica had filled me in on some of the excruciating dating experiences she'd had before she met her boyfriend, Zack, and I had dreaded having a similar fate; but I was definitely enjoying this first date.

Erick was visibly nervous throughout most of it, and even knocked over his entire cup of coffee in my direction. The poor guy was so embarrassed, but thanks to my ninja reflexes, he only splashed my leg a little. We sat and talked for about two hours before deciding to part ways.

We could have stayed there for another couple of hours, but he had to head out to meet his daughter. We talked a bit more in the parking lot and when I went to leave, I leaned in for another polite hug. This time, though, I was met with a long-lasting full-body embrace, which confirmed that yes, he did in fact have a great body. His parting words were, "I really hate to leave and end something so good." All I could think about was how I wished he'd press that amazing body against me again. My mind started to wander to thoughts of him pinning me up against the side of my car and kissing me relentlessly. Then we'd ignore the fact that it was broad daylight and we were in a public parking lot, and we'd grope and fondle each other like…

Whoa! Down, girl! Down!

I told him that "they" say it's best not to have too much of a good thing and I went on my merry way—completely sexually frustrated, but grinning ear to ear all the way home.

CHAPTER 12
MEETING MICK

I went home from my date with Erick and spent the next couple of hours on the phone with Mick. There was something about him that intrigued me, and I really wanted to meet him before I agreed to see Erick again; but he never even hinted at meeting face to face. I conferred with my dating advisor and she told me that I shouldn't spend more than a week chatting with someone before meeting them in person.

Gawd, Mick. Ask me out!

Sunday—nuttin'.

Monday—nope.

Tuesday—nada.

On Wednesday (one week after we first started chatting), I sent him a message and invited him out for a drink after work. I didn't hear back from him until I was already on the bus and almost home. He was in his car on the way home from being in training all day, and had only just then received my message, so we decided to meet for a late dinner at a restaurant near my house.

I arrived first to secure a nice booth by the window so we could chat without being in the main traffic area of the restaurant. As I waited for Mick outside, I saw who I thought was him as he drove through the parking lot and back out onto the street. I was hoping that if it was him, he was just taking another go at finding a parking spot, and wasn't leaving at the sight of me. I was right on both counts. What was the first thing he said to me? "I betcha thought I saw you and ran for the hills." It was a nice ice-breaking comment, and we went inside.

Then he completely caught me off guard. "You lied to me."

"Excuse me?" was my shocked reply, and I could feel my face begin to burn.

"You lied. You told me you were 5'7" and a brunette."

"I *am* 5'7" and I said that I had auburn hair. Check my profile."

Some cop he is—can't even remember the particulars of a perp.

Although the conversation flowed somewhat smoothly, it did feel like I was on trial. He kept giving me "cop-eyes," which made me even more nervous than I was already. I quickly discovered that Mick liked to take every opportunity he could to make a joke at my expense or to make me question something I had said or done. Maybe that was *his* way of pacifying his nerves.

After refusing to allow me to even split the cost of the tab with him, he asked if I wanted to go for a drive. He drove me to a spot with a beautiful view of the city, and we both agreed it was sad that I had never explored such areas of our city before. How ironic that the person who moved to the province so recently knew more about it than the one who was born here.

We returned to the restaurant parking lot and talked until after two in the morning. I was really enjoying my time with him, but as we headed into hour seven of our date, I had to pee so damn badly that I *really* wanted to leave. No. I *needed* to leave. He asked me if he could see me again, that coming Friday, to which I agreed. We parted ways without a hug or kiss, but he did put me in an arm-bar hold at one point. Don't get the wrong idea, though—he wasn't a violent man. He knew I had recently achieved my black belt in tae kwon do, so it was just for fun. I quickly learned that those quirks came often and out of the blue with him.

For the next two days, Mick played on the weaknesses I'd told him about—namely my panic attacks and fear of crowds—and sent me messages in an attempt to make me more nervous about our upcoming date. He made comments about going somewhere where many of his co-workers would be, or insinuated that we'd be doing some sort of physical activity. He knew that I was shy, intimidated by trying a sport that I didn't know how to do and also had trouble being in large crowds, so he was doing his best to freak me out as much as possible. This did not invoke fear in my heart, it only made me more determined to get sweet revenge for the telephone joke.

Any one of my family members or coworkers can confirm that you do not want to be on the receiving end of one of my April Fool's gags. Over the years, I finessed my techniques and became notorious among my friends and family; those closest to me feared for their safety as that dreaded day approached each year. After a certain point I stopped playing tricks altogether, because the paranoia that they put themselves through each year was far more effective than anything I could possibly come up with. So, with a few years' worth of unused pranks in my pocket, Officer Dublinie was about to experience a doozy.

Although one of my talents is using a variety of character voices, I called Brenda at work and asked her for a favour so that there would be no chance of my voice being recognized. Brenda agreed and I proceeded to write the script for the voicemail message she would be leaving on Mick's machine. I knew he was in training all day, so we had the perfect window of opportunity.

> "This message is for Mr. Mick Macintyre. It's Louise Turner from the Telecan Security and Fraud Department again. Mr. Macintyre, this is the third and final message that I will be leaving before taking action against you and disconnecting your telephone services. As previously stated, we have received numerous reports of harassing calls coming from this number and you have until the end of the business day today to return my call. Again, this is Louise Turner of the Telecan Security and Fraud Department. I will be in the office until 5:00 p.m. and can be reached at 777-555-1234. Again, Mr. Macintyre, this will be my final communication with you before initiating legal action against you. I strongly suggest that you return my call."

I only wish I could have heard the actual message, but Brenda can put on the most amazing "don't mess with me" professional voice, so I'm sure it was incredible. She made sure to block her number before calling, because the number I gave her to leave was actually for *Dial-A-Prayer*. I used to call that number every day as a child and would listen to the friendly message that always began with, "Hi, friend. I'm so glad you called..."

I figured Mick would get home, listen to the message, call the number, and realize it was a joke. I guess I overestimated him. Just before I was about to leave work and go home to get ready for our date, Mick called me. He asked how my day had been and what I'd been up to. I told him I had just finished spending about a quarter of a million dollars for the company's new server equipment in Guatemala and was relieved it was all over. He then asked, "Is that all you've been up to? You haven't been playing any tricks on anyone today, have you?"

I said, "Did something happen? I swear I haven't done anything." I made sure to sound sincerely clueless about his accusation.

Apparently, Mr. Super Cop called the phone company directly and asked to speak to Louise Turner of the Security and Fraud Department. After being bounced from person to person for close to half an hour, he was informed that there was no such person nor a department of that name, and was asked what number he was told to call. He gave the number to the customer support representative, who put him on hold for quite a while before returning to the line attempting to stifle her laughter.

"Umm. Mr. Macintyre, we've called that number and, well… Mr. Macintyre, it's for some sort of recorded prayer message. Sir, do you know of anyone that may have wanted to play a prank on you?"

Mick immediately thought of me.

After he told me the story (which I punctuated with intermittent gasps and "Oh my gawd Mick's"), I said, "Do you know what this means?"

"Nooo… what do you mean, do I know what this means?"

"Oh, Mick… what this means is… you really have to be careful of who you play pranks on because it might come back and bite you in the ass!"

"I knew it was you!" he shouted, and started to laugh uncontrollably.

He then informed me that it had hit too close to home because, when his ex-wife moved out, she changed the address on his utility bills and then didn't pay them when they arrived, resulting in both his water and electricity getting shut off. I felt horrible. No, not really. This was by far my best prank ever, and I wondered if there was some way to patent it.

When he picked me up that night, he admitted that it was the best prank ever and said he might want to use it on someone one day. I must admit, I gloated outwardly for the entire evening. I was so proud of myself.

Prior to our date that day, Mick had continued to tease me via text message about what we were going to do that night. Before I left the apartment, though, I told Daniella that I was confident I knew what we were doing for our date, and wrote it on a piece of paper and tucked it into my back pocket to reveal to Mick later. To be honest, though, if I ended up being wrong, I wouldn't have told him about my guess. We arrived at a hotel and he pretended he had reserved us a room, but I didn't let him get a rise out of me. I simply said, "Thank gawd! I'm long overdue for a new bathrobe."

We approached the top of a flight of stairs, and I saw a mat on the floor that had the logo of the comedy club we were going to. Halfway down the stairs, as he began to gloat about surprising me, I said, "Umm, Mick, hold on."

I reached into my pocket and handed him the folded piece of paper that had "Comedy Club" printed on it. He couldn't believe it and searched the rest of my pockets for more guesses. He said that maybe I was the one who should be a police officer. I began to gloat one more time.

It was the worst comedy show either of us had ever seen, complete with a monologue about online dating—*awkward*! Despite our internal squirming, though, it did not mar our enjoyment of each other's company.

We had a bite to eat (and I forced him to let me pay this time), then we went for a drive, and then sat in the car and talked for hours again. He told me that he really liked me and wanted to see more of me. He was such a sincere gentleman, and, although I hadn't even wanted to respond to his initial message, I was game to get to know him more. That's when he leaned in for the first kiss. It was nice and gentle, and I felt a touch of warmth inside. Nothing to write home about (nor steam up the car windows), but it was comforting. We kissed for a while, and it was about one in the morning when he asked if I felt comfortable going to his place because sitting in the car was getting too uncomfortable for him. I agreed and told him that I trusted him, but secretly, I really just had to pee again—my body is not built for these marathon dates. *Damn you, infantile bladder! Damn you!*

Our gentle kissing session escalated into something far more intense in his bedroom. Although I didn't find him physically attractive, there was just something about him. Something that was enough to give me the freedom to make out with him with gusto. I was fuelled by severe sexual frustration, but made sure that my jeans stayed on. My mind was racing during the entire session because I was quite perplexed at my behavior. One minute, I couldn't imagine even kissing a man I wasn't in love with, and now I was ready to tear him apart. I didn't feel anything close to this with Phil. My experience with him was just plain awkward. Maybe the anti-Veronica was stepping into the forefront. As much as my loins ached (okay, so that sounds like some line out of a cheesy romance novel, but it was true), I was able to keep us standing firmly on second base. What I really wanted to do was get right down to business and relieve my pent-up emotions. I think I had achieved the equivalent of "blue balls" by this point. But I held my ground.

At about three a.m., I got a call from Daniella, who had been pacing the apartment and worrying about me because I wasn't answering my cell phone. While we were out, my phone was on vibrate and I thought I'd feel it if it rang; but my jacket pocket was not tight enough against me. Now hours had passed since she first tried calling me, and she was livid.

I told her to go to sleep and assured her that I was fine and had not been chopped into little bits and left in a dumpster somewhere. But I felt horrible. What kind of mother was I for doing that? After some more passionate second-base play, Mick and I fell asleep chatting, and he took me home at about seven that morning.

As we pulled up to my place, I said I had something for him and asked him to wait in the car while I ran in to get it. When I came back with a gift bag, he appeared visibly weirded out that I had bought him a gift after only two dates. His look of relief was obvious when he peeked inside the bag and saw that it was just some homemade chocolate mousse. He'd told me he loved chocolate, so I prepared it as a reward if the date went well (I think we can all agree that it did) and also as a peace offering for my telephone prank. He dug right into it and began to moan with pleasure. Yup… another victim of my amazing chocolate mousse. I was feeling very smug again.

We parted ways and I collapsed into bed to sleep off the sexual aching and general fatigue. I was as giddy as a teenager.

CHAPTER 13
MANAGING THE BUTS

When I woke up from my nap, I took my profile down, as did Mick, and we made the agreement to see each other exclusively. Erick noticed my missing profile and sent me a text message asking if everything was alright and saying he hoped my disappearance was not because of something he'd done. I told him that I'd met someone I wanted to get to know better, thanked him for his time, and wished him well in his search. The day after I met Erick in person, as wonderful as he was, I realized that I just didn't want to get involved with someone with the ex-wife baggage that he was burdened with. It made me very sad to hear that, although Madison was not his biological child, Erick was being forced to pay child support for her in addition to alimony for his ex. Would I be spending my days footing the bill because she was soaking him and living the good life? I had a very uncomplicated separation situation, and didn't want to have to deal with someone else's complicated one.

Jessica was very happy for me when I came in to work that Monday, and she could see how I was beaming from my time with Mick. I was so glad she had bullied me into contacting him.

Mick and I couldn't see each other all that often, but I guess that's a good thing when embarking on a new relationship. I really loved my time with him, even though the majority of it was spent lying and watching TV because he was so exhausted from work. I understood and supported him, and I loved how safe I felt whenever we were together.

One of the biggest commonalities between us was that he also had trust issues. Ever since his wife cheated on him with his friend, he didn't trust anyone anymore. Because of how our similar wounds had bonded us, for the first time in my life I was starting to feel as though I could trust a man. He, on the other hand, had a ways to go. I made a conscious effort to go into our relationship without judging or comparing him to my exes, and let the cards fall where they may.

But it was hard. I asked him one day when he was going to trust me and he said, "It's not you. I swear it's not because of you." I explained to him that *that* was what hurt the most—that he was damning me because of what someone else did to him.

One day I was helping him put away laundry and my Type-A side asked if he'd mind if I organized his closet and drawers a little better—he gave me carte blanche to do so. During my clean up, though, I came across some greeting cards. I'll be honest, I was a very curious soul and still somewhat untrusting, so I read them. They were from women he was involved with after his separation from his wife, women who gushed and gushed and gushed about how wonderful and romantic he was and how much they loved having him in their lives. My hands began to tremble at how much I was invading his privacy, and my stomach lurched when I read those heartfelt messages. All I could think was, *When will I get to meet this man? When will Mick make me swoon like the others?*

Although I enjoyed myself when I was with him, something nagged at me. Why was it that when he kissed me, I felt *nothing*? Do you lose all your endorphins once you turn twenty-five? *Am I dead inside?*

Whatever it was, I came to accept that I would never feel the mind-blowing passion and desire for a man I had felt when I was younger. Sex was sex. What I'm talking about is that deep burning ache that you feel for someone at the beginning of a relationship. You know that feeling you get in every ounce of your being if you have a passing thought about him, or if you hear his name, or his voice? Or the instant electricity that surges through your body when his hand touches your face. I resolved that I was old now and my loins didn't have it in them anymore. Oh well… there's always chocolate, right? *Mmm… chocolate…*

Besides, Mick was weird.

Is that mean to say? No, really, his behavior bewildered me at times. Here's an example.

He called me up one night before heading to bed and asked if I wanted to go out for dinner the following night after he took his daughter back to her mother's. I agreed and made sure to be ready for the time he said he would come pick me up. The time came and went, and I started to get sincerely concerned. I called his house and his cell phone (which he rarely remembered to turn on or even take with him), but I couldn't reach him. Three hours later, I finally reached him on his cell and he chirped, "What's up?"

"What's *up*? I've been waiting three hours for you to come and pick me up! Where are you?"

"I'm out with my buddy Jeff. I was going to call you when I got home to see if you wanted to go for a coffee."

"Well, I was waiting for *you* to pick *me* up for the date that *you* invited me on!"

"When did I say that?"

"Uh, when you called me last night."

"I was half asleep. You should have known better than to believe anything I say when I'm so exhausted."

I was livid and hung up.

It wasn't the only time something like that happened. He would often ask if he could call me on a particular day or time, and then days would go by before I heard from him.

I'm not a hysterical woman, but because of Mick's line of work, I sincerely worried when he didn't call when he said he would. At one point I needed to reach him and left him five voicemail messages in the span of a week. No, I'm not a stalker; Mick was a licensed electrician and owned his own renovation business before he followed his dream of becoming a police officer, and an associate of mine needed work done at two of his restaurants. It would have been easy money, and I was trying to give him first refusal of the gig; but it was very time-sensitive.

Anyhoo, I thought it was the coward's way of dumping someone, so I drove to his house… and felt my stomach lurch at the sight of his car in the driveway. I called his house, but he didn't answer. I almost drove away, but then turned around and marched up to his door to confront him. I rang the doorbell and he answered looking bewildered and surprised.

My first words to him were, "Why did you have to do me that way, Mick? What did I do to deserve that?"

"What are you talking about?"

"Why couldn't you have just been civilized and called or emailed to say that you didn't want to see me anymore?"

"What are you talking about?"

"You told me a week ago that you would call me later that afternoon to make plans, and now it's been a week and you haven't returned any of my calls."

At this, Mick expressed sincere remorse for his behavior, and claimed that he had in no way meant to make me think he wanted to break up with me. He was in a funk because of his depression and his ex-wife, and had just isolated himself from the world. We talked for a couple of hours, and as usual, he made me feel safe and at ease. I had seen his antidepressants sitting out before, so I did believe him; but I have to say, I really hoped he would get over himself soon and stop letting his ex's actions stunt his happiness. I kept pushing these shortcomings into the back of my mind, because in many ways, Mick brought out the best in me. One of those ways was by making me love cooking again.

Being married to HV 2.0 robbed me of my passion for cooking and baking—I would come home from a long day at work to find a ton of dirty dishes in the sink and strewn about the countertop, and the first words out of his mouth would be, "What's for dinner?" I'd have to spend the better part of an hour cleaning up the kitchen before I could even consider starting dinner. I soon hated cooking and stopped doing it altogether.

Mick allowed that passion to flourish in me again. He worked so hard that I enjoyed providing him with a hot meal to come home to. I'd prepare dinner at my place and eat with Daniella (or leave her a portion, depending on what her schedule was), then bring dinner to Mick with one extra portion for freezing. He enjoyed my cooking so much that it gave me incredible pleasure to be able to give that to him.

One day, I planned something extremely special. I had spent the night with him and arranged to take the next day off work. He didn't know about the day off, but we planned to meet back at his house that evening, so he gave me a spare key since I would be getting back there before him. I left his house and parked around the corner, waiting for him to leave. The minute he left, I went back in and began to execute my grand plan.

He wasn't a slovenly man by any means, but his house needed a little TLC because of the long hours he worked. I cleaned it from top to bottom and prepared an amazing meal complete with an expensive bottle of wine I'd bought to complement my culinary masterpiece. Then, the *pièce de résistance…* I'd brought over a package of one hundred tea lights, and put them everywhere. As the time neared his arrival I feverishly lit all of them and lay in wait to see his reaction. I had never done anything like this for anyone before. The entry and front room looked romantic and serene.

When Mick walked through the door, I heard him say, "No way. No way. You have got to be kidding me." I appeared in the doorway of the kitchen and he said, "I can't believe you did this." He walked across the room and kissed me in a way he'd never done before. I knew that I had affected him to his core.

We had an amazing dinner and I spent the evening listening to some of his many hilarious stories about his new career. I loved listening to his stories, and although I hadn't known him that long, I felt so proud of him. After dinner, he asked if we could lie down for a little while to digest before our evening activities and my payment for a job well done. He fell sound asleep and I lay there debating whether or not to wake him and take my payment. Being the lady that I am, I let him sleep. Did it bother me? Yes… yes it did. I was looking forward to the full-meal deal. I never told him how much it hurt me, though, because he woke up in the morning (after I had already left for work), realized what had happened, and expressed so much remorse that I couldn't stay mad. He also made me promise that I would never recreate "The Night of 100 Candles" for any other man.

Even though he helped me renew my passion for cooking, he was also responsible for some major downsides of our relationship. I was working hard at losing weight and getting back into shape, and was finally starting to feel better about my physical self. Then Mick asked me one night if I'd ever considered breast augmentation.

What? Is he serious??

Although that's what I shouted in my head, my answer to him was a simple "No, I'm happy with my double-D cups."

It wasn't just a one-time comment, though; he asked time and time again, to the point where, without telling him, I consulted a plastic surgeon. The doctor thought I was nuts and said I had beautiful breasts that needed, at most, a lift rather than an augmentation. I had always thought about getting a lift done after I was finished having kids, so at least my curiosity about the procedure was taken care of at the same time.

So, five hundred non-refundable dollars and one consultation later, I decided that the surgery's thirteen-thousand-dollar price tag was not for me. But the seed was once again planted that I just wasn't good enough in any man's eyes.

Day after day, Jessica kept telling me to end it because of the turmoil she saw me going through at the hands of Mick's erratic behavior. I kept making excuses because I really enjoyed myself when we were together. But finally one day, after yet another unfulfilled promised left me stood up and worrying he'd been shot, I decided I'd had enough; and the next time he called me, I told him as much.

"Veronica, I've told you before that you can't take stock in things that I say when I'm tired."

"All you ever are is tired. So I'm supposed to just spend my time having zero expectations about a balanced relationship with you?"

"You think our relationship is unbalanced? I thought we have a great time together. I love being with you."

And I loved being with him, but it wasn't enough anymore. I had lately come to realize that the scars Mick's wife had left him with would never heal fully enough for him to let me in.

"We just have to find our groove. You just have to be patient with me."

"I'm sorry, Mick, but I just don't have it in me right now. I'm obviously not ready for this myself."

Is breaking up with someone supposed to be this exhausting?

Mick asked if we could still have a friendship, and in truth I wanted one too; but I didn't initiate any conversations after that, and only politely answered his emails and texts that came every few days.

After ending things with Mick, I was again haunted by my feelings for Phil. I had previously come clean with him about Mick. He said he was happy for me, but our friendship became strained. I told Phil that I realized my thoughts of being in love with him were more that I was falling in love with the *idea* of him. He had certain quirks that I didn't think I could live with, and the distance didn't allow us the opportunity to get to know each other casually anyway. When I was at his place during the summer, I had looked at him and thought, *This man is forty-five years old and set in his ways. Can I truly be happy with him?* A very large shadow of doubt loomed over me. It still loomed now, but I had an inexplicable soft spot for Phil. I also feared that the soft spot was in fact just the old Veronica thinking she was unworthy of true happiness and incapable of living a full life without a man in it.

Phil still tried to talk me into moving to his province—for Daniella and my future, not for a potential relationship with him. Daniella still held her ground and refused to move, but it renewed that consideration in my mind. Our latest home was proving to be a nightmare because we were probably the only two in that building who didn't smoke pot. We were forced to keep all the windows shut because of how constant it was. Also, the kids that Daniella was associating with were beginning to leave a lot to be desired.

It was a very confusing time because of how unhappy I was with my life, so even though I had broken it off with Mick and was trying to distance myself from the friendship he wanted, I called him and asked if I could come over to talk… *as a friend.* I told him about Phil, and the prospect of moving *because* of him, but not *for* him. Since he knew that one of my main drives for moving was that I could not afford a mortgage in my city, Mick told me he could teach me how to get a mortgage in our area and do quite well with what I was earning.

Guess what? Yep, we jumped right into the sack and started seeing each other again.

About a week later, he accused me of lying to him. I was staying over at his place, and Daniella was staying over at a friend's house; but he thought I was lying about her whereabouts. He had always criticized me for leaving her home alone overnight to be able to spend the night with him, and he thought I had left her at home this time too. As it turns out, she *had* gone home shortly after I got to Mick's place, because she couldn't handle how much her friend's parents smoked. But it bothered me that he had no faith in me, and there was something deeper at the root of that. Although I had always justified it in my mind, my leaving Daniella alone didn't sit well with me either.

She's fine. She's thirteen years old and in a secure apartment building across the hall from the building managers. The only time I'm away is when she's asleep, so what's the big deal? I was left alone from the age of ten.

Deep down, I knew that it was a big deal, and I felt like a horrible mother for doing it. So selfish. I realized, once again, that I did not deserve happiness because I had made the commitment to be a mother. I just had to get through the next five to sex… err, *six* years, and then I could start my social life again.

The last straw this time around fell when I was at a birthday party for a co-worker at a restaurant near Mick's place. I looked amazing and was a little sauced up, so I called to see if he was up for a visit so that I could satisfy how completely good I was feeling. He was home alone watching TV but told me that he was too tired. Although I've never been good at initiating intimacy, I tried to beg with a little bit of integrity… and was shut down. He explained that he wouldn't be good company and asked if we could put it off for another night. I agreed but felt completely humiliated. I sent him a message the next day to work out the details and didn't receive a reply for two days.

Our second go at it didn't last as long this time, but it helped me realize something very important—I was not going to settle anymore. No more *buts*. I was not going to be with a man unless he was "the one." This time I opted not to be a coward and broke up with him face-to-face. The whole time I was talking to him, he kept kissing me and stroking my face and telling me that he just needed time. Mick was visibly upset by this break-up, and I left him standing in the doorway in tears. The old Veronica would have melted at the sight of that, but I had to be strong and walk away. I couldn't stay on his emotional roller coaster anymore. There was no room in his life for a woman, because he was still a giant, open, seeping wound from being wronged by his wife. He was choosing not to heal.

I have to admit, though, although Mick's behavior caused me a lot of emotional turmoil, he did help me learn so much about myself. A sweet, sweet man—just not the man for me.

So, to summarize:

Erick—A good-looking, sweet guy with a huge heart, good looking, soft and very likely kissable lips, good looking, and an amazing body, but unfortunately, not-so-amazing baggage. Did I mention that he was good looking? So good looking…

Mick—An honest, faithful, and kind man, but tormented by the wrongdoings of his ex-wife.

Two wonderful men, both a part of my learning curve of who I truly was and how I wanted to live my life.

Phil—I dunno. I really don't know at this point.

CHAPTER 14
TIME TO GET PICKY

Begrudgingly, I continued to spend my evenings window-shopping for the man of my dreams... The One... HV 3.0.

I used to joke that I was married for six years the first time, almost ten the second, and I'd "get an easy fifteen out of the next one."

Although everyone always laughed when I said that, I realized it was not what I wanted. I wanted to spend the rest of my life with one man. I never wanted to get married again, but I did want to share my life with only one man. Phil and I had discussed marriage and children—not with each other, but with a future partner. Would either of us ever want to get married again or have another child? We both believed that if we knew we had found our "the one," and it was important to them, we would take either or both plunges wholeheartedly.

I was still very iffy on the child issue, though. I had purposely had Daniella at a young age and wanted to be done having children by the time I was thirty. I was thirty-seven at this point, and the thought of having another baby really didn't sit well with me. I wanted to be young and vital for my children and grandchildren. Selfishly, I also wanted to be able to have a life with the man of my dreams that did not involve diaper changes and annoying school functions. I'd done my time with the parent advisory boards, baking dozens of cookies, taking other people's snotty-nosed (and I mean literally snotty-nosed) kids on field trips. Blech. I was done with all that.

Now, after spending almost a month back on the dating site since splitting up with Mick, I was becoming increasingly frustrated by the messages I was receiving, so I decided to take a different approach: contact the ones that *I* was interested in. What did I have to lose, right? What's the worst that could happen? They could delete my messages without replying and further slam, trounce, and stomp my self-esteem into the basement. Meh. What the heck. It was worth the risk.

Although I was flattered by seventy-eight-year-old Virgil who felt that I was the love of his life (and he let me know on a daily basis for two weeks until I finally blocked him), and the droves of men under 5'6" who felt they were put on this earth for me, I always wrote back to each and every one saying:

> Thank you for your kind words.
>
> I am, at times, reminded that I am too honest and open; but I choose not to change that part of me. I'm really glad my profile comes across well, because it is definitely a reflection of who I am.
>
> Thank you again for your message and good luck in your search.

For the most part, they responded and thanked *me* for taking the time to respond. Most of them also pointed out that most people would have probably just deleted their message, maybe without even reading it. I couldn't do that to someone. That was just too mean.

Now that it was time for my new plan of attack, I started narrowing down my searches by the following criteria:

Astrological compatibility: Do I believe in this? There's a huge part of me that does, and every astrological personality profile I have ever read has been bang-on with my stubborn Capricorn self; so why not trust that someone, somewhere has figured out which signs are actually compatible? I discovered that I was so not compatible with HV 2.0, but technically should have been compatible with HV 1.0 (a Virgo). Despite my mismatch with HV 1.0, Virgo and Taurus were my new targets.

Height: 5'10" and above. A total non-negotiable now. Although my father was shorter than my mom, I wasn't so accepting. As I mentioned before, when I'm around people who are shorter than me, I feel like an ogre—complete with hunchback and hairy moles on my face. For once, I wanted to feel feminine, petite, and delicate. Definite non-negotiable.

Age: Erick was my age, Mick was six years older, and Phil a full nine years my senior. Nine years was too much. Then again, I guess it might have boiled down to the spirit of the man. But in general, I needed to be more realistic and stick to an age range of two to six years older than me.

Children: The men my age had proven to be very disappointing in the sense that they still wanted more children. At that point, I had pretty much concluded that I was not willing to dust the cobwebs off my uterus, but would consider men who had kids of their own. If their profile stated "Wants more children," I would move on to the next one. "Undecided" could be a possibility, though, because it might mean that they were like me, and didn't want kids but could be convinced if it was really important to the other party; or that they would accept being a stepparent to pre-existing rugrats. The clarification would have to be early on in the communications.

Seeking: My ideal was men seeking a long-term relationship, but I would also accept dating. Jessica advised me to knock my seeking status down to dating because it was less intimidating to men and wouldn't make them think I just wanted an immediate rock on my finger. I agreed, but always gave the long-termers priority.

Distance: Had to be within twenty-five miles if possible. I was probably more flexible on this one than most of the other requirements.

Profile pictures: I fell prey to being sucked into a conversation with a photoless user once before (remember the homophobic Californian?), and couldn't get stuck in that web again (no matter how well the conversation flowed). I spent one marriage repulsed by the sight of my spouse (HV 2.0), so I needed that physical attraction to be there this time. Although I myself have not been bestowed with a face or body that would grace the cover of a fashion magazine, I knew that I needed to feel as though my mate was guy-candy to me.

Body type: I'm not perfect, so anything from average to athletic would be just fine. Within reason, of course—not athletic in the sense of spending six days a week in the gym for hours on end. I wanted to be with someone who liked to be active because I was tired of spending my life on a couch watching endless movies and TV shows. It was another element of the new Veronica that I wanted to explore.

But was I dooming myself to a life of loneliness? Was I going to die alone due to my pickiness? One of Daniella's friends told me once, "Don't worry, Mama… you'll always have me." As sweet as the comment was at the time, I really couldn't imagine the company of that multi-pierced teenage girl being enough for me. Yup… I'm going to die alone.

Now, it was time to start my new approach. I bookmarked all of the eligible bachelors that met my picky criteria and began to wade through their profiles. Some were very brief and to the point, some gave a little too much information, and some just tried way too hard. A select few really intrigued me, though.

CHAPTER 15
THE FREE TOASTER OFFER

There was one little thing I found somewhat intimidating about looking at the men I was interested in: at the bottom of each profile, it stated how many people had that person on their favorites list. I think the highest I myself reached was about thirteen admirers. Most of them were either old or vertically challenged, and the remaining few didn't have photos (and I didn't even want to imagine what they might be doing in their mother's basement while they looked at mine). So what is an average woman to do when she's intrigued by a man who is on fifty to two hundred favorites lists?

Do I just tuck tail and settle on my soul mate, the septuagenarian Virgil? Or do I man up and send a message to this Casanova of the dating world? I decided to take the plunge; but I knew my message had to really stand out. It was like applying for a job—most employers pay little attention to the resume, but a candidate will intrigue them with a strong cover letter. This is what I came up with:

> *Hi there. I just wanted to take a moment to let you know that I was very intrigued by your profile and we seem to have quite a bit in common. Unfortunately though, I am a little perplexed at something I saw, or actually, didn't see in your profile. Don't get me wrong, I find you to be an attractive man, but I have read through your profile three times and cannot find where the free toaster offer is that would justify why you are on so many women's favorites lists.*
>
> *If the toaster offer is still available, I would definitely be interested in taking advantage of it.*

Once my hands stopped shaking (literally), I became pretty darn proud of myself for my unique way of standing out from the rest.

My theory was correct; the strength of a cover letter never fails to get a candidate in the door. I received responses from all five of the toaster messages I sent. It was unanimous—they all loved the approach and were now equally intrigued by me. The conversations began to flow and it looked as though I might not die alone after all.

First there was Drew. He was 5'11", lived just a stone's throw away from me, and had an obviously great physique. He had two children and listed his occupation as Controller. That's a good thing. Smart, strong, and active. We began to have some great chats until he said,

> I get my kids every weekend from Friday to Sunday and they are my life (they are four and six) and I give myself to them exclusively when I am with them. I also like to work out seven days a week for four hours each day. Staying healthy and fit is very important to me.

Wow. What a dedicated man. A devoted father and incredibly committed to staying healthy… but wait. Let's do the math here. I was never good at logic problems, but I think I can figure this one out. If he works Monday to Friday, let's say nine to five, and works out for four hours each day, would that be from four to eight in the morning, or six to ten at night? Or maybe six to eight during both the a.m. and p.m. to break it up a bit? When would he have time to shower me with affection, woo me, and sweep me off my feet? Would I only be able to spend time with him if I doubled as his spotter at the gym? Okay, well at least we'd have weekends together, right? Oh, wait, that won't work either… he's under *parental lockdown* every weekend, remember? Okay, so… why again are you on this site?

Next!

Barry… Magnificent Barry… Beautiful Barry. Great body. A little intimidating really, but we're the anti-Veronica now. You go girl! I'd never been attracted to a man who shaves his head, but it was obvious that he had the potential to have a full head of hair, and I love thick hair. As for the goatee, I can live with it; but I'm concerned that what they say is true: Men with facial hair are hiding behind a mask.

Barry? Are you actually insecure deep down inside? Maybe you were the runt of the litter, and didn't blossom until you were in your twenties; maybe you were the victim of multiple swirlies in school, and have thusly shaved your head so that you can survive a swirly somewhat unscathed.

Yes, these were all scenarios my inner voice considered. I was analyzing too much, I knew that; but remember… no *buts.*

Barry had a twenty-one-year-old-daughter and he loved her dearly, but not in an obsessive way like our friend Drew, the pumped-up accountant. No small children. Yay! Now we're cooking with gas. Barry really made me laugh and he asked if we could meet for coffee that weekend. I was definitely keen to meet him and accepted his invitation. We were going to touch base the following day to nail down a location.

The next day I did not receive a reply to my *Good morning! Hope you have a great day!* message, even though I saw that Barry had been online a couple of times already. Oh well, people get busy. No worries. Another day passed, though, and nothing. On the third day (the day before our date), I went to send him a message and noticed that all of our messages were gone. What does that mean? I still wasn't too familiar with all the nuances of the site, so I searched his screen name. Barry had closed his account that morning. Um… ouch. What the hell does that do for a woman's ego?

I went to my mentor, my sage, my confidant—Jessica. I explained the situation to her and she informed me that it was quite a common phenomenon in the world of cyber-dating.

"People communicate with multiple prospects at the same time and then when they meet someone they are serious about, they hide their profile or close their account altogether if they really feel that they've found *the one.*"

"Why wouldn't he send me a message to tell me, though?"

"Veronica, I keep telling you, you are too damn nice. People aren't like that, especially men. They're cowardly and take the easy way out."

How rude. Fine, I'll move on to Isaac the artist.

Isaac is not like Samantha's artist Sebastian. Isaac's art sells for over a million dollars apiece. When I originally saw his profile, I was not interested in him because he lived about an hour away, and out in the country to boot; but he had a link to his website so I went to see what he was all about. I was blown away by his work. He worked with steel and created the most breathtaking items, so colossal they could only fit in a barn. His creations really impressed me, and I visited the site often to admire the craftsmanship.

Isaac's profile kept catching my eye because he was constantly changing his main picture, so I wouldn't realize it was the same person until I clicked on his actual profile. One day, after admiring his work for quite a while, I decided to follow my motto of, *When someone does something that positively affects you, tell them.* So I sent him a message:

> Hi there. I just wanted to send you a quick note to comment on your artwork. I've gone to your site many times to admire the talent, intricacy and originality of your pieces and I think they are amazing. I see that you no longer have your link listed in your profile, but I did bookmark it to see what future works you had in store. Congratulations to you on the sale of your most recent. Cheers! Veronica

I actually signed my name to that one because I was sincerely just sending him a note to tell him how positively his art affected me. Nothing more. Don't look at me in that tone of voice (another famous Veronicism)… I swear it's true! Isaac wrote back later that day and thanked me for my compliment. He said he'd removed his link because he was concerned that women would be attracted to him for the price tags of his pieces, and he didn't want to attract gold-diggers.

> Hi Isaac. It's truly a shame that you have to hide something that you must be so proud of because of the unwanted attention it might cause. I totally understand though. But I'll be honest with you, I wouldn't be after you for your money—but actually your dog—black Labs are my favorite!

Isaac loved that line and continued to communicate with me. Geesh. My words were like candy for these guys who I would normally be too intimidated to approach. If only I could stay on this side of the screen, I'd have so many fulfilling relationships. Isaac was a nice-looking man (and fit my astrological and height requirements), but our conversations just didn't flow and they soon trailed off to nothing. About a year later I saw a newspaper article about him on his site (yes, I was still going to admire his work), including a photo of him and his obvious significant other. Good for you, Isaac!

Mike was the general manager of a well-known mid-range restaurant chain in the province. From my experience in the restaurant industry, I knew that the coin he'd be pulling down wouldn't be anything to sneer at. He far exceeded my height expectations and was built like a tank. I could see myself cuddled up in his big strong arms eating food that I didn't have to cook while we watched a chick-flick after a long, hard day's work. One of his sorta-kinda *buts* was the distance. It wasn't unreasonable, but wasn't ideal. I decided to just see where it would go.

I loved talking to Mike. He made me laugh so much. Not in an "I'm just a man-child trying to hide behind my humour" kind of way; our conversations just flowed. I could tell that my words had an equally positive affect on Mike, and we decided to meet. He gave me his cell number as well as his work number, and said that if I felt comfortable, I could call him the next day to make arrangements. I replied that I would and started to get those nervous butterflies in my stomach again.

The next morning, I went to the site to wish him a good morning and let him know the approximate time that I would be calling. Mike? Mike? Where did you go? Conversations—gone. Profile—gone. Seriously. What the heck is up with these "toaster" guys?

As much as Jessica tried to convince me that it wasn't *me*, it was just the name of the game, I was still hurt. I was starting to get fed up… and worn down. I was starting to believe I would definitely be dying alone.

A couple of weeks later, though, I had a thought. A thought that would come to haunt me.

What if Mike took his profile down because he felt that I was his soul mate, and he was waiting for my call? And now, weeks later, he would see that I was still on the site and had never contacted him. Did I drop the ball? Did I miss out on the man of my dreams because of a misunderstanding? Did I squelch his self-esteem so much that he didn't have the confidence to repost his profile?

It was too late now, because I'd already discarded his numbers. I guess it just wasn't meant to be.

Well, on to Scott, the fifth of the "toasters." Scott is a cool name, a name that only hot guys ever have. He was no different; he had a crotch-rocket (a racing bike) and was tall, dark, and handsome. I have always been anti-motorcycles, but seriously, when a guy *that* hot shows interest in a Plain Jane like me… you gotta look into it.

The conversations with Scott were easy, and he was very enthusiastic. But I couldn't quite match that enthusiasm; he was doing most of the work, and we both knew it. I don't know why my aversion to motorcycles caused me to shut down so quickly. My theory is that I was either scared I might eventually lose him to an accident, or I subconsciously felt that he was just too cool to want someone like me in his life. Whatever it was, I was struggling with fully letting myself go.

As hot and cool as Scott initially seemed, he too had a *but.* He had recently decided to return to school. It was a four-year program and he was extremely excited about this new chapter in his life. His life as a nurse. Although I've always been one to sniggle at the thought of a male nurse, I was still excited for him. What I was not excited about was the prospect of dating a broke student. It's not that I was looking for a Sugar Daddy, but I wanted… no, I *needed* to be with a man who could stand on his own two feet financially. Although Scott did his very best to convince me that we should meet, I thanked him for his time and went on my lonely way.

That would mark the end of the five toasters. My strategy to stand out from the rest had yielded results, but it just wasn't the right formula for the moment.

Dying Alone: The Saga Continues.

CHAPTER 16
LIFE CHANGES

It was the end of October now; sixteen months had passed since my separation from HV 2.0, and five months since I first started communicating with Phil. My break-up with Mick and my subsequent toaster experiment had made me realize that I still had many emotional scars in need of healing before I could successfully be in a relationship again. It wasn't fair to subject anyone else to my knee-jerk reactions. Until I could figure out how to curb my untrusting nature and feelings of inadequacy, I resolved that I should probably just follow Jessica's advice: invest in a "toy" and keep an eye out for sales on batteries. It was a world I'd never delved into before, but maybe it was of value at this juncture in my life. Who needs a man when you have the Energizer Bunny?

I continued my friendship with Phil, and I'd be lying if I said there wasn't still an ache inside me over the *what if* of our relationship that could never be. Phil proved to be a good friend, but my misery and loneliness continued to consume me, more and more each day.

Maybe I would just let Random Dude from Apartment 24B woo me. I had turned him down gently one day when he cornered me after I got back from a 25km run/walk. (What a great time to ask me on a date—when I'm all sweaty and gross.) But if he wanted to dine with me when I looked like *that*, maybe he'd give me a second chance. Ugh… romance in the ghetto. I think I'll pass. Sorry RD 24B.

Then one day Daniella shook me to the core. I came home from work and she said, "Let's do it. Let's just move away." I was completely shocked and speechless—and scared. I guess Daniella had finally seen the direction that her friends were heading in and realized what a dead-end life we were living.

I called Phil and gave him the news. He was completely ecstatic, and we began to plan. Although I was not moving to the other side of the country for Phil, there was still that nagging *something* in my head that got my hopes up a little. I was in the middle of renovating and moving my company's office, and silently vowed to see the company through that before I left. Daniella and I decided that we would move during spring break, so at the beginning of December, I took a preview trip to our future hometown to meet with recruiters and look at houses.

When I arrived at the airport, Phil was waiting at the carousel for me, and the look on his face made me feel as though he really did have feelings for me. I know that I looked pretty damn good too—I was down fifteen pounds from the first time we met and was also having a bloody-good hair day. I felt a wave of emotion come over me as he wrapped his arms around me.

Oh my gawd. I really do think I'm in love with this man.

Enter the confusion once again. *Oh cripes! Back on this damn roller coaster.*

The week was wonderful. Phil was his usual sweet self and I felt like I was home. I made dinners for us and his sons and it felt like one big family. Even his dog loved me and one of his sons confirmed that she normally never acted that way towards people… *especially* women.

But… oh, there was the *but.* Phil and I shared his bed that week—platonically. That confused the hell out of me. He was passionate at the airport and then we had a very satisfying encounter after my bath—an encounter that left me looking forward to a week of further perks. Then he acted like my buddy for the rest of the week that I was there. I didn't ask him about it, but I was completely confused. And that wasn't even the big *but*!

The big *but* happened one morning when I woke up to find him gone. I lay awake waiting to hear some noises to indicate his whereabouts, but the house was silent. I went into the spare bedroom where my luggage was, and he was in there on his computer. When I wished him a good morning, he shot up from his chair and almost lunged toward me. His abrupt reaction is the only reason my eyes darted to the computer screen for a split second. He snapped at me and shooed me out of the room. What was he doing? He was on a dating site. The way he reacted made me realize that the *buts* were really starting to mount with him.

During that week, I also got to meet Samantha face-to-face. I took a nauseating two-hour bus ride to meet her for lunch at a great little shi-shi foo-foo restaurant. We talked for hours and it was like we'd known each other our entire lives. We laughed and we cried, and I was so looking forward to having this wonderful relationship upon my actual move. She lived about three hours away from Phil, but it was apparently a beautiful area on a lake, and we talked about the weekends that Daniella and I could come up and spend with her and her two chocolate Labs. My future was really starting to come together.

The flight back home was a torturous one, because my mind was racing about everything and anything. Although there were so many *buts* about Phil, I kept ignoring them in the hopes that he'd just accept me as the one and only woman in his life. I was, once again, working towards sacrificing myself in order to become someone that I wasn't.

But I couldn't do that anymore. During those five hours on the plane, I came to realize that Phil and I would never be a couple. I finally realized, without a doubt, that I was only in love with the *idea* of him.

The realization that, despite all of these emotions, the move was the right thing to do came when my plane landed and I discovered that home was no longer home to me. I stepped out of the airport and unexpectedly blurted these fateful words out loud: "Aww f—!" I was so done with this place.

Even though I made my decision about my future with Phil on the plane, my loneliness and fear of the unknown kept drawing me back to that same emotional place with him. As the days passed, and he was obviously still very actively dating, I became bitter again. So I decided to get out of my funk by taking action of my own. I changed my dating profile to use his postal code (it was the only geographical point of reference I had for the area) and took a look at what guy-candy his city had to offer.

Apparently, I was candy for the men of his city; the responses I received were overwhelming. I can't really explain how I felt, but I was surely feeling a little more validated than before. The messages from definite non-candidates were dealt the usual copy and paste *thank you blah, blah, blah*, but there were some that got my attention.

One of those was Max. Max was a chef and father of two, with a pretty uncomplicated divorce situation. Although his kids were younger than I wanted to deal with, he seemed to have things under control. I explained to Max that I didn't actually live in his city, but that I was moving there in April of the following year—he was willing to wait and get to know me more cyberly.

We took the plunge and spoke on the phone, but it didn't flow as well as our written messages had. Then the *but* came up. Max was a smoker. Ugh. I had forgotten to put that on my list of non-negotiables. Of course, he claimed that he could quit for me, but I explained to him that he had to quit for *him*.

Max even proposed that he fly to my city and drive over with me when I moved. As sweet as the offer was, I told him, "Max, you're a parent. So you can probably agree that me explaining to my teenage daughter that I will be driving across the country with a complete stranger, would not be the most stellar example of good parenting." He realized how creepy it sounded and dropped the topic. Smoker man. Ugh. This was not going to work for me. Time to wean him and wave goodbye.

Duane, Duane, Duane. Seriously… who really spells their name that way? But I couldn't use that as a *but*, as that was his parents' fault. Duane was not an unfortunate-looking man, but not one that I looked at and uttered the phrase, "Mmm, now *that's* what I'm talkin' about!" His photos suggested that his fashion sense was similar to that of HV 2.0; but that is something we could work on together. We could eventually abolish his "mom" jeans.

Duane was very enthusiastic about me, and I was very optimistic about him too (especially since his baggage was acceptable and he claimed to be financially on track in his life). He lived about an hour from Phil, but Phil's area was not the be-all-end-all of locations, so I was flexible. I decided to take that plunge and talk to Duane live, because I was really enjoying our cyber-clickage.

Then I heard his voice. Sigh… I don't think I mentioned that looks come third to an amazing voice and great hands for me. Unfortunately, Duane's voice suited his name. It was a nasally whine, and I really had to think about whether I could spend the next fifty years listening to that.

I soon began to daydream about having a freak kitchen-utensil accident whereby both of my eardrums were punctured by two flying shards from a broken wooden spoon during an enthusiastic sautéing session. The odds of that were slim, but I was trying to be flexible. Trying to be accepting. Trying to ignore a *but.*

Although Duane was doing his very best to convince me to move into his basement suite rental (and he was already starting a collection of tree ornaments for my first Christmas there, since he knew that I had just donated my tree and all of its ornaments to a less privileged family), it was time to wish him well and focus on my move.

Oh, hello… Who the heck is that gorgeous man?

CHAPTER 17
BRANDEN

"Outdoorsie" caught my eye and I found myself going to his page just to stare at his photos. He met so many of the requirements that were on my newly created list. But would Pretty Boy talk to Plain Girl? I doubted it, but I read his profile anyway, and it went something like this:

> Good day! The complexity of compatibility between men and women is very well-known in society, and dating profiles are really just a formation of pixels on a computer monitor. I hope you will take a few minutes to complete my survey. It will surely help give you an idea of whether or not we could be compatible. (FDA and PETA approved, no humans or animals were harmed in the creation and testing of this survey.)
>
> * NOTE * Before you spend time taking the following survey, I would be remiss if I did not mention a reality check of the most unromantic kind: I love the area I live and work in, and have multiple family commitments close by; so if your postal code is further than 40km from mine (and you are not willing to relocate), then we are not likely to be a match. This, unfortunately, is a non-negotiable for me and will probably save a handful of you time by exiting out of my profile now.
>
> If you:
>
> - think the best things in life are free: add 35 pts
> - have ever been caught shoplifting: deduct 12 pts
> - find men who are handy a turn-on: +15

- loathe cooking: -30
- smoke: -20 (and just stop taking the survey altogether)
- view getting a full body massage as foreplay: +15
- view getting a full body massage while talking, watching TV, or listening to music, is a favourite treat: +30
- enjoy taking drives with no set destination: +10
- have enjoyed taking drives over previous partners: -25
- have a temper: -15
- enjoy angry make-up sex: +15
- enjoy nature and outdoor activities: +30
- were able to return previously shoplifted items without being caught: +10
- have a high sex drive: +35
- lose your communication skills when you're upset: -20
- have ever posed nude: +15 (but mail me the photos, and I will ensure they don't fall into the wrong hands)
- can name two brands of camping equipment: +10
- love to kiss: +40
- are guilty of spontaneous gestures of affection: +35
- are overcome by lustful urges towards strangers at a bar: -15
- know what an "Eskimo Roll" is: +10
- can demonstrate an "Eskimo Roll": +50
- are comfortable wearing a bikini: +20
- are comfortable sunbathing topless: +30
- enjoy a variety sports: +10
- like kids, but are not interested in having more: +25

If you have scored above a hundred, and think that we might be compatible, then I look forward to hearing from you. Please also note that I do not reply to "winks"— you need to actually send me a message to express your interest.

I laughed so hard at his profile and was drawn to him even more. I knew full well that Pretty Boy was out of my league, but I answered him back just the same.

I've always lived by the philosophy that if someone affects your life in a positive way, you should let them know. Well, your profile really made my day. LOL Although I scored a strong 200 on your quiz, I don't actually live in your area to demonstrate an Eskimo Roll (which I am fully aware is not a type of Sushi).

I currently live in another province, but am moving to your area in April. Again, I just wanted to say a quick hello and tell you that your words really made me laugh. A nice breath of fresh air.

Good luck in your search. Veronica

Apparently, it is true that trying too hard only drives people away, because whenever I didn't try at all or express any desire for a connection, the men flocked to me (like moths to an aloof, uninterested flame). I was confident that had I expressed interest, they wouldn't have given me the time of day. I guess I know how to subtly stroke a man's ego and make him wonder if he would be good enough for me to be interested in. Yes, Branden was good enough; yes, he wrote back to me; and yes, I had to look up what an Eskimo Roll was.

Talking to Branden was like talking to someone I'd known my entire life. He took his profile down and committed himself to getting to know me better. I was flabbergasted and overwhelmed and flattered and giddy. *Pretty Boy likes Plain Girl. Pretty Boy likes Plain Girl!*

Branden was a chiropractor with his own practice, and had also written a highly respected book in his field. I'm sure it was impressive in the chiro community, but it was definitely way over my head; I was just excited about a lifetime of free back adjustments.

Free or not, I just hope he's not a "bone cruncher." That would be bad.

Anyhoo, Branden had two children (Chelsea, 6; and Adam, 8) who lived with their mother about forty-five minutes away from him. His practice was a few minutes from his house, which is why his profile emphasized conflict for anyone who didn't want to relocate to his area.

Branden's ex-wife was apparently a nag. He claimed that he could never do anything right in her eyes. He told me about the time that he hung the Christmas lights on the house while the temperature dipped below minus twenty-five degrees. What did she say when he came back in from hours in the cold? "I'm so sick of those lights. Why can't we get new ones like the other neighbors have? It's so embarrassing." She craved a world of materialism that he could not provide and that did not interest him. So she started surfing for a new mate and was cyber-dating while he was at work every day. One of the biggest problems between them was that she couldn't handle his insatiable sexual appetite (all I could think was, *Bring it on, soldier!).*

We were cyberly inseparable over the next few weeks and spent hours on the phone together every night. Every time I saw him on webcam, I got butterflies in my stomach and feelings in other areas that I hadn't felt in a long time. I was hooked for sure.

I told him that if he was half as perfect in person, then I would know I had met my "the one." I could talk like that with Branden, and he spoke the same way towards me. We talked about our future together every day. Although his voice didn't match his face in the way I'd hoped it would (something deep and smouldering would have been nice), I could definitely live with it for the next fifty years. Was there a *but*? Nothing that I could really pinpoint since I had never actually met the man. I was on the express train to Loveville and I began to ache to meet him in person. During one conversation, he said he wasn't sure he could wait that long to meet me. Four months was a long time for him to put his life on hold on the off chance that we might be a match.

Wait… that sounded really cold. I don't remember exactly how he said it, but it sounded way more eloquent than how I said it here. So with that, I made the decision to leave earlier than our previously planned spring break departure so I wouldn't risk losing him. When I initially decided that Daniella and I would leave on the first of February, it was for purely selfish reasons—the main one, of course, being a certain six-foot-four chiropractor—but also because I was reaching my breaking point with my job and couldn't get out of there soon enough. I then discovered the schools in that province are on semester schedules and would actually begin on the first of February. *Perfect.* A perfect—and valid—excuse for uprooting us three months early. Now, to find a place to live.

CHAPTER 18
THE MOVE

Now that I'd committed to moving up our departure date by three months, I needed to find us a place to live. The search was daunting because I didn't know the areas at all and I couldn't seem to find any good listings for the areas Phil told me to target. Phil would do drive-bys of rental houses for me whenever I found one in his local online paper, and before he knew about Branden, I asked his opinion of the city that Branden lives in. He said it was a great area and that I should go for it if I found something good.

On the day of my 38th birthday I found an amazing rental property, but it confused me. The ad stated that it was in Branden's community, but the postal code indicated a totally different area. I sent the address to Phil and he duly went on his customary drive-by. A little later in the day, he asked me to call him. That wasn't like Phil. We mainly communicated by text, instant message, or email—this must be important. When I reached him, he asked "Was the address 386 or 836?" Phil was aware that I had a slight form of Dyslexia that caused me to frequently transpose numbers, so he thought maybe I'd confused the street number. I confirmed that it was 386.

"Holy shit, Beatrice! You've gotta go for this place. I went to 836 and it had a car on blocks out front, but 386 is a gorgeous new high-rise downtown. You've got to jump on this place!"

I got so excited that I replied to the ad immediately even though I found it a very odd listing.

Although the photos looked like something out of a magazine, the content of the ad made me scratch my head. The owner claimed to be a pastor who was on a missionary trip abroad, but his Irish-sounding name did not match up with the broken English that the ad was written in. Suspicious, I contacted *Pastor McMurphy* to ask for a time that Phil could meet someone to see it. The good pastor informed me that I just needed to send him two hundred dollars and I could have the keys.

Sigh… a scam. Ugh! Was I ever going to find something?

A few days later, I found a listing in Branden's area, so I asked him how he felt about me living four minutes from him if things didn't work out between us. He said he knew things *would* work out, and to have me so close would be an absolute blessing. Seriously... how could a woman's heart *not* melt at hearing something like that?

Since this place wasn't near Phil's house, I enlisted Branden's help, and he met with the owner of the basement suite. I trusted his judgment, and told him he could put a deposit down if he felt it was suitable. Apparently, he did, and I officially had a place to live. That same day, I had a nice long talk on the phone with the owner, Patricia.

Patricia was in her fifties, twice divorced, and now in a relationship with a man who she met... wait for it... on the internet! She had a grown son who was a chef, but had lost her daughter to cancer when she was nine. She seemed like a very nice woman and was touched by my story of new beginnings. We talked (and cried) together for a couple of hours before hanging up. About an hour after our conversation, Patricia called me back and said, "I'm sorry, I can't let you live in my basement with your teenage daughter."

My heart sunk... now I would have to begin the search again.

"After what your daughter has been through, I can't let her live in those conditions. So you two are going to come and live upstairs with me!"

I was floored. I was speechless. I was a coward and said yes. Although her home was beautiful and clean, I did not want to live with a roommate. But I've never been good at saying no, or dealing with conflict, so I agreed and justified it with the fact that I wouldn't have to invest in furniture just yet. Besides... I *knew* that we'd be living with Branden in the very near future, so this was a more economical "do-for-now" solution. I was excited about my future with my "the one," and couldn't believe I'd had to fly across the country to finally find him.

Soon after our housing situation was solved, Branden gave me an ultimatum of sorts. He knew about Phil and our past and wasn't happy about it. He felt that Phil had ulterior motives and told me outright that he didn't think he could accept Phil in my life. We talked extensively about it, and I put up many arguments to defend my position. Branden had a way of breaking down situations so that they made sense and appealed to my love of logical thinking; and I couldn't deny that, were the shoe on the other foot, I wouldn't be able to handle a situation like this either. I did some deep soul searching and sat down to write Phil an email.

Dear Phil,

First off, I want to thank you for changing my life. Little did I know what sort of life could be out there for me and Daniella to live. Regardless of how our relationship began, and has played out, you have been such a wonderful friend through all of it.

I have been corresponding for over three weeks now with a man I met online, Branden. My look-see on the site was, at the time, solely out of curiosity and with zero intention of contacting anyone. I had not planned to think about dating again until I was settled in town; after all, my timeframe was still aimed at mid-April and it would have been unreasonable to think that I had time to redirect my focus onto that and also unreasonable to string someone(s) along for that long. The reason that I did not tell you about him was that: 1) It could prove to be hurtful to you; 2) It is my private life; and 3) I have yet to meet the man and, as we both know, there are no guarantees.

The past few weeks that Branden and I have been communicating consist of hours upon hours of daily phone calls in order to get to know each other. It isn't just banter and casual conversation, but very deep and thorough talks in an effort to get to know each other as best as possible. The majority of the probing and learning is led by him as he does his best to learn everything he possibly can about me and my past. It is pretty clear to both of us that we are each other's "the one." But also, I am realistic (as is he) and neither of us want to make any bold statements until we meet in person. The level of communication that I am able to have with him on paper or on the phone is something that I've never experienced before in any relationship (cyber or "real"). Ironically, though, this time it is me who is guarding my heart; but his intentions for our future together are very clear. A future that I am very excited at being a part of.

Writing this to you makes me feel as though I am being very hurtful, but unfortunately, I have to be detailed so that you understand the motives of what I am about to say.

You know how special you have become to me over the past few months, but I also don't know whether or not you are really able to be an unconditional friend because of our past. I believe that I have been nothing but supportive of you finding your "the one," (e.g.: the old flame that cropped up, or going onto more in-depth dating sites), but I don't know if you could be supportive that way to me.

It is very clear to Branden what my feelings are for him, and he no longer has worries of my possible wavering devotion, but he is not comfortable with a friendship between you and me. You can call it insecurity on his part, but I don't think many people would be comfortable with the situation. You and I discussed this before. What would we do if one of us found our soul mate, and that person could not accept our friendship? We agreed that, if we were such true and sincere friends, we would have to accept the other person's decision, wish them well, and go our separate ways.

Thank you again for everything that you've been to me, and I hope that you can understand and accept that I have to do this for the sake of nurturing my relationship with Branden.

Much Love—Veronica

After receiving the email, Phil called me, argued his case, and was crushed that I was firm in my decision to stop all contact with him. Branden was shocked and floored that I did what I did, and became even more excited to meet me after seeing the commitment I was already making to him.

During my transition period, Branden continued to be my rock and voice of reason. I couldn't believe I had such an amazing man in my future. One of the biggest hurdles that he helped me through was my job. On January 3, 2008, I sat down with our company's CEO and told him that I was moving. The company was in a very shaky state and couldn't afford to lose me financially or emotionally, so I made him a proposal. I said that I would stay on as the office manager, but from our site office (which was in my new province). I could perform eighty-five percent of my job remotely, and my assistant would be my *body* when I was gone. He agreed that it was a great idea and I continued planning my departure for the next month.

Three days after our discussion, the CEO entered my office, shut my door, and slumped into the chair across from me. With an ashen face, he informed me that I must hand in my resignation effective January 31. He said that they would keep me on full-time contract for two months, and then one month half-time. He offered no explanation, but said I would get to keep my laptop after the contract was complete. I was in shock. I knew the company was in a transitional state, but I hadn't realized it was that bad. It was only later that evening, while talking to Branden, that I had my "aha" moment. Our bonuses were going to be agreed upon on February 8. Mine was to be twenty-five thousand dollars. That money was my moving money and I was banking on it. I came to the realization that our vice-president of Human Resources (the department *I* created) was doing his best to look good and save the company a handful of dough. He'd done this before. If I had just stuck with my original plan to move in April, I wouldn't have cost myself my nest egg—my moving money and the starter for a down payment on a house. I was so mad at myself and completely devastated; and I couldn't recover from the betrayal.

It was Branden who lovingly made me realize that we are all just numbers, no matter how much blood, sweat, and tears we give to a company. He opened my eyes to the truth of the world, and I felt like a changed woman after that. Although I was twenty-five thousand dollars poorer, I was grateful for him; it was one more reason that I couldn't wait to start our new life together.

Two weeks before our departure, I contacted HV 2.0 and asked him to meet me at the court house to sign our divorce documents. Why did I cave and do all the work for the lazy weasel? Because I didn't want any future ramifications once I left the province.

When we met at the courts I made sure to look amazing. I was down thirty pounds from the last time he saw me and was wearing slacks and a sweater that completely emphasized my bangin' hot new body. Did he notice? Oh, yes siree Bob, he noticed. Outside of his comment of "Have you lost weight?" I could see the look on his face. He definitely wanted a piece.

After the papers were signed, stamped, paid for, and in the safe hands of the clerk, I informed him that Daniella and I were moving away. He was shocked and made it very clear how upset he was that I hadn't told him earlier.

"Andrew, I haven't heard from you in almost a year, so why are you acting so wounded? You have absolutely no involvement in Daniella's life, and you don't contribute a dime—even though you are legally her father—so what do you care? Really, why the hell would I think that you cared?"

Needless to say, Captain Victimo could not formulate an argument for being completely pathetic, as usual. Almost a decade wasted with that idiot. I still couldn't stand to look at him because the face that I once found so handsome only had a permanent look of whine on it. Done, done, done! Goodbye, Professor Whineypants.

Captain Victimo vs. Professor Whineypants. I think I should write a graphic novel about those two characters. Hmm… what would their super powers be? Captain Victimo's cape would be made from a petal-pink baby blanket and he'd have lightning-fast responsibility-avoiding reflexes. Professor Whineypants would be perpetually sucking on a candy soother that hung around his neck and plotting his world domination by creating a potion that would turn anyone into a diaper-bound crybaby after one sip. They'd make a movie out of it and it would be bigger than the *Spy Kids* series. Who would play these characters? I adore Giovanni Ribisi, so I wouldn't want to insult him by throwing his name out there to play Professor Whineypants. I just think he'd completely embrace the necessary personality spectrum of crazy professor all the way to whiney, snivelling twit. As for Captain Victimo, that's a tough one. Maybe Jack Black or George from *Seinfeld.* I'll have to think about that one for a while.

Did I just go on a tangent? Sorry, I don't think I mentioned that I am, at times, completely distracted by my vivid imagination. As I was saying…

Moving day arrived, and the silence between Phil and me hurt my heart. It just didn't feel right not being able to share all of this with him, since he was ultimately the reason all of this had come to pass. Regardless, Daniella and I sold (or donated) all of our material trappings, packed our suitcases (and the cat), and headed off on our new adventure… our new life.

We arrived to the worst snow storm that the province had seen in decades, and it took us an hour and a half for a taxi to come and get us at the airport. I have to admit, though, that the drive was beautiful. Everything looked so peaceful underneath a thick blanket of snow. It definitely wasn't how I remembered it from years before with HV 2.0. I missed Phil already, and sent him a text to tell him we'd arrived. Needless to say, I didn't receive a response.

We pulled up to our new home, shell-shocked and tired, and all I could think about was that Branden was only four minutes away but I wasn't going to see him until the next day. I felt so impatient and so excited to finally be with him, and we decided we would meet in a little coffee shop at the strip mall at the end of my street.

The next day, I nervously trudged through the knee-deep snow to the coffee shop. He wasn't there yet, so I went to the washroom to make sure that the snow storm hadn't wreaked havoc on my hair. When I came out from the back of the store, he was there—he was so much taller than I imagined, and he dressed less stylish than I imagined too. He turned around to face me and I thought, *Oh... really?* He wasn't the smoulderingly hot guy on the video camera—the one whose looks caused my own daughter to say, "Holy crap. He's hot!" He was plain... kinda dorky-looking, actually. Oh well... he had won my heart when the physical was not an option, so he must be the one.

It was awkward but comfortable being with him. After about half an hour, he leaned over, in this public place, and kissed me like I'd never been kissed before. I melted. Wow. Forget the bushy, unkempt eyebrows and the mismatched outfit... wow... wow... wow. I think he just blew my socks right across the room. Apparently, I'm *not* dead inside. After a couple of hours at the coffee shop we moved our conversation to his car. In mid-sentence he stopped me and said, "I'm sorry, but I *must* feel your skin on mine." He took my hand and placed it on his warm stomach and then kissed me—kissed me hard and long. We made out like teenagers for about an hour until we were both ready to explode. He had to leave, though. He had to pick up his daughter for skating lessons. I walked... no, I floated back home, aching to feel his touch again.

As the days went on, the physical passion between Branden and me was undeniable. It was now clear that endorphins don't die when you get older—you just have to be with someone that can stir them in you. My, oh my, was I ever stirred. My sexual hunger for him was insatiable, but something was nagging me about him; something wasn't quite right. I kept sloughing it off as just the getting-to-know-you phase, but talked to Samantha about it all the same. Branden had little childish quirks that irritated me (and reminded me very much of some of HV 2.0's traits), but I tried to convince myself I was just being a snob.

One thing about our intimate relationship that was difficult for me was that he was... well, *overly* endowed. I'd never seen or been intimate with a man of such... umm... geez... how do you talk about something like this without wanting to hide under a table? As much as I was sexually stirred by him, after an hour of passionate play, I began to think, "Oh gawd... is he going to stop soon? I don't know how much more I can handle." I thought I would get used to it, but it never got easier for me. I even had brief thoughts of "No wonder his wife left him." In addition to that, he liked a lot of oral gratification. By "a lot," I mean that it could have become a very lucrative part-time job for me. This was a huge struggle for me too. And to top it all off, he liked to "give back" and make things all about me. Most women would thoroughly appreciate such an unselfish lover, but honestly, he wasn't very good at it; and he took offence when I'd say, "It's okay. I'm fine. You don't need to do that." It was about as erotic as watching someone make a ham sandwich. But despite my sexual reservations about him, I muddled on thinking that we'd find our groove eventually. Or... I'd become wheelchair-bound.

When we went out for dinner on Valentine's Day, the host at the restaurant stopped us and said we were the most "in love"-looking couple she had seen the whole night. If a complete stranger could see this, then what was I having reservations about?

I dismissed the ongoing feelings of doubt.

Then one Friday night, three weeks after Branden and I first met in person, I confided to Samantha that I was really having reservations about the whole thing. From all I told her, she agreed that I needed to talk to him. Even though we'd only been together for a brief period, there was no point in dragging it out if the *buts* were starting to mount.

The next day, he planned to take his brother fishing. I left him a voicemail asking if he would like me to make dinner for us, but I received no reply for the rest of the day. I wasn't upset or concerned, because I knew that his brother lived quite a distance away, and assumed that he'd decided to spend the whole day with him.

On Sunday morning, while I was driving with Daniella, Branden called and asked if it was a good time to talk, and I stupidly said yes. He told me that it wasn't working for him and that it was time for us to move on. I was shocked, but not surprised. His reasons for the incompatibility made me laugh inside, but I silently agreed. You probably want to know what those reasons are. Get ready for this...

Branden felt as though we were sexually incompatible. Amen to that! Although I had the drive, I just couldn't handle the mechanics of it all with him. But the second reason made me angry. He didn't feel as though he could ever be involved with someone who had children. *Are you kidding me? You have two!* I guess his little spoiled brats were the axis that the world spun on. The only part that really bruised my ego was that he had his profile back up by noon that same day. *Wow. Some mourning period.*

What was the next thing I did? I called Phil. I had been living in his city for three weeks now and it never felt right not having him in my life. I kept hoping that I'd accidently run into him somewhere, because then I wouldn't technically be betraying Branden by seeing him. Phil was cold and distant on the phone, but agreed to meet me for a coffee.

Phil definitely didn't let me off easy and made it very clear how much I'd hurt him. I could tell, though, that he still had feelings for me. I didn't feel the same way, and worried that I would allow this to happen just because I wasn't good at saying no. Time would tell; now that we lived in the same city, we could see if this would be a friendship or something else. I did still want him in my life.

That evening, I picked up Daniella from her friend's house and we went over to Phil's to watch TV with him and Jake. Daniella and Jake got along moderately well, but it was how open and relaxed she was with Phil that really blew me away (this was the first time they met). We all know that cats and kids are the best judges of a person's character, so it was clear to me now that Phil really was a good guy.

CHAPTER 19

DOE-EYED GIRL—HONESTY ABOVE ALL ELSE

Although Phil and I were talking every day again, nothing was moving forward in terms of a romantic relationship. I guess he was controlling the situation with his walls strongly erected. I was still of the silent opinion that he was not who I wanted romantically, so I wasn't stressed by it; I just enjoyed spending time with him as a friend.

Time to hit the cyber-world again, and with my new location and my new outlook on "no buts"—because of the Branden situation—I revamped my profile. Here is what launched my popularity in my new hometown:

> Doe-Eyed Girl—Honesty Above All Else
>
> I am a very efficient person, so in order to save you time, I have provided my details in point form, and if they intrigue you, the details are listed below at length. No, I'm not THAT much of a Type-A personality, but I thought I'd combine both popular ways of writing a profile into one—you can either skim the points (and reference the ones that you want to know more about) or sit down with a cup of coffee and spend the next three hours reading all about me. You see? I'm great with flexibility and appealing to different personality types.

Me:

1) honest, patient, caring, sweet
2) divorced, no baggage (maybe just one cute little carry-on that I will tend to forget to bring with me all the time)
3) single mom
4) responsible, considerate
5) active and health conscious
6) semi-homebody, a bit shy, socially presentable
7) physical
8) sense of humour, feisty

You:

a) honest, gentle
b) fit, active
c) humorous (conditions do apply)
d) tidy, clean cut
e) financially responsible
f) passionate (kinda super, totally, really important)

Me:

1) I'm probably the most honest, patient and caring person you'll ever meet. I am a server of people and love the opportunity to do things for the people I care about. Unfortunately, this has also been a negative trait of mine because I tend to give too much and lose sight of the things I should do for myself. Working on that balance. As for being "sweet" it seems to be the most common descriptor that people use with regards to me.
2) After fifteen years of marriage and almost two years solo, I've done a little dating (and by little... I mean... really, hardly any at all), but mostly spent my time learning more about myself and how to live a life of better balance. I have recently made a very drastic, yet positive, change to my life and am enjoying this new chapter (yup... totally meant to keep you in suspense). I have no overbearing ex living across the street or

fighting me for custody. Nope... no baggage... just my cute little carry-on tote. What does it look like? Well, I'd rather reserve disclosing the potential contents at this point in time.

3) I am the mother of an incredible fourteen-year-old. Yes... I used the word "incredible" with respect to a teenager. I have spent over fourteen years working hard to ensure a great relationship with my child so that we have unconditional love, communication, and respect for each other.
4) I am young at heart, but very responsible and considerate. I take pride in representing my employer to the best of my ability; and make an effort to positively affect the people around me. As a human being, I would prefer to sacrifice my comfort or happiness, if I can make someone else's better.
5) Used to study martial arts and am coming back from a couple injuries, so I'm only now beginning to ramp up my physical activity (currently per week - cardio 5x, weight training 2x, and boot camp 3x). UFC championships? No, you won't see me in the octagon... but I don't mind trying new activities and staying fit and healthy. I am not about living a life of alfalfa sprouts and granola, but I just eat balanced so that the occasional Snickers bar (or butter tart, or cookie, or Maple Blondie, or...) doesn't have to leave me feeling guilty.
6) Give me my PJs and someone to snuggle with and I'm happy to stay home; but the girl in me also loves to get dressed up for a nice dinner out. I like to talk a lot (I try to contain it), but more in an intimate setting; as I tend to get a little overwhelmed in large crowds. Ironically though, people always say that they wish that they were as confident and outgoing as me; so either I fake it really well, or am not as shy as I claim to be. LOL
7) I am very tactile, but not clingy. I love to touch, massage, scratch, hold hands, cuddle, kiss, and nuzzle. Although I can scale it back depending on the partner, it is a big part of

who I am. If you don't like to be touched, then I'm probably not the one for you.

8) I do have a sense of humour and I am not above mocking myself; but in the face of formal situations, I am the picture of perfect behavior. I tend to have a sarcastic sense of humour, bordering on twisted, but you can definitely dress me up, take me out, and have no regrets. The flexibility of my personality allows me to be relatable to all demographics. I was recently informed that I must add that I'm feisty.

You:

a) Honesty is probably the biggest deal for me. I would rather be hurt by the truth and have to deal with it, than be devastated later when I find out about something that was hidden from me. I think I was Sherlock Holmes in my previous life because I always uncover the truth. That's a hint at the contents of my carry-on baggage. I am a very calm and gentle person, so arguing is something I avoid at all costs. If you have a hot temper, I trust you will reserve that to your couch-side coaching during HNIC. You'll notice that I didn't say that you had to be patient, though... I have enough of that for both of us.
b) Not looking for Mr. America or the UFC welter-weight champ, but it would be nice to know that you care about your health. If you're my "the one," then I'd like to know that I can keep you around for a long time. If your six pack resembles more of a pack of Jell-O pudding, just remember—"Everybody loves Jell-O pudding!" So don't be so hard on yourself.
c) As with my sense of humour, I do love someone who doesn't take themselves too seriously. A balanced sense of humour is great, but needing to be the trickster 24/7 is bad. Once in a while I would like to have some time with the serious, more sensitive side too (romantic traits would be great too... actually... it would be pretty awesome... I've never experienced

romance before, but have heard good things about it).

d) I would prefer someone who is tidy. You don't have to be a neat freak, but when your underwear starts to walk across the floor on its own, I may give you a disapproving look. You care about your appearance. Not in a metrosexual way, but in a showered-shaved-and-nice-shirt-and-pants way.

e) Your finances are under control. I'm not looking for diamonds, furs or a Sugar Daddy; but don't ask to borrow twenty bucks from me or ask me to get a second job to support your couch habit.

f) Then there's the big one—passion. I hope that with the chemistry that comes with a successful connection, you are not opposed to being physically and emotionally passionate. Please refer to my personality trait #7 for ways to reciprocate in order to guarantee that I always have a smile on my face.

First Date

I probably don't have time for jetting off to Mont Saint-Michel this week, so maybe something casual so that we can chat and see if there's enough chemistry to lead to having a real first date.

Would my profile's facelift draw the attention that I was looking for? Was I able to properly convey who the true Veronica was? The messages started flooding in, so I think the answer would be *yes* to both questions.

Granted, I did get a couple of messages that said my profile was too long, but obviously, those individuals didn't actually read the opening remarks to understand that they could have stopped at the point-form descriptions. Those individuals had just made it very clear that they did not fall in the category of a prospective HV 3.0. The rest of the messages were overwhelmingly complimentary, and I had my work cut out for me now.

Men's profiles tended to err on the side of skeletal (at best), but I was of the opinion that if they read my profile and saw we had something in common (height requirements allowing), they were due their shot. After all, since I was a single mom and could not afford the pricy cougar-print cat suits for my hindquarter-flaunting photo shoot, these guys were judging me based on my words and my big brown eyes.

Patricia proved to be very persuasive when it came to me actively dating again after breaking up with Branden—she hated Branden from the moment she met him. The cat hated him too, and, as I said before, that is usually the best way to judge a person's character. I think Patricia was living vicariously through my cyber-dating, and she made me contact people that I didn't want to contact. She drove me nuts, actually, as she sat next to me looking at the profiles. Then Rico happened. And Walter. And Graham. And Fred.

A distorted photo of what appeared to be a somewhat handsome man beside a crotch-rocket motorcycle would bring Rico into my life. Rico was younger than me, but sent me a very enthusiastic message, for which Patricia convinced me to reciprocate. We exchanged a few brief messages and then, very soon, spoke on the phone (due to Patricia's forceful coaching). The call lasted eight minutes and was extremely uncomfortable.

Rico worked in a health food store by day and was a bouncer by night. After speaking to him live, I realized that he went against every single thing that was on my list of to-haves. I wrote him a quick note and thanked him for his time, and went on my way. From start to finish, my "relationship" with Rico had lasted one hour and twenty-six minutes. *Ugh... Next!*

Now Walter. Six years older than me, well-established, blurry photo, so easy to talk to. Walter was a plumber by trade and had done very well for himself. So much so that he only felt the need to work three days a week. He was married for twenty years and they had simply grown apart and gone their separate ways. They were never able to conceive children, so his baggage was almost non-existent. We very quickly began speaking on the phone, and his voice made my heart very curious. He had a deep, manly, comforting voice that made me swoon inside like a little schoolgirl. Regardless of the fact that I hadn't really seen a photo of him, I loved our conversations and really wanted to meet him. I pictured us at his cottage, walking his dog through the woods. The simple life. I craved the simple life. Like Mick from my hometown, he never brought up the topic of meeting, so on St. Paddy's Day (after more than a week of talking), I asked him if I could buy him a green beer. He agreed to meet but insisted on dinner instead.

I saw him standing outside the restaurant and he was tall, dark, and... umm... tall, dark and... umm... old? Unattractive? But he was tall... and we got along great on the phone.

Give it a chance, Veronica. You fall in love with the heart and soul first, and then the face becomes more beautiful. Just give him a chance.

Don't get me wrong, Walter did not have a face that would make small children cry; but I felt no attraction at all.

I sat at the table with my arms crossed, and he repeatedly reached across the table to make some sort of physical contact with me. He was gaga for me and made it clear by the way he looked at me and gushed about how gorgeous and perfect he found me to be. He was so sweet, and as he talked, my mind began to wander.

There's got to be something you like about him, Veronica. Well, he has beautiful blue eyes… but do I really want to see that body naked? Do I really want to wake up next to that for the next fifty years? Maybe if I just close my eyes and let his voice overcome me, then it would soften the reality of the visual. Belly button lint. Why did the image of belly button lint come to mind when I thought of him naked?

At the end of our date, I agreed to a second. I mean, think about it… if you have a great connection on the phone and in writing, there's got to be something there, right? *Right?* I wasn't so sure anymore. I soon came to realize that my comfort level and ease of communication with these men did not necessarily signify a legitimate connection, but the fact that I was becoming more comfortable in my own skin. I was falling in love with Veronica. Falling in love with Veronica for the first time in my life.

My phone rang one day, and it was a woman.

"Who's this?" she asked.

I was stunned. "Um… you called me. Who is *this*?"

"This is Sofia. You were talking to my boyfriend on the phone."

My mind began to race. The only two men I was communicating with were Phil and Walter. Had one of them lied to me about being in a relationship with someone else? "Could you be more specific, please? Who is your boyfriend?"

"Rico. You were talking to my boyfriend Rico on Thursday, weren't you?"

Rico? Rico… Rico…

"Ohhhh. Rico. The guy from the dating website? Yes, I was. We spoke for about ten minutes, and—"

"It was eight actually," she interrupted.

"Okaaay. Yes, about eight minutes, and then I sent him an email saying that I did not want to communicate with him any further."

Long story short, Rico was into older women and was looking for a Sugar Mama. During my conversation with the distressed Sofia, she handed the phone to him and said, "It's for you." I heard him ask her who it was, and she told him it was a good friend of his.

Rico came on the phone and I said, "Hey Rico, it's Veronica... Veronica from the dating site."

I think I heard him pee a little. "Uh. Ohhh..." was his reply.

"Rico, your girlfriend called me. Good luck with that." And I hung up.

The ever-distressed Sofia proceeded to call me three more times that day. During one of our heart-to-hearts, she told me that she was going to break up with him once and for all because she was tired of his cheating. She said that when she'd first caught him online, he told her he was helping his friend try to catch his girlfriend cheating. I decided to lay some heavy words on the angst-ridden Sofia.

"Sofia, promise me that you'll never go back to him. No matter how good the sex is... have some self-respect and never go back to him."

"Sex?" she said. "We don't have sex. He won't have sex with me because he says that I'm too fat."

I think she heard the audible thud when I hit the floor. What the *hell* are these women doing to themselves? I don't know how I managed, but I got off the phone from Sofia and never answered her calls again.

I told the story to Walter, and we had a great laugh when I admitted that I thought he had lied to me and actually had a girlfriend. We had another great conversation and set our next date—walking his chocolate Lab, Bella, the following Sunday. But when Sunday arrived, I realized that I could not lead this man on. He was too sweet, too kind. I sent him a message and told him I couldn't see him again, and wished him well. I felt like a coward doing it over text message, but I just couldn't "face" him over the phone.

During all of my dealings, I was discovering that men popped up in threes, so while I was communicating with Walter, Graham and Fred were also in the wings. You're probably doing your man-math and thinking, "But what about Rico? That makes four. Your theory is flawed." Seriously... should we even count Rico? I think not. My theory still stands. They always come in threes.

My written communications with Fred were equally as stimulating as with Walter, and he made me laugh so much. Fred had two small children who now lived in Scotland with their mother. She was his high-school sweetheart and had gone off the deep end one day and snuck them out of the country. As much as Fred missed his kids, he was not willing to subject them to the turmoil of being ripped away from their mother, so he let them stay with her with the conditions that his mother (who lived near them in Scotland) would be permitted a very active role in their lives. Fred used to be a fireman but had left that career to become an engineer. He made a ton of money and bought a huge house and all the material trappings for him and his then-wife. After her meltdown, he realized that he just wasn't happy. So he sold his home and followed his dream of becoming a paramedic. I respected him for that, but couldn't help thinking, "Six-figure income to minimum wage... really?" I saw his photos and he was not my type at all, or even appealing to me, but our connection was real. Graham, on the other hand, described himself as handsome, so I believed him and thought that maybe he just wasn't photogenic (his photos were of him in a lobster bib with butter smeared all over his face and hands) and that there was indeed hope for a physical attraction this time. Graham was amicably divorced and had a ten-year-old son with whom he had a very tight relationship. He was an accountant at a global chocolate distributor (that part got me really excited... free chocolate!). He wasn't as easy to talk to as Fred, but I did enjoy our communications. Here's where I get weak and lose all sense of reason. Graham was Irish, and Fred, Scottish. Accents—my arch nemesis.

The written and telephone banter with both of them simultaneously continued until one day, one of them called and I didn't know which one it was. I hated myself for that. I knew then that I had to pull the plug on one.

Even though I wanted to meet Fred first, my date with Graham was going to happen sooner. He had been travelling with his son and, even though I reached a point of not wanting to meet him because of my superior connection with Fred, I agreed to keep the date. How could I say no to a man who called me, long distance, from a ski hill while on vacation with his son? I can't be *that* cold.

Graham and I met for a casual hike at one of the same places Branden had taken me. There I was in my expensive hiking boots (Branden was the outdoorsy one, remember, and encouraged me to buy them) and my corporate dressy coat. I'd say that things were awkward, at best, but then I slipped and fell hard on a patch of ice. Graham just stood there and stared down at me. *Awkward!* I'm sure that my face went flush, and it hurt so damn much. I was no longer in the mood for this. Once we navigated our way back down the trail without me breaking my neck, we went to a coffee shop near my house and I realized that I had *zero* connection with this person. Then, out of the blue—meaning, *totally* off-topic—as we sat in that bustling coffee shop, he brought up a conversation about tattoos that he had had with his son. He slammed the idea of body art, and as I sat, grateful that my two large ink jobs were well covered, I thought, *cheque please.* Besides that, I could no longer stand staring at the price tag he'd forgotten to take off his "jumper," It was a crystal-blue pullover that I'm sure his mother picked out for him. It just screamed mama's boy. I couldn't take it anymore, so I looked at my watch and said, "Oh shoot! I promised my daughter that I'd take her to the mall to get supplies for her science project." Yeah right… like Daniella *ever* actually did her homework. Whatever. He'd never know the truth.

I guess the painted lady really was *all that* because Graham asked me on a second date. The coward that I am said yes, but I sent him an email the next day thanking him for his time and cutting my little tattoo-phobic friend loose.

Fred, in the meantime, lived about two hours away, but was moving to my city for his new career, so our plans to meet were delayed due to geographical challenges. So what happened next? Stefan cropped up. Oh my gawd… this was starting to make my head spin.

CHAPTER 20
JUGGLING

Stefan contacted me and had a slightly off-color profile. His humour was a little odd, and he was pretty darn specific about what he didn't want in a woman. I gathered by his words that he had been around the block a couple times with dating sites and had some interesting encounters. Thankfully, I did not have "big bucked teeth that looked like Chiclets," because apparently he had an aversion to that. Oh well, some people just don't have a flair for writing. We'll give him a chance.

He wasn't anything special to look at (a little intense-looking, actually) but I had never let that stop me from giving someone a chance. Oh wait. Look at where he lives. That's an hour away. No way. No way. No way.

But wait a minute, Veronica... what if he's the one? What if you miss out on the one because you won't drive a few miles?

My stupid inner voice was driving me nuts. No way.

I responded to Stefan's message and thanked him for his very enthusiastic words, but told him that the distance was just too great. Stefan wrote back promptly and argued that if we established that there was a connection between us, we would be daft not to investigate because of a few miles separating us. He further informed me that sometimes sacrifices can be worth the prize. Not having a backbone, I agreed to give him a chance.

Stefan and I began to communicate feverishly through the site because he was actually away on a family trip to Turks and Caicos for three weeks. After about a week of banter, he asked if he could call me to see if there was a connection between us over the phone. *Seriously? The dude wants to call me from Turks and Caicos?* I rationalized that he probably had a really good long-distance calling plan, so I agreed. We spent over an hour on the phone... seventy-five minutes to be exact. I made him laugh so much (as I did in my messages to him, but I never feel as though LOL or ROTFLMAO really counts), and he said that he could sense something between us. He was even a little racy with his innuendos, but for some reason it didn't make me feel uncomfortable. He said that he couldn't wait to meet me and wanted to meet at a halfway point at a popular steakhouse.

I asked him, "Are you sure you want to make that kind of time commitment? I'd be fine with just meeting for coffee."

"Are you worried about me spending the money? Don't worry about that, I think you are going to be a very good investment."

"I didn't say that I was worried about the money. I said *time commitment.* If we don't click, then you're stuck with me for at least an hour. I'd be fine with a stale donut and cold coffee sitting on the bumper of your car."

He laughed hard at that comment, and told me that now he wanted to meet me even more and that he wished his vacation was over already. He was firm about the restaurant date, so I agreed to meeting him there two days after his return.

Did I mention that during all of this, I was still talking to Fred? The connection between Fred and me was growing stronger by the day, but there was just *something* about Stefan that made me want to meet him first. I had a feeling, so I put Fred off for a little bit longer.

Oh wait… are we still at three? No, I think we're short someone. I guess it's time for Lorenzo. I'll have to keep you in suspense about Stefan since he's still in Turks and Caicos, so we'll move on to Lorenzo.

First, for some background: Phil has two sons, Jason and Jake. When Jason's birthday was coming up, I thought I'd surprise him and bake for him one night. I packed up all of my supplies, and Daniella and I went over to his house. Phil was working that night, so it was just me and the three kids. I think young Jason fell in love with me that night. I came over to bake just for him and no one had ever done that for him before.

Jason wasn't your average fourteen-year-old boy—he was actually pleasant to be around—so doing something like that for him was an absolute pleasure. He was the son that I never had and had always hoped for. My sweet little son-by-association, Jason.

After I finished baking, Jason, Daniella, and Jake went upstairs to watch TV, and I sat down at the computer to continue with my online obsession. An instant message popped up to request a chat, and it was from someone new. I went to look at his profile and it was really nothing to write home about, and there wasn't a damn picture either. Was I going to allow myself to get caught in a conversation with Quasimodo again?

What to do. What to do?

Enter *Veronica is a pushover* example number two thousand, three hundred twenty-three.

Lorenzo and I proceeded to have a nice chat for over an hour. It was a nice chat mainly because I made it clear that I was not taking on any more talent at this point in time. I also made it clear that we could have friendly chats but that there would be no meet 'n greet. After that hour, I bid him adieu to pack up the kid and go home, and he informed me that he was enjoying our conversation so much that he hoped I'd come back online to continue. Although I was tired, I agreed. I have to admit, it was nice just chatting without getting tangled up in any love strings.

Lorenzo and I messaged until midnight and then he asked if we could talk on the phone. We proceeded to spend three hours on the phone. It was a great conversation and I really liked talking to him—although, at times, his thick accent made him a little difficult to understand. He was intelligent and funny and really helped give me some insight into the online dating world. We talked about my trials and tribulations so far, and it was nice to get a man's perspective on all of this—a non-biased male opinion—because the cyber-dating scene was starting to wear me down.

Lorenzo was Italian and moved here only two years before (he moved here to marry his now-estranged-psycho wife). He was highly, *highly* intelligent and also highly frustrating in that he analyzed everything I said. Being the bigger person, though, when I got frustrated with him, I would mock him for his foibles with the English language (and he'd let me); so from early on in our cyber-friendship, I referred to him lovingly as the "Damn Italian."

I told him about Stefan and Fred, but also explained how I had put Fred on the backburner because I really wanted to meet Stefan. He urged me not to leave Fred hanging, but hoped that Stefan was all that I was hoping he was cracked up to be.

Lorenzo and I proceeded to chat daily, and he'd call me while I was driving home at night so that I had company in the car. I'd pop my headset on and have lots of giggles to make my commute go by quicker. I could see Lorenzo becoming a good friend. Maybe one day we would meet.

The day finally came that I was to meet Stefan, and I was nervous. More nervous than usual, because this date involved driving to an area that was totally foreign to me. Driving to an area that was totally foreign to me while it was *snowing*. Why would it decide to snow in April?

Some might think that I'm exaggerating for the sake of entertainment value and would say, "Gimme a break! The woman has a navigation system.

She's just being melodramatic." Well, no… no, I'm not. Let's pause for a moment so that you can fully understand how difficult it is for me to find my way out of that proverbial paper bag.

I am known as "The Queen of Lost," so, GPS or not, things can get challenging for me. I purchased a GPS just before I moved to my new province, but before that, I was on my own. I was thrilled the day that the internet introduced map sites because then I didn't have to sit in my car trying to find where the AH165 quadrant was on the micro-printed map in my glove box. I am also the type that has to turn the map so it is facing the direction I am driving in. Needless to say, I have never once been asked to be the co-pilot on a lengthy road trip. But here's a perfect example of how bad I am directionally.

Every Tuesday for about two years, I had to drive from my house to a client's house to pick up documents to prepare for the following week. They lived about forty-five minutes away and across four towns. I would reach their home without incident (except for a handful of times that I was too timid to change lanes and risk cutting someone off, and subsequently missed my exit). The trek back home—in the dark—was a totally different story. For some reason, I could never remember what exit to take and always took the one that sent me across my least favorite bridge and approximately ten miles out of my way. So ninety percent of every Tuesday, I sat on the side of the road having a panic attack and attempting to prepare myself for the trek *back* across that same damn bridge. On average, the return trip took me ninety minutes. Yes… I'm dead serious.

Then there was the time (about a month after I moved to my new province) that Daniella and I decided to go shopping in town. After our successful shopping day, I set the GPS to "Home" and let her guide us back to our safe-haven. Gina (the name that I gave my GPS) guided us through a few of the bustling downtown crack-whore-infested streets with apparent confidence until she told me to drive straight into the side of a building. I could only go left on the one-way street, but Gina was adamant that I drive straight into the twelve-storey building that stood ahead of us. I turned left, knowing that she would sputter "recalculating" in that condescending tone we had grown accustomed to in the past month, and she took me around the block to the same spot and informed me that I was expected to go straight. Well, I guess I thought that if I kept turning left, she'd clue in to the fact that I wasn't going to go that route and would finally alter her course (this was before I discovered the "detour" option). Umm… yeah… not! I dissolved into tears and called Phil. He "drove" with us over the phone and guided us to safety. To this day, I cringe when I see that building.

So now you understand why panic sets in so easily with me when it comes to navigation. Let's return to my story of meeting Stefan.

Sure enough, I got lost. Gina (that belligerent GPS) informed me that I was now sitting on top of the restaurant. Well, unless the restaurant was ingeniously disguised as an old, run-down gas station with boards on the windows, I was pretty sure that my destination was still yet to be reached. I drove back and forth a bit until I finally stopped at a not-run-down gas station to ask for directions.

They had no idea.

Well, they had an idea, but it was wrong, so I got lost again. By the time I found the place, I was fifteen minutes late and sweating like a whore in church. I pride myself on my punctuality and cannot stand the thought of being unaccountable to anyone. So now, on top of first-date jitters, I was worried about unsightly armpit sweat stains. I did my best to compose myself and walked into the restaurant with my head held high.

As I approached Stefan's table, it sincerely felt like I was walking in slow motion, and when I saw him for the first time, my thoughts were, *Oh... really?* I had hoped that maybe he just wasn't photogenic and would be better-looking in person. He was chatting with the server, and then turned (again, in slow motion) and locked eyes with me. I could see that his words trailed off, and he looked mesmerized. So much so, that the server turned around to see what he was distracted by. I knew that I was having a good hair day, but this was awkward and I could feel my face go flush. "Are you Veronica?" he asked. I nodded silently and slid into the booth across from him. The next thing he said was, "Oh my god. Your photos don't even do you justice. You are absolutely gorgeous."

Gorgeous? C'mon... no one has ever used that word with regards to me before. Never. Is this guy for real?

I was hopeful that the red sweater I was wearing would offset the fact that I was probably going to spend the evening experimenting with all of the hues of red one's face could possibly turn. Shy Veronica now sat in on our date. I felt like an overwhelmed child.

As we talked, Stefan never stopped looking at me in a way that made me feel as though he was licking me with his eyes. No man had ever looked at me that way. As flattering as it was, I could feel my face and ears burning constantly.

During one of our communications online, he said that he was a very blunt man who would not waste anyone's time. If he didn't feel that there was a connection, he would make that clear. Also, he never *ever* kissed a woman on a first date—not even for a polite farewell. Ironically, just as I was thinking about those comments, he leaned across the table and planted one on me. He was lightning fast, so I didn't even know what had hit me until his lips were pressed hard against mine. *Insert red face.*

He apologized for being so forward and said that he just couldn't go another moment without knowing "what those lips felt like."

Would it be rude to spend the rest of the date hiding under the table? Oh my gawd. This man is too intense.

At one point, I excused myself to use the washroom, because the combination of wine, nerves, and an infantile bladder was getting the best of me. But I didn't want to get up. I wanted to stay hidden behind the table so that he couldn't look at the rest of me the way he had been looking at my face all evening. As I mentioned, I was wearing a red sweater, and I paired it with a tight-fitting light grey pencil skirt. I knew full well how amazing the subtle ruffle made my ass look, and the four-inch heels showcased my lean, muscular calves. I could feel his eyes burning through me as I walked towards the restroom. *Do I have to go back? Can I find a way to walk back without watching him watch me walk across the restaurant? Maybe I can time it like Mrs. Doubtfire did during the restaurant scene of that movie… I'll just hide behind a waiter and then slide back into my seat when he least expects it.*

No such luck. His eyes were glued on me as I walked back to the table. It felt like I was walking in slow motion again and I prayed that I wouldn't slip and make a fool of myself as I tried to navigate the slippery tile floors on nervous, shaky legs.

I lost count after that of how many times he lunged across the table to kiss me, and he eventually came over to my side of the booth and couldn't keep his hands off me. He wasn't groping me, but repeatedly caressing my face, hair, and hands; then he pulled me in closer for even more kisses. I felt so uncomfortable being faced with a level of passion that no man had ever shown towards me.

Don't get me wrong, I do like PDAs; but this was over the top, and I felt horrible for our server and the rest of the wait staff that kept walking by. Our… his… our… no, *his* behavior was so over the top that our server finally asked if this was our first date (due in part to how Stefan greeted me with "Are you Veronica?"). I lied and said no. I explained that we'd been together for four years and did this role-playing to keep the passion alive. The twinkle in Stefan's eyes after I said that just made things even more awkward.

Was I being overly polite and shy by allowing him to be so outwardly affectionate to me?

Was the old incapable-of-saying-no Veronica rearing her ugly head again?

Or was I truly feeling a strong attraction to this man regardless of my lack of attraction to his face?

He did have great hands, and I'm definitely a sucker for great hands. Voices and hands—would I ever find the perfect combo? HV 1.0: Spanish accent, great hands (until he, out of anger, slammed his own hand in the car door and mutilated two of his fingers, rendering his hands visually disturbing to me); HV 2.0: great voice (when he wasn't in a state of "whine"), but stubby sausage fingers (I spent almost a decade avoiding looking at them). HV 3.0 needed to have both.

Stefan's voice was nice (but he was Romanian, so that's probably not an accent that would make me swoon, should I ever have the opportunity to hear him speak his mother tongue), and his hands were great. This hand-voice combination definitely flew with me. But the face… hmmmm. Maybe I'd grow to love it.

We closed the restaurant and stood at my car to say goodbye. Despite the fact that I had parked right at the front door (in clear view of the restaurant staff as they closed up shop), Stefan was all over me. He pushed me hard against the side of my car and kissed me like it was our last day on earth. His hands were everywhere. Since he was pressed up against me, it was clear that his feelings were sincere. *Very* clear. Although our actions were definitely warming me up inside, I was shivering from standing outside in the cold and snow for so long. Stefan asked if I felt comfortable sitting with him in his car. Regardless of how aggressive he had been all night, I felt as though I could trust him (and his mini-van was parked in a visible area under a light, so I figured I was okay). He turned the heat on in the car, and then we both turned the heat on. I was shivering in a different way at that point. We spent the next couple of hours in his warm car, and the connection between us was obviously very strong. Yes, we did actually talk a bit more, but I'd say that the scales tipped heavier on the making-out side of things. I was sincerely shocked at my behavior on this first date, and questioned if it was because I was sincerely attracted to him, incapable of saying no, or just so bloody horny that I couldn't contain myself anymore.

I was right to wait to meet Fred; I now knew that I wanted to get to know Stefan a lot better. *A lot* better. He asked if we could have another date two days later (Friday), so that we wouldn't have to worry about getting home early to go to work the next day (it was now three in the morning). I agreed and we went our separate ways. I felt so comfortable with him that I really didn't want the date to end. Neither did he, and he made that *very* clear. We had to *literally* tear ourselves away from each other, and the burning loin thing was back in full force.

Over the next two days I received a lot of flattering messages from him. He said that he'd never, ever met a woman as incredible as me; that he didn't think any other woman would *ever* be able to measure up to me; and that I had really overwhelmed him by how I made him feel. Wow. Again, no man had ever acted this way towards me. His enthusiastic words were now making me think that the *but*—the distance—maybe wasn't a *but* after all.

I learned a lot about Stefan at the restaurant that first night, and was really looking forward to the dinner he was going to make me at his house on Friday. He told me that he and his brother ran a creamery in his community and that, as a part of our meal, he was going to treat me to a variety of cheeses they produce. So, feverishly, I began my trek to his home after work on the big day. Fifty minutes to get home, half an hour to freshen up, and then the hour-long commute. I was praying that the GPS (and his directions) would get me there without incident, since he lived in a rural area.

Gina the GPS did right by me and I arrived with only one incident of lost which was quickly remedied by a u-turn. Had I not seen his mini-van in the open garage, though, I would have thought I was actually lost.

His house, or should I say his *sprawling estate,* stood before me. The bay doors were open on his multi-car garage, revealing a Ferrari sitting inside. I sat stunned for a moment and was ready to tuck tail and run. He's wealthy.

He's wealthy?

Crap.

I had long since grown tired of dealing with the egotistical behavior of wealthy men in my career over the years, so I surely did not want to take something like this on. I would much rather be with a man who is money poor, but time wealthy. He had seen me by this point, so I had to go forward. I entered into our second date with my excitement replaced by guardedness. My walls were totally up now.

Stefan had a wonderful spread prepared, and we sat at the kitchen table and talked for hours. He told me all about his past, his scars, and his baggage.

Stefan had been married for a total of eighteen years. He met his wife shortly after he came to Canada and they had an idyllic marriage at first. After the birth of their two boys, she began to work at the family retail store (Stefan always felt that a wife should contribute to the income of the home) and their relationship became somewhat strained. They, like many couples, fell into a pattern of work and children and lost sight of the passion and connection they'd once had. He continued that, because he felt as though there was something very special between us, he wanted to confide something about his past that he had never told another woman. Something for which he was utterly ashamed. I prepared myself for the worst and began to mentally plan my exit strategy.

Stefan claimed that he had always had a very high sex drive and, when the intimate relationship between him and his wife began to wane, he asked her how she felt about attending a *swingers* event. Although she was hesitant at first, he promised her that they would just go and, if she felt uncomfortable, they would leave. They didn't leave.

Week after week, they attended the events and Stefan participated with gusto. He felt invigorated and alive, and his desire for his wife returned. Their intimate relationship reached a level of passion that they had never experienced before. He remembered one night very clearly, though. As he was actively having intercourse with another woman, his wife was in the bed next to them with that same woman's husband on top of her. Stefan watched his wife as he continued to pleasure himself with the other woman, and he noticed a distant, almost dead look in his wife's eyes. He had been so selfish in satisfying himself all those weeks that he never once took notice of his tortured wife. She never complained or shied away from the activities, and he never bothered to ask her how those activities made her feel.

After that night he didn't ask her to return to those events and watched her slowly begin to change. She was obsessed with her appearance and told him she wanted to have breast augmentation. Stefan, like most men would be, was onboard with her request and was thrilled with the final results. With the change in her appearance paired with the change in her attitude, his passion for her grew even more. She was far more sensual and seemed to exude confidence. He loved it. But something didn't feel right. There was a certain coldness coming from her and he just couldn't put his finger on it. He attributed it to her usual resentment towards his long hours at work. Until he found a receipt on the lawn that must have fallen out of the garbage. It was a receipt from a local motel. A cash receipt for a room.

Stefan became consumed with jealousy and paranoia and rifled through her drawers and purse whenever she was in the shower or away from home. He finally planted a tracking device in the trunk of her car, and his suspicions were sadly proven valid.

He followed his wife to a nearby motel and watched as she met her lover and they entered the room. Then he waited. Then he did what you only see in movies: he crept up to the motel room door and listened for what seemed like ages. He could hear them making love. He could hear her wild moans of pleasure. Like any good scorned husband, he banged on the door until her lover opened it. He stood silently in the doorway and stared at her as she lay huddled under the bed sheets. Without saying a word, he left. Devastated. He knew that this was his fault. Her exposure to the world of swinging had changed her. Had made her feel unworthy and driven her into the arms of another man. He felt single-handedly responsible for the demise of their marriage.

As he told me his story, I looked deep into his eyes and I could see that he was truly opening up his soul to me. The old, insecure Veronica would have wanted to crawl under a table or run as far away as she could from something like this. She would have thought, *I wonder how long before he expects me to allow him to watch other men have their way with me?* But all I could think about was the beauty that was radiating from him and taking my breath away. I could feel my heart racing and I just wanted to hold him close to me and make love to him. The face that had first disappointed me now seemed so beautiful, and I could feel my heart going somewhere that I was pretty sure it had never been before. This was only our second date, though, so how could I be feeling so intensely about a man?

Was the old "ten fingers, ten toes… yes, I'll marry you" Veronica rearing her ugly head again?

After filleting himself to me, Stefan told me he thought for sure it would be the last time he ever saw me. He was shocked and overwhelmed when I told him I felt closer to him than ever. The connection between us was so strong now that I dared ask myself if I thought I'd found "the one."

We had an amazing night together and I literally floated the whole way home the next morning. Yes… I said the next morning. That night we discovered another thing that we had in common—equally insatiable sexual appetites. I had never jumped into bed with someone so quickly before, but it felt so right with Stefan. Was I ashamed? A little. But if what I did was so wrong, why did it feel so right? Wow… sorry… that *totally* sounded like the cheesy lyrics of a song. Why did I feel as though I could be myself around him?

His emails to me were always so amazing and I really couldn't find any *buts* at all. I had confessed to him that, had he shown up to our first date in his Ferrari, I don't think he would have had that second date with me.

The Ferrari… oh, the Ferrari.

Upon starting my new job after my move, I was quickly befriended by Paulo, who worked for one of my bosses. Paulo was a couple of months older than me and we got along like we'd known each other for years. He was a real sweetheart, and there was no confusion about the boundaries of our relationship. We were buddies, and we both knew that. Mostly due to his work-related travel, he had never experienced a serious long-term relationship. I assured him that I had been married enough times for the both of us and hoped that he appreciated my public service of saving him a lot of pain, grief, and alimony. Paulo became my shoulder. On a weekly basis I kept him up to speed with the torture and turmoil that I was putting myself through in the dating world. One of those sessions included my question to him about the Ferrari.

"Paulo, I'm in a bit of a pickle. I went out on another date with the Dairy King (our little nickname for Stefan, the dairy mogul), and he came and picked me up in his Ferrari. Well… I really have no interest in cars and I don't know how to handle this situation. If I act as disinterested as I am in his glorified phallic symbol, then he might take that in one of two ways. One: that I don't care about the things that he's passionate about; and two: that I'm pretending to be nonchalant because I want him to think that I'm disinterested, but actually just want him for his money."

Paulo interrupted me with a good hearty belly laugh—this was not the first time he'd seen me go into a paranoid tailspin.

"Then," I continued, "If I act all enthusiastic and gushing about his stupid road rocket, he'll think one of two things. One: that I don't really care, but am acting that way so that he'll buy me stuff; or two: that I'm faking the enthusiasm and am really not interested in his passion at all. I don't know what to do."

The amount of time that it took Paulo to stop laughing felt like an eternity. He sympathized with my dilemma, though, and told me to be straight-up with Stefan: tell him that cars really weren't my thing, but that I didn't want to insult him and make him think I wasn't interested in his passion.

I took Paulo's advice and came clean to Stefan. He laughed just as hard as Paulo had and told me that what I just said (and had been stressing over for days on end) only made him more attracted to me than ever. If there had been any doubts of my honesty up to that moment, I think that conversation ended them all.

On our next date, I met him at his house and he took me out for dinner at a beachside pub. During the long drive to our destination (in the Ferrari) he told me about why he had the Ferrari. It had been a childhood dream of his from when he still lived in Romania. As a boy, he'd sneak into the stands at the race track and watch the cars for hours. There was a Ferrari there and he vowed that, one day, he would own his own. So, to have achieved that goal was huge for him. He then said, "Now that I've achieved that, I think I'd like an S-500 next."

"Wow," I said with sincere surprise, "You totally don't come across as a pick-up truck kinda guy."

Stefan almost drove off the road laughing and said, "Not an F-350. An S-500!"

"Is that a Toyota or something?" My question was truly sincere.

Stefan abruptly pulled the car over and gently cupped my face in his hands. After the most amazingly passionate kiss, he informed me that an S-500 was a Mercedes of some sort, and that I had officially reached angelic status in his eyes. He told me that he was falling hard for me. We had an amazing night together and I knew that I was falling in love with him.

CHAPTER 21
TIME TO PERCH SAFELY ON THE FENCE

In true Veronica form, what began as floating on Cloud Nine soon became the fast descent to hard Earth. My relationship with Stefan was beginning to torture me, for a few reasons.

The distance—After a while, I got tired of always meeting him halfway in restaurants. It was so public that we really couldn't have intimate conversations with all the interruptions from the servers trying to do their job. And eating out all the time meant that he was spending a ton of money. I didn't care how much money he had, it just wasn't necessary.

I asked him one day if, on our next date, I could just come to his house and cook dinner so we could relax and get to know each other better. After the first time I did that, I knew he pretty much had a Veronica addiction. He loved my cooking and I introduced him to dishes he'd never tried before. I loved doing it too. He was so Type-A that he'd be cleaning up as I prepped, so there were no dishes for me to do when the food was ready. That, in my eyes, is a dream man.

But after an exhausting week at work (and 4:30 wakeups to exercise every day), the commute to and from his house on Friday nights was taking its toll on me. A couple of times, I had to pull over and take a nap because I was falling asleep at the wheel on the way home. Stefan, like Phil, felt as though his teenage boys were naive to their father's extracurricular activities. Therefore, I was expected to drive home each night. Except there was one night that I didn't think I could make it home alive and asked him if I could stay if I *promised* to be gone before his sons woke up. He agreed, but I was slowly starting my climb to safety on my proverbial wall again.

Self-worth—There were two other dates that didn't sit well with me either. On the first, we went out for dinner and fawned all over each other as usual. By the end of the date we were both so completely aroused that we needed to find somewhere where we could satisfy our cravings. Stefan's location of choice was the back of his minivan in a parking lot next to a police station. Yes. A police station. It was a satisfying encounter, but I felt like a horny teenager hiding from my parents. Seriously… a police station? Sigh…

The second date was similar; after eating dinner at a restaurant near our first-date steakhouse, we were raring to go and went across the street to a hotel. They were full. All of the hotels were full because of some hockey convention in town. Hotel after hotel turned us away, and I realized how Joseph and Mary must have felt. Well, they might have had a bit more of an important task to attend to, but you get what I mean.

We finally found a place with a vacancy that wasn't too far from my house. The young man behind the counter began to check us in and said, "Mr. Moldoveanu?" Stefan's face went ashen and he quickly stammered, "It's okay, I'm separated." When we got to the room, he explained to me that the boy was part of the youth program he ran at his church. No one knew that he and his wife were separated. After our passionate romp, Stefan told me that he needed to get home, but I could keep the room for the night. Wow. Way to make a woman feel like a dirty secret. A dirty whore? I wasn't sure what I felt like that night, but I went home to my own bed.

Time poor—Stefan worked very long hours, so we only saw each other once a week. He even cancelled one of our dates because he was so tired. I wasn't surprised, because I'd had a nagging feeling he would.

Unable to commit—Although I told him that I was fine with not being in a committed relationship (I was trying to be the anti-Veronica, remember?), my feelings for him were becoming so strong that I knew I wanted more. His wife's infidelities had made him gun-shy—I was sure it was the reason he was holding back.

During one conversation, he assured me he was not seeing anyone else. I believed him in my heart of hearts, but couldn't compute why he spent his lunch hours on the dating site. Was it just a way of stroking his own ego, to know that he was getting messages from more women? If that was the case, then why did he update his photos and tweak his profile every few days? It made me very confused. His words to me in person and on the phone and in his emails sounded so pure and sincere, but his actions away from me were so contradictory. Why couldn't he call or write to me on his lunch hour?

The distance, again—I had just moved Daniella to this province, so how would she feel about moving to a rural community if Stefan was the one? I was not the only person in this equation, after all. I'm pretty sure she would have been miserable; I just can't see Daniella being happy as a farm girl.

Is this really me?—Although I thought I felt like I could truly be me for the first time with someone, I realized after a little while that I was gradually tweaking myself for Stefan's sake. Little comments about his preference of things made me change how I did certain things, but I never realized it until, one day, he asked how well I tanned.

Although I come from a Middle Eastern/Brazilian mixed heritage, my skin reflects only the English/Scottish/Irish part that my mother contributed to the recipe. Stefan told me one day that he looooooved deep, dark, tanned skin. So did I, for that matter, but that's not the point of this. With that comment, I proceeded to take a step into the world of spray tanning. Long story short, once was very much enough and I had to hide my streaky hands from him on our next date. A very large light bulb was now shining brightly over my head.

In a conversation with Lorenzo the Damn Italian one night, he tried to pour some logic into my brain. He told me that he felt the reason I was still on the dating site was that I was unsure about the Dairy King and my feelings for him. He was partially right, but the real truth was that because Stefan made it clear that we were not exclusive, I was doing my best to play the game as well. A game that, I soon discovered, I was not very good at. At all.

During my time with Stefan, Fred was persistent. Did you think I'd forgotten about Fred? No, Fred was in the wings the whole time trying to convince me that we should meet because we were "meant to be together." I agreed to meet him one night for dinner and I ended up having the best laughs I'd had in a long time. My face and stomach hurt by the end of the night from laughing so much.

Unfortunately, though, the first nail in his coffin was that he could have been the hand twin of HV 2.0. Blech. Sausage fingers. It was the first thing I saw when I entered the pub, and I was ready to turn around and leave. Yes, I am *that* horrible of a person. There are very strong emotions attached to a man's hands for me; hands represent the man's strength and capability to provide for his family. I guess it stems from my cavewoman psyche—the whole hunting and gathering thing. Well, his hands repulsed me, and the thought of being touched by them... ugh... made me shudder.

We had a great date but I made it clear to Fred the next day that I felt no romantic connection between us and planned to pursue my relationship with Stefan. He begged to differ and begged and begged and begged. I told him that I could be his friend, and nothing else, so we continued a friendship online. I even told Stefan that I went on the date, and he said that because we were not exclusive, I didn't need to tell him those kinds of things. But I couldn't imagine not telling him. It made me wonder, though… was he not telling me things too? Was he truly busy at work or was he busy getting busy with other women?

One night, during yet another long instant messaging conversation, the Damn Italian berated me for not replying instantly to those that had messaged me on the dating site. I told him that it felt like no matter how I did this online dating thing, I was doing it all wrong. This topic was starting to get old, and his constant criticism was making me agitated. No, scratch that. It was making me totally pissed off at him.

Ironically, while we were chatting about this, I received an email notification from the dating site that a message had come in. It was some random man (whom I had never had contact with before) asking me to meet him at "The Langston." I asked Lorenzo if he knew what The Langston was, but he had no clue. I looked it up online but could find nothing. At the same time as I was doing this, and talking to him, I was also booking a flight for my mother.

So picture this: I'm messaging Lorenzo, while booking a flight online, while discussing the itinerary with my mother, while balancing the phone in the crook of my neck, when another message comes in.

> Well… thanks for answering. At the very least a simple yes or no… mighty respectful of you.

I could not believe it. He gave me *four* minutes to reply and then came back with that? Do these people honestly think that when a message comes in, life just stops? What if, at that very moment, the phone rang, or someone came to my door, or I had a raging case of Montezuma's revenge because I had just flown back from a week-long missionary trip through the Congo? Does one bring the laptop into the bathroom in such a case? Is it rude to disembowel yourself in front of a complete cyber-stranger? Oh my gawd. These people are insane.

> I'm sorry, I didn't mean to come across as rude. I was on the phone with my mom booking travel for her. I guess I should have multitasked a little better. :) My sincerest apologies for seeming as

though I sloughed off your invite. I will decline, but I do appreciate the offer.

Figured as much.

I was stunned. That four-minute delay in my reply may have saved my life. If *Random Dude #362* flipped his lid after a four-minute delay, what were the chances that I would end my night chopped into little pieces in the dumpster behind The Langston? That was my argument to Lorenzo that night, and boy, did he give me a hard time. He continued to ride me about the fact that I was seeing someone who I claimed to have strong feelings for, and still dangling a carrot out on the dating site.

Although I knew what was truly deep in my heart (and I knew that the more I argued with Lorenzo, the more it was a case of "thou doth protest too much"), I proceeded to write twenty-six Dear John letters that went something like this:

> Thank you so much for your kind words and the time you took to email me. I am so, so sorry for taking such a long time to reply, and hope that it did not come across as rude or dismissive. I feel horrible that it's taken me this long. Not that I need to explain, but I have been burning the candle at both ends with my job, motherhood, and fitness schedule, and have just not had the time to sit down to reply.
>
> I am at times reminded that I am too honest and open; but I choose not to change that part of me; so I'm really glad that my profile came across well to you, because it is definitely a reflection of who I truly am.
>
> I am tucking my profile away for now, as I would like to take some time to get to know one gentleman better.
>
> Thank you again for your message and good luck in your search.

During my next messaging session with Lorenzo I let him know what I had done.

Okay, I think I am no longer an asshole anymore. I just hid my profile and wrote twenty-six Dear John letters. I apologized profusely for the delay and wished them all well. Was that okay?

I cannot believe you... Did you change your messenger picture for that purpose?

Did I do it wrong? As for the picture, no, I just changed it.

LOL No... You did excellent... That angelic look in your new photo does match what you did... Anyhow... you know... I can't believe that you actually listened to me...

Why wouldn't I listen to you? Have I ever claimed that I was all knowing?

Well... a lot of people are so full of themselves that they don't accept a good suggestion... I am not used to such a nice personality...

I'm just trying to do right by people because that's how I want to be treated. That's all... I just can't stand the thought of hurting anyone, whether I know them or not.

If you were here... I would give you a kiss... (in appreciation)

Awww... thank you. That means a lot. You know... whenever I write those letters, about 80% of them write back and thank me for doing that. Tonight, I got a message from one guy who asked me why I would "bother" and "what does [he] care." That really hurt my feelings. It wasn't necessary.

I tend to get overly sensitive about things, and this instance was no different. It didn't matter if I received handfuls of positive responses from my messages, I always allowed myself to get stung by the one negative comment. It's a part of Veronica I've never been able to change. Then again, maybe it's a part of Veronica I shouldn't try to change.

That night, Friday, May 9, 2008—almost three and a half months after moving to a new province—I decided that it was time to take a step back from all of them—Stefan included.

Time to focus on finding a new school for Daniella.

Time to focus on finding a permanent place for us to live.

Time to discover what Veronica truly wants for her life.

CHAPTER 22
DEAR JOHN 26

Good intentions can be met with equally good failures. At least my desire to take a step back was sincere, but it seemed as though fate had other plans for me.

By the time I sent out the Dear John letters, it had been more than a week since I'd last seen Stefan. Again, he cancelled our date because he was just too tired.

Is he telling me the truth? Or did someone else catch his attention?

A few days later, he hid his profile; now I was thoroughly confused.

Did he hide it for me? Is he ready to only focus on me?

On one occasion, during one of our many passionate and heartfelt conversations (no, I'm not being sarcastic… they really were amazing talks), I told him that if he wasn't "the one", then the next guy would be perfect. He laughed and said that, for him, there could never, ever be another woman that even came close to measuring up to me.

It was conversations like that that made me fall deeper in love with him. The distance, though… the lack of regular communication… the long hours… his lunchtime cyber-hobby… those were the things that made my stomach churn when I was away from him.

There was one more thing about Stefan that could be considered a *but*—he was a hunter. I found this out on my first visit to his house, when he took me on a tour that led into his semi-unfinished basement. He had recently gutted his basement and dug further under his property to make it larger. He took me around one corner and it looked like he was making a bowling alley—*Great… ugh… dude's a bowler.* But then he informed me that it was for target practice. His own private shooting range. Oh my gawd. I was on the fast track to falling in love with him just because of that. It was always a secret desire of mine to learn how to shoot properly—now I'd found the man who could teach me. I instantly drifted deep into my imagination and envisioned a sultry and seductive night. I'd be wearing a tight sweater, short skirt (to emphasize my great legs, of course), stiletto heels, and protective eyewear, with a Glock 17 firmly gripped in my hands. Stefan would be standing behind me with his torso pressed against mine, one arm around my tiny waist (it's tiny in my fantasies… don't judge!), his hot breath on my neck, and his other hand guiding mine toward the target. Yes, just like in the movies. I imagined us slowly, gently squeezing the trigger together, and the kickback of the gun firing shocked me back into reality. I hadn't heard anything he'd been saying and now I only had one thing on my mind.

Once I came out of my erotica fog, Stefan took me around the next corner to see the home gym, office, theatre, recreation room, and then finally… the trophy area. There, standing before me (literally *standing*) were a fox, an elk, four ducks, a goose, and a moose or Snuffleupagus of some kind; in addition to the heads of a variety of creatures on the walls. I burst into tears and Stefan's face went ashen. He quickly ushered me out of the room and assured me that he didn't do any game hunting anymore, only duck hunting.

Duck hunting.

Duck hunting?

Duck hunting?

I used to have pet ducks, so the thought of duck hunting to me was the equivalent of kitten hunting. *Oh my gawd.* How was I going to handle this aspect of him?

Over time, I started to accept that part of Stefan and even added my own desperate logic to it. When he and his sons went hunting, they gave their kill to the local farm hands. They were a group of immigrant families that tended the farms in that area, and they would clean and freeze the kill to feed their families for the year. I rationalized it as being a beautiful gesture that he did every year, and that way I could support him in his hobby.

To show my support, I went and bought a cute little purple duck-call thingy and tucked it away to give to him on a special day closer to hunting season. Did you know that there are many different kinds? The litany of questions the guy at the store asked me was insane. Thankfully, once I gave him all of the details I could remember, I did end up getting the cute little purple one I wanted.

I started fantasizing about what our blended family life would be like. He and the boys would spend the day hunting and then come home tired and cold to my special homemade hot cocoa and a warm house smelling of wonderful foods made with love. I would reward my brave hunters and treat them like kings. Little did I know then that I would never share a duck hunting season with my brave warrior.

After sending out the Dear John messages, I started to receive multiple email notifications that messages were waiting for me on the dating site. Since my profile was now hidden, I knew they were the replies to those messages. Being the curious soul that I am, I would log back in, read each message, smile at how sweet they thought I was, and log off again.

Of the twenty-six men who replied, there were three (like I said before, they always come in threes) who really couldn't take no for an answer. They were in no way offensive or pushy, just hoped that maybe I would reconsider my choice to step away into the arms of one man.

They were Tony, Steve, and Greg.

Before I sent the rejection message to Greg, I looked at his profile and saw that he was 6'2", Virgo, lived in my area, didn't want any more kids, and had salt and pepper hair. Although his photos were totally unappealing to me (he actually reminded me of one of my cousins… blech… although he resembled my second-favorite cousin… blech nonetheless), I thought,

Why?

Why now?

Why is Mr. Six Foot Two Salt and Pepper Virgo contacting me now when I'm walking away?

Months of messages from Messrs. Five Foot Four Chubby Bubby and now I get *this*? But then there was also the amazing profile that he had posted for himself:

> Im back again, and just looking to find a simple, yet compassionate,woman to begin a relationship with. An easy break down of me goes by the words that i live by, a motto per say:
>
> LIFE is short
> LOVE truly
> KISS slowly
> FORGIVE quickly
> SMILE from the HEART.
>
> Its that simple..."

Honesty is that best policy with me and that goes both ways. Looking for a woman thats athletic to thin build and will only respond if you have an "up to date" picture,

Want to know more just ask... im easy going.

All the best to you in your search for happiness...

Oh, brother. His skeletal profile and grammatical, spelling and punctuation errors made it easy for me to click send on my letdown letter.

Forgive me for exposing my snobbery, but if a person can't even take the time to capitalize the "I" in "I'm," let alone put in the apostrophe, then why should I waste time on him?

"Per say"? I won't even go there.

To be perfectly honest, I think I was trying to find any reason I could to justify shelving the guy. I'm really not that mean, I just wanted to protect my heart from further hurt. A scared little turtle afraid to stick her neck out.

Anyhoo, all three men were tall, had astrological signs compatible with mine, and lived close to my area. Steve had actually been on my favorites list while I was still in my old hometown and then disappeared for a long time. Now he was back and just as devastatingly handsome as ever; and since I was really questioning my feelings for Stefan, I fell into conversations with him... and Tony... and a smattering of banter with *The Greg*.

Although my initial interest was in Steve (the physiotherapist, 6'6", divorced, eight-year-old daughter), Tony soon became the frontrunner, and Greg trailed in a far, distant, abysmal third place. I loved talking to Tony and we really clicked in all of our messages.

Tony: 6'4", athletic build, Cancer, owned a mid-sized auto parts distribution company, had kids in their late teens. Soon we started messaging privately and he called me his "Cutie Pie."

Awwwwwww.

Very quickly, Steve became a little... *a lot*... too enthusiastic and sexual in his messages. I was starting to get a bad vibe about him so I let our messages trail off into nothing. Goodbye, Mr. Yummy Pants... hello again, silver foxes.

Tony, on the other hand, was still raring to go after three days of communications, until he said, *I just have to go make a phone call, can we chat more in a bit?*

We had just finished talking about our kids and filling each other in on their details. I knew that we were getting to a point where he'd ask to meet me, and I was getting really nervous. Excited, but nervous nonetheless.

I never heard from Tony again.

He had previously added me to his instant messenger list, so I'd see him online, but he never messaged me. I let Tony go by the wayside and removed him from my instant messenger contacts. I didn't allow my feelings to get hurt with that snub, but it still made me wish that people could just shoot from the hip.

So now I just had Greg… and Stefan… and Fred (who continued to cyber-stalk me).

I received a couple of base-touching messages from Stefan, and my agreement with Fred was that we could speak through messaging only, and only as friends. I thought I made it clear to him, and I thought he understood. Apparently not.

My initial banter with Greg began innocently when he questioned why I was back again. *How did he know that I was coming back?* On this particular site, when someone is on your favorites list, you can see when he or she last logged in. It's quite a handy tool for stalkers and frazzled femmes who want to establish if their Dairy King is still spending his lunch hour cyber-flirting instead of calling or emailing her to tell her how much she means to him. And breathe.

Disclaimer: Much of the English language has been harmed in the making of this story.

For those of you who have a dominant Type-A personality, please note that none of the grammar, punctuation, or spelling of *Greg "Mr. Shakespeare" Silver Fox*'s dialogue has been altered in any way. You, too, may enjoy the agitated, twitchy feeling I experience with the muck and mire of his fou-fou talk. In response to Greg's query about why I kept coming back to the site, I wrote:

> My profile is hidden, but I still receive email notifications when someone messages me, and since we have corresponded in the past, you will always be able to see my profile until I physically delete it.
>
> You worried me though, because, once in the past, when I thought my profile was down, I

had actually jiggled something and it was still up. Thus the reason that you saw me before. :-D Thought I had done it again. LOL

But to answer your question, no change in mind. I'm still overwhelmed and sitting on the proverbial fence. You will note that I haven't deleted your messages... that would be a subtle hint that I am not "un-intrigued." I'm just overwhelmed by all the attention and sitting high upon my safe little fence while I regroup.

So on that note, I will retire for the evening. Thank you for popping your head in again though.

His reply was filled with drippy stuff in an effort to come across as sincere and deep.

Sit as you may, and do as you must.

Just a joy to wonder:

as it is a joy to rise to shine, for with no sun, it is only us that makes the day bright.

SMILE FROM THE HEART!

Veronica, i hope that fence that you are safely perched upon sits comfortably, for i would not like to see such a fair maiden hurt from the elements?

Have yourself a wonderful day full of greatness.

Oh lord. Is it just me, or did you just throw up a little in your mouth too? "Have yourself a wonderful day full of greatness." What the *hell* is that? Who says stuff like that?

All I could picture was some sort of door-to-door evangelist saying that. Is he just priming the pump so that he can lure me into his cult of ill-grammared religious zealots? Am I the only one who reads it that way? Instead of expressing my disdain at his frilly words, I replied:

OMG! LOL

You brought me back in here for THAT! LOL

Oh Greg, with such fluffy words like that, I cannot help but be careless upon my perch knowing that I have such comforting padding awaiting me below.

Very charming. Very charming.

Did I find it charming? No, not at all. But I didn't want to burst the little bubble in which he was floating faaaaaar above the planet that we lived on. But what did my words do? They only encouraged him more:

I'm very confident that i would be below ready to catch you as you jump into my arms.

A shared smile and a soft embrace as i slowly lower you to asure your feet, we are still on earth. Flights of fancy and sunsets to chase, the horizion is endless, only time is to make the beginning. When is the only question, as only now dreams can fill the moments...

Sweet dreams to you Veronica.

Beautiful eyes and a smile to match.

Why?

Why?

Why?

Why did he have to compliment my smile?

The thing that I loathe most about myself is the thing that he loves. Ugh...

What can of worms have I opened?

Okay, if he wants to play it fluffy, I'll hit him with a taste of his own medicine:

I had to go and look at your profile just now to see what your profession was. So does that mean that you are the "supervisor" at Hallmark? Or a distant relative of some famous poet?

As my bleary eyes linger upon the screen I am taken to a distant place in my mind that is filled with the softness of the morning breeze and the strong, yet gentle arms of a caring man. In that state, I can close my eyes and imagine the warmth of the sun filling my soul, and the beat of his heart soothing me with its rhythm.

That is about as good as it gets for a woman who's been up for twenty hours after only three hours' sleep.

Sir, why oh why do you try to lure me away from the safety of my perch?

There.

Take that!

Stick that fluff in your pipe and smoke it. Oh my gawd, when will this sugary talk end so that I can have a normal conversation with this man? Well, by the following, you'll see that I was nowhere near the light at the end of my cyber-fluff tunnel:

As your bleary eyes rested in a soothing sleep. Calmly rested high atop your safe perch, all well known that the world surrounds you to new realms. Glorious images painted to a sky, with wings to flight as they soar in the morning breeze.

What more could your heart ask; rhythm in time as the hand that holds, a joint union travelled down your new found destiny, never to look back...

Good morning, nothing lost only gained...

Im Greg, not Sir, lol

Okay, this was getting ridiculous now. Rather than cutting the cord, I was willing to allow this man to redeem himself and become normal.

Well Sir Greg, :-p

You obviously have me intrigued. Maybe you could tell me a little more about yourself.

You're of European heritage, what exactly? I'm a mutt myself - Middle Eastern, Brazilian, English, Scottish and Irish.

I'll let you fill me in on what you're comfortable with, and you are welcome, in turn, to ask what you like (if there was something that I actually DIDN'T put in my profile LOL).

The baton is back in your hands.

There. Maybe Mr. Shakespeare can show his true colors now.

Well now Ms. V,

Nice to hear of your mixture, im guessing you get your dark hair from your Middle Eastern roots, your verse from the Brazilian and the way you express yourself ever so delightfully from the Irish roots? No need to answer those responses, lol.

European roots, yes, both my parents are from Hungary, i am born here. I also speak Portuguese fluently, but no Brazilian blood in me. I actually lived there for 3 years, and learnt the lingo point blank. I'd love to learn Spanish one day, but all in time...

As the baton twirrrrrrrrls, i am in alittle bit of a hurry and must fly like the wind to my brothers house, it is my little nephews birthday today, he is officially 2 today, big party on Saturday.

I am truly intrigued with the way you write and express yourself, no lies to that comment, its impressive. Not one liners and the lalalalalalalalaa shuffle.

I will definetly get back to you, by all means.

As you questioned the supervisor role, no its not for Hallmark, but have been recommended to script my poety for publishing, lol. All in time i say...

Someone had recommended publishing that stuff? Oh boy.

Thank goodness this wasn't all happening in person, because he would have won the wet T-shirt contest after being soaked by the sarcasm that my words were actually dripping with. For a moment, I thought that maybe I was just being too cynical and judgmental; so I went back and read our conversations again... nope. I still found him to be just as annoying as before.

Actually, my dark hair comes from my hairdresser. I'm actually a frustrated redhead. It's more auburn now, but I decided to go very dark for the winter. It's salon-enhanced red again for the summer. I was a carrot top as a kid, but ironically, it did not come from my Scottish or Irish heritage, it is from the M.E. side of things.

As for the Spanish, I don't think you'd have any problem learning it since you already speak Portuguese. That's how I learned to speak it, because my second language is French.

My eyes and my literary follies have always been what people like about me. My beer belly and eleventh toe are the things they don't like. So at least I have some traits that balance me out a bit. I do also have a very sharp sense of humour, so if you're uptight and serious all the time, you might consider closing this chapter.

When I write it's my form of freedom. It's hard to be eloquent in the moment sometimes, so my creative outlet comes into play here. I am a very visual person, so when people speak, I see their words as images; therefore, I too try to paint a vivid picture with the words that I say or write.

Have a wonderful time with your family, and I look forward to learning more about you. I loved it when my daughter was two, but four years old was my favorite age. They're still your baby, but yet you can communicate more effectively with words at that point. I also love that they are like little bobble heads at that age. Big eyes, big head, little bodies. I adore her as a fourteen-year-old too, but I miss that little girl. Okay, I better go before the old lady gets all sentimental.

Veronica

Fingers crossed that he was uptight and serious so I could end this banter and continue my house-hunting in peace. I really get tired of how polite and nice I am when it comes to humoring people, but I would rather be the one cast aside because of their choice (and then whine about how mean they are). I will let you continue reading without my negative commentaries. And yes, his punctuation, spelling, and grammar continue to be untouched… my apologies to *them thar Type-A folks.*

RED, oh so very interesting... one of my favorite colors, and not to say that to attract your attention. All my kitchen walls are painted red, including the cieling, and i have alot of base accents throughout the house, ooooooooh! wowwwy. lol I find red as a passion and enhancement to life...

Im impressed as to you bragging about the beauty of your beer belly, true sexy at heart, lol. As for the eleventh toe, now thats impressive, any relation to "Mork", Nanoooo, Nanoooo. In a foot to foot of sense, very cute though.

Sob as estrelas nos encontraremos... enquanto isso, boa noite minha linda... doce sonhos

Ps. Had a wonderful family time, its always pleasant within these gatherings and memories to last a life time.

Assim, good night Veronica, Ronnie, V, which ever if preferable to you.

você também pode ser fofa...

A redheaded Capricorn... pretty scary by most people's standards. Fortunately, I am not a typical Cappy, so no lives have been lost with my temper and there are no ex-husband body parts strewn carelessly in the woods. I'm a very peaceful, calm and loving person (unless I'm in tae kwon do, and then that's when all the cap-fury is expelled).

I must warn you that I need to use an online translator to read Portuguese. I find it much easier to read Italian actually. The translator did not like how deep and poetic you were being, but I was able to get the gist of it.

Well, my daughter's computer decided to turn itself on and do updates, which woke me, scared the hell out of me, and now I'm wide awake. So, I am off to the gym and then TGIF!

I hear it's supposed to be a beautiful day. Have a great one!

VJ (thought I'd throw another one in there)

Well, early to rise catches the glare special to another eyes. The opportunity to watch a sun rise is always empowering and lifting to any day. Its truly nice to hear from you so early in the morning... you gave me a special smile.

As for the Capricorn characteristics, not worried at all, even though you know Tai Kwon Do. Now that would be interesting to witness, thumb wrestle shall we, lol

I will refrain from the portuguese dialogue for the time being... hope the workout was a good release and empowering to kick start your day. Yes, TGIF.

Im off to a new training session today, a new adventure ahead of me. My saddle mounted and guns are loaded, (would never use one, just the expression of intensity).

Ok VJ

Have an amazing day, and keep that beautiful smile going, "SMILE AND THE WORLD WILL SMILE WITH YOU".

I'm glad I could put a smile on your face this morning in my groggy state. I do enjoy getting up early for my exercises because it's my quiet time. No one at the gym but me and my music. 3a.m.... it's not often I get up and stay up that early, but I don't mind once in a while.

I had to sign a legal document once I received my black belt that stated that, because I am a registered lethal weapon, I may not use my skills for anything but self defense. Therefore, I don't think I can indulge you in the thumb wrestle. You could call the authorities and tell them that I was using brutal force on you and put me away in the pokey for many years to come. They'd believe you too, because what 6'2" man, in his right mind, would admit to having his ass kicked by a scrawny girl.

I've used a gun... and it's quite empowering. My use was for protection in Central America, but I have always wanted to go to a firing range for fun.

The smile on my face never leaves, but as the day wears on, and I am at the end of my rope dealing with unnecessary human ignorance, it just gets bigger and bigger. After all, the easiest way to get at someone's jugular is with your teeth bared.

Boy... I really sound like a very violent woman. Really I'm not. Can't even kill an insect (they must be caught under a glass and put outside).

So, you still owe me a bit of a bio. If it so pleases you, you may do so at my private email below so that I don't have to keep coming back here.

Isn't the day always great when the smile never leaves your face??? To deal with human ignorance can be frustrating yes, i know how you feel... dealt with alot of it in my life. But, we maintain a straight face or justice in ourselves and must accept and forgive the victim of demoral. Once you witness or experience to your nature someone of sorts, it best to just repeat the phrase:

"I SEE PEACE, I SEE LOVE, I SEE BEAUTY". Acknowledge the acceptance the others are unaware of, we are equal not peasants of another race non existant of this earth.

I truly would not want you to be any other than who you are today and yesterday and of course not to the future. I know you have morals and a great respect for humanity and all living things, why would you be something you are not? I am not looking for a fantasy of any sorts, nor superficial dream... i would want you to be exactly who you are and no other.

I am impressed that you have self defense training, very important in todays world, i guess all depends on the destiny of our travels. Yet, this would inhance your well being and an added bonus. Mind, body, spirit as i say it, important.

Hope your day was successful, sorry i didn't respond this morning, i did read your last response, but was running late to respond.

It was a dream of mine to study martial arts when I was a teen, but I was so shy that I couldn't get up the courage. I even tried convincing my daughter to do it with me when she was about five. Then when she was seven, she came with me to take some friends' kids to their class and she was blown away. I couldn't start because of my job commitments, but I enrolled her. She is a second-degree BB (I'm only a first degree... pout... pout), and I have had great peace knowing that when she's at school she is not going to be taken advantage of. Honestly, in this day and age, I think all women and children should have that training. I'm not crazy, nor am I violent (if you saw me, you would never guess that I have that skill-set), but if it were to come down to it, and my life or someone else's was at stake, I would not hesitate.

Murphy's Law kicked in today and, of course, while everyone was leaving early for their long weekend, I was still there two hours later than I should have been. Then my plans for this evening were cancelled, so I'm trying very hard not to pout. LOL Okay... no... I'm pouting. LOL Maybe a nice cliché bar of chocolate will pick me up... nah... I'll just pout. I have brunch plans with my friend from out of town on Sunday, so I'll just count down the hours until our girly gabfest. That'll perk me up.

But it was nice to come home after too long of a day to a nice, cheery message. Thank you for that.

The One and Only - Ronnie :-D

P.S. No need to apologize for the late reply.

Im always thrilled to send a cheery message to anyone, especially a morning message by email or text, truly enjoy it with alot of insperation, aslong as a person appreciates the time and efforts. You probably just can't understand how much that gives me great pleasures. Yes, i am a true extorovert. About 80% extro and 20% intor, i do have to think of myself as well no??

Anyways, i am truly sorry to hear that your long wkend plans fell through to the deep end, and notice that you are still swimming or rowing with some paddels anyway. But, no need to pout, regardless of the outcome, we are still all young at heart and things will become as you wish, just manifest it, and witness. SO BE IT, AND SO IT IS!

Chocolate eh? LOL, I have said this many times, and its sad to the fact: "A woman that craves chocolate... lacks affection ". No offense, but the comfort is yet peaceful and comforting without menace, i guess?

Please don't get yourself down and be cheerrrrrrryy! Yaaaaaaaaaaaaaaaah! I am sure there is much love that surrounds you not witnessed yet?

Not meaning to pry, but a question-how are things with the gentleman that you have given a chance with coming along? You don't have to answer this if you think its non of my business, and i respect your privacy.

Lacking affection? I snorted when I read that. LOL Understatement of the year, my friend. Actually understatement of the past two decades. LOL

As for my gentleman caller, I am regrouping. I've taken a step back for the time being.

So what kind of fanfare are you up to this weekend? Time with your kid(s)?

Would have been reallllllly cute to hear you snort aloud, lmao. But, not to laugh at your situation, i know how you truly feel, been there done that,with all honesty. Oh well, everything happens for a reason. A true shame that life is sometimes and what life brings to us.

REGROUPING? Don't understand, why the stepping back? Have you pick-up some strange signs or vibes not to your liking??

For the fan fare, not too much, just a bunch of friends heading out. Im actually going to celebrate a career move. A total revelation and passion that has been growing and unseen for much of time. Yesterday was my last day as Supervisor, and no not at Hallmark. That would of been a great job of interest though. In my past i have been Project Supervisors, Shop Foreman, Lead Hand and who ever to the best of my ability and passion. Well, that passionate candle has burnt itself out unfortuanatly. But, not so, i have an awesome hands on ability that will never lack and will continue to give help to any that request or that i see are struggling. Always willing to give a helping hand and make someones life easier if accepted.

I have turned may passions to sales at the moment, and what a feeling. I will be selling air purification systems for the home evironment. I believe it with all my heart and see it as the wave of the future, we all need it, clean air that is. We can't control the pollution and VOCs but we can try at least to purify the air that we breathe daily at home. I say think now, too late later...

As they say "If you don't pay for it now, you will have to pay for it later." That is in reference to our health. So many people are in denial/ opposed to taking care of their bodies, and not realizing that when they're older they will have to deal with medications and technologies to save

their lives. I had to leave my air purification system where it was when I moved here, so I'm looking forward to finding a permanent/semi-permanent residence so that I can install one. I had an amazing unit and it always helped me sleep so much better. I never woke up feeling stuffed up or headachy.

I study nutrition and health as a hobby, so I'm very passionate about taking care of this temple that God has blessed me with. I want to be healthy for my daughter and my future grandkids. My view is, it's not about how you look in a pair of jeans, it's about allowing your body to run efficiently.

I applaud you on your new career path. Although exciting, it must be a little intimidating at times. Then again, I don't know how men process and handle things. I just moved to this province three months ago to find my inner peace. I have no family here, and only one friend (who I've only known a year), so at times it's scary and overwhelming. Sometimes it's hard to be bulletproof in the face of my daughter. Sometimes I wish I could be a girl and just cry my eyes out when I get overwhelmed. I used to watch "Extreme Makeover: Home Edition" every Sunday (before we moved here), so that when things were feeling overwhelming, my daughter just thought that it was the show that was making me cry (I'm a big crybaby when it comes to that kind of stuff). The reasons I would watch it were: 1) To stop wallowing in self-pity and realize that I have it a lot better than so many people; and 2) To bawl my eyes out without my daughter knowing what was really causing it. It was good therapy for sure.

As for the gentleman caller. No strange signs or vibes. It's a distance thing (an hour away) and he's very busy with his growing company. I'm not getting the time that I would like, but I'm not selfish enough to stand and jump up and down and say "Look at me! Look at me!", as I understand the workload and responsibilities he has. I am very gun-shy about the dating scene, and taking my time to properly assess what it is that I would like for my and my daughter's future.

I have actually been married twice (six years for the first and nine for the second), and rushed into both. There, my dirty secret is out. I do believe that I did everything in my power to make those marriages work (the second one, for sure). I have spent the past fifteen years reading probably every self-help and PMA book out there to learn how to be a happy, kind, and well-balanced person. Fortunately, I was gifted with the ability to be truly honest with myself, so I was able to see where I needed changing and tweaking. I really like who I've become and am just looking to one day share my denture cup with someone who allows me to be me in every single way. I had to pretend to be something that I'm not for too many years. I won't lose sight of 'me' ever again. For the first time in my life, I'm comfortable in my own skin.

Was that TMI?

WOW, you are a woman of my own heart, really, and thats scary for me to read your words at heart.

Your comments of the Extreme Makeover; i was exactly the same, wouldn't hide a tear of the blessing that are passed on to well deserving individuals of life. I once possed a question to my ex, yet at the time to my wife... i said: "i would love to volunteer my time to a causes like so, and would be very prided to the fact to help a well deserving family in need. Would you do such a thing, i asked?" Her response was no with a true smug look on her face. I tell this with no lies, and not because she is my ex, but to me at the time my heart litterally drop a mile.

His last message struck a chord in me that made me believe that maybe there was something salvageable underneath all of that fluff and horrible grammar and spelling. *Damn it, damn it, damn it! Why am I letting him win?*

After a few more brief messages back and forth, I was finally able to convince him to switch to emailing me on my private email address… you know… the one that has a stupid name and you only give it to strangers? Six days of banter and getting-to-know-you chat until he finally asked me to meet and we exchanged cell numbers so he could call to make arrangements. Although I was intrigued, I really wasn't interested in meeting him. My heart was closed up, and besides that, he had yet to really sell me on him. But I agreed, because: 1) I'm a wimp and incapable of saying no; and 2) I figured that he'd meet me and realize we had nothing in common and I could go back up on my fence and keep safe.

I told him that I had a toonie burning a hole in my pocket and would join him for a coffee.

Well, instead of calling me, he sent me fifty text messages in *one day*. No, I am not being melodramatic for the sake of entertainment… I actually counted them! Daniella always laughed at me while watching me try to text, because I am the type that has to count out loud when pushing the buttons for the corresponding letter (complete with tongue sticking out of the corner of mouth). It was frustrating to say the least. During that day of texting, Greg took me out for a walk with him (cyberly, that is), and I felt something come over me and wished that he would ask me to come along. I quickly slapped myself in the face to wake up from the strange fog of loneliness and longing I was suddenly feeling. Instead of asking me to join him then, he invited me to meet the next evening (Sunday) for coffee and a walk.

On Sunday afternoon he sent me a text asking if I wanted to meet him earlier than originally planned. I was just sitting at home in my jammies working, so I agreed to meet him an hour from then. Then my phone rang. When I saw the number (although I had yet to record it in my phone), I knew it was him, but I didn't want to pick it up. I quickly realized that, since I was meeting him in an hour, it would be rude not to. My stomach did a flip-flop and I engaged the call. The next thing that happened completely threw me for a loop.

I heard his voice for the first time and a warmth washed over me, to the point where I could feel my face go flush. It was almost as if he was standing behind me with his arms wrapped around me, surrounding me like a warm blanket. That feeling of a strong man behind me, holding me tight, while nuzzling his warm face into the nape of my neck. Kissing me ever so gently, ever so slowly, as his hands began to move tenderly to…

Veronica! What are you doing? Snap out of it!

Greg gave me directions for our meeting and it made me laugh aloud. We were to meet at a parking lot behind a hotel close to the boardwalk where he had walked the night before. All I could picture was parking behind some seedy motel by a dumpster so that he had some place to dispose of my remains after he chopped me into pieces. I shared the visual with him and the sound of his heartfelt laugh warmed me even more. I could feel my face go flush again.

I went and got ready for our date and was about to leave when Daniella said, "You're going out like *that*?"

"What? I look fine." We were only going for a walk, so I had put on my black yoga pants and matching jacket. What was her damage?

"Seriously Mother. Could you *at least* brush your hair and put on some makeup?"

"Listen, Daniella, if he doesn't like me for who I am, then screw him. I'm not out to impress anyone anymore."

Daniella proceeded to force me to make a slight effort. So I brushed my hair, put on mascara, and left for my one and only date with Greg. How much cosmetic prep work do you need to do to go, drink a coffee, rip off a Band-Aid and be done with it? Sigh… the things we do to appease our children.

CHAPTER 23
MEETING GREG

I'm not sure if I was truly nervous, but I know I was a little on edge because of having to find my way to a location I'd never been to before. *Did the cyber-guy give me "girl" directions? Will I be circling for hours?* Regardless of the fact that I had my trusty—but belligerent—GPS, I will remind you that I am, after all, the Queen of Lost, and can outsmart even the most advanced navigational system in order to get myself completely turned around.

I pulled into the parking lot of the hotel and it was exactly how he said it would be laid out, and there he was in his car. *Now* I was really nervous. I pulled up beside him and raised my hands in a gesture of victory. I didn't know what else to do—I hate hellos and I hate goodbyes—I had to break the ice somehow.

He was already standing outside of his car when I got out of mine, and I was so grateful I was wearing my sunglasses to mask the look in my eyes, because I did not expect to be so taken aback by his appearance. He was wearing a dark blue windbreaker that looked amazing against his olive skin and silver hair. He was so tall and so solid that I just wanted to wrap my arms around him. The term *wow* was actually uttered very clearly in my mind. The photos on his online profile were headshots, and his hair was considerably longer—the man in front of me was clean cut and freakin' gorgeous.

Nervous? Yes. We now have confirmed nervousness. We have lift-off!

What started as a rip-off-the-Band-Aid-and-never-talk-to-him-again meeting took quite an unexpected turn. For the first time since I started this whole cyber-roller coaster, I was looking at a man whom I found to be quite... well... scrumptious. Remember beautiful Erick? Good, because Greg's gorgeourifickness made Erick look like Gomer Pyle. I can't believe I considered settling on Gomer when I could have Adonis. *Holy crap! How am I even going to be able to string together simple sentences on this date?* I was completely gaga and tongue-tied.

We popped into a coffee shop to grab our drinks, but I really didn't want anything because I knew we'd be walking for a while and didn't want my infantile bladder to embarrass me. I ordered coffee, and he, a mint tea.

Mint tea? Mint tea? I wanted to order mint tea. Why didn't I order mint tea? Why is he ordering mint tea? Is he trying to put on airs? Is he trying to come across as Mr. Suave and Sensitive? Grrr! I really want mint tea. I can't change my order now—that would seem lame. Ugh... I really would prefer mint tea. Pout.

We walked along a lakeside path and Greg talked just as much as I did (it was so refreshing, as I was used to more one-sided conversations from previous dates). I felt comfortable around him. We talked easily and I found myself acting like me. The me that only Daniella ever witnessed.

Greg was excited. As he'd told me in one of his previous messages, he had just quit his job as a foreman at a company that made custom store fixtures to become an independent salesperson for a residential air purification company. He was so excited and spoke about it with such passion—he told me so many facts about air purification that I finally let him know he was preaching to the choir. I spent years as an independent contractor for a company that marketed, among other things, air purification systems.

I really enjoyed listening to Greg. It was nice to keep my mouth shut for once and just go along for the ride. We walked for over an hour, and there was never a lull in the conversation. It wasn't constant chattering to fill awkward silences—it was sincere conversation that flowed. Finally I had met the real man under the fluff. He spoke like a regular guy—the Shakespeare-on-crack from the cyber world didn't make an appearance.

I found out that English was Greg's second language (his family immigrated here from Hungary), which explained the grammatical disconnect of his written messages. I felt slightly ashamed—maybe it wasn't insincere fluff after all... maybe he was doing his best to rise above his linguistic limitations. Whatever it was, I'd met the real Greg now and liked what I was seeing and hearing.

As we came close to reaching our cars again, he asked if we could stop so he could use the washroom.

Thank gawd! I won't have to suffer needlessly.

Hold on a minute. A man needing to stop to use the facilities? Do you think he has an immature bladder too? Have I met my soul mate?

Upon entering the washroom, I was quite dismayed to see that the blustery winds had wreaked havoc on my hair and that my eyes were bloodshot from all the fresh air. Honestly, I don't remember the last time I'd gotten that much fresh air. Since I moved here, I'd pretty much been a shut-in. Okay, let's be honest… before I moved here, I'd pretty much been a shut-in.

We got back to our cars and stood and chatted even longer. I kept changing positions to get him between me and the strong winds. The man is built like a brick shit-house, so he made a great windbreaker for me. He asked if I wanted to continue our chat in my car, but I told him I was fine. Shivering uncontrollably, but fine. After talking for probably close to another hour I finally agreed to take shelter in his car.

Inside the car, we talked for *another* hour, and it was still so comfortable. I kept looking at his mouth. My gawd. He had the most amazing lips and I just wanted to know what they'd feel like on mine. I will admit that I missed much of what he said because I was mesmerized by his beautiful lips and that gorgeous, perfect, gleaming white smile.

Suddenly my phone chimed. I apologized and told him I'd let Daniella know that she could call me if she needed me. It was actually a text message, but not from her. It was from Fred—the stalker—as he so fondly became known as in our household. I scanned it quickly and saw the key words can't live without you… you're all I can think about… we were meant to be together. I apologized again and looked at my watch. It was six o'clock, and I told Greg that I still needed to get home and pick up Daniella to go grocery shopping.

We talked for another hour. I just couldn't find a way to leave (remember, not good at goodbyes). I really couldn't read him very well either. He seemed somewhat aloof towards me, but was very polite and kind nonetheless. As I started to get out of his car, he caught a glimpse of one of my tattoos. Well, that led to a new branch of conversation. Finally, at seven o'clock, I told him that I really had to go before Daniella disowned me. I thanked him for the conversation and coffee and wished him a good evening.

Driving home, I thought about the four hours I had just spent with Greg. I kept recapping the new memories and each one made me smile more than the last. I had enjoyed my time with him so much. It was so comfortable and so… so natural. It felt as if I'd known him for years.

When I got home, I quickly ran into the house to relieve myself (yes, *again*) and tell Daniella I was home so we could scoot off to the grocery store. She asked me how the date went and I said, "It was fine. He was really nice and really easy to talk to."

"Are you going to see him again?"

"I really don't know. I didn't get a feeling from him either way. I really don't know."

When we got into the car, it wouldn't start. Not a click, not a chug, not even a gargle. The only thing I could think of was to call Phil.

He didn't answer.

Phil and I usually only email or text each other, so if one of us calls the other, we know it's something important. Since he didn't answer, I figured it was because he was working and couldn't. What to do? Then a thought came to me. I remembered Greg telling me that he'd started restoring a pick-up truck at one point in his life.

I sent him a text message that said, "What does it mean when you try to start the car and it only makes a *click-click* noise?"

As I waited for his reply, I reached one more time to try to turn the car on. Just as I turned the key in the ignition, my phone rang and scared the buhjeezus out of Daniella and me—we both screamed. Laughing and shaking, I answered the phone—it was Greg. He went over a few things that it could be, but basically, because it was the Sunday of a long weekend, I was dead in the water.

I thanked him very much for his help and apologized for disturbing him. He replied, "No problem. Anytime. Talk to you soon." I hung up the phone and said, "Well… I guess I *will* be seeing him again."

That night I talked to Phil. He felt horrible for missing my call but was out of town with a date. I whined to him about my confusion over all my dating woes, and, since my car was dead as a doornail, he came and picked me up for a platonic sleepover at his place.

Phil's house was always such a comforting place to be. You could even see the peace in Daniella when we'd have our blended family gatherings. The next morning, Phil and I went out for brunch and he got to witness firsthand the attention Greg was giving me. The texting was non-stop. Not annoying, but constant.

The attention he was giving me and the level of communication was somewhat overwhelming, and it scared the hell out of me. I knew it was what I wanted in a relationship, but I didn't know if I wanted a relationship yet, let alone one with him. My head had gotten very fuzzy with this recent addition to the Stefan equation. Sometimes even Phil made the situation worse, because even though it was established that we would never be anything but family, his actions suggested that he didn't want me to be with anyone else.

I met Greg later that evening for another walk. I didn't want him to know where I lived, so we met at the same strip mall where I'd first met Branden. Behind that mall ran a trail that spanned for miles, so that was our venue of choice. As we walked and chatted, there were the little high-school touches and shoves and tickles. Then at one point he said, "Look! Bunny!"

Oh cripes. Here we go again. Enter fluffy fou-fou Greg.

Miles down the path, when a deer ran out and he said "Look! A deer!" I saw a twinkle in his eyes and realized that *Goliath Greg* was just a big fuzzy teddy bear. Well... more like a gorgeous silver fox.

I don't know how long we walked before our hands bumped one more time and he took the opportunity to hold on. It was so *high school* that I felt seventeen again—in a good way. In a *very* good way—right down to my toes, including some key areas in between.

Then I got confused by his signals when we stopped at a nearby coffee shop to warm up and chat some more. He wasn't touchy-feely anymore, he was almost standoffish; and I was definitely thrown off. Once we headed back towards my house, I figured it was safe to let him know where I lived, so I let him walk me all the way home. As we stood outside under the street lamp, he made a few gentle attempts to kiss me. Right up there with hellos and goodbyes, first kisses make me want to run and hide. Each time he'd lean in, I'd get overwhelmed with shyness and do a *tuck-and-weave* to avoid his advances.

This is so embarrassing. I'm a grown woman and I can't even kiss a guy.

Finally, I reached up and laid one on him.

Remember that "am I dead inside" question I had back with Mick? Well, even though I thought that Branden and Stefan had reignited that passion in me, this was a different feeling altogether. What I had felt for them was purely sexual; it wasn't like this at all. The minute Greg's hand touched my cheek, I felt an electricity surge through my body as if he had recharged my soul. At that moment, I was very relieved that I wasn't a man... if you know what I mean.

We spent the next few hours in the tightest embrace, kissing like reunited lovers. Although I felt nervous and self-conscious about the whole process (and the chance of neighbors seeing us), when he held me tight, it became *very* apparent that he was a *big* fan of my lips. Again—if you know what I mean. Wink wink, nudge nudge. Wokka wokka!

I didn't want to leave him, but I'm so glad we had nowhere private to go, because I don't know if I could have controlled myself in secluded surroundings. He finally left at two o'clock in the morning, and I could not function. He had definitely found a place in my mind and I did not want to be away from those arms or lips.

The next day, I was able to get my car towed, but was stranded and couldn't go to work. Early in the afternoon, I received a message from Greg asking if I would like a kiss. I replied, *Do you mean—do I want x's and o's, or do you mean a real kiss?* A real kiss is what he wanted, and he drove twenty minutes to come and claim it.

When he walked into the house, the shyness came over me again because he looked incredibly gorgeous and smelled amazing.

Why is this sweet and incredibly good-looking man giving me the time of day? I've only ever attracted frogs… how have I suddenly gotten a prince?

Overwhelmed? That was an understatement.

He came in and sat on the living room couch and Leopold (Leo), our cat, instantly jumped onto his lap, plopped himself down, and started purring and making bread on him.

What? Leo hates all men. Is this a sign?

After I shooed Leo away, I got my kiss. Two hours' worth actually. My intention was to receive a few lovely kisses and then go for a walk before Daniella got home from school. What actually happened was that she walked through the door as I was straddling Greg on the couch while we made out like teenagers. Fast as lightning, I threw myself off of him and sat innocently beside him as his eyeglasses went tumbling to the floor. There was a stunned silence and then I said, "Daniella, this is Greg."

They exchanged polite hellos and then Greg went to use the washroom to compose himself. Daniella said, "Is he the tow truck driver? And… what happened to your face?"

Oh thank gawd, she hadn't seen anything. Phew. Not so phew was the fact that a very large area around my mouth and chin was bright red from the combination of our very passionate kissing session and Greg's razor-sharp two-day stubble. I was mortified. It looked like I had been beaten up. I very coyly explained to my daughter that we had been kissing *a little.* The following days would see my chin begin to peel, which I explained to coworkers as being a sunburn from working in the garden over the long weekend.

Greg and I went for a nice walk before he headed out to meet up with his boys, and we spent the entire time giggling like teenagers and smooching and cuddling every few steps. We definitely had a strong compatibility (and a strong physical connection as well), but did I want this? Was I ready for this?

Were his arms strong enough and soft enough to catch me from the leap I would have to take from the safety of my high perch?

While Daniella and I shopped later that evening, the sweet text messages started coming in from Greg. As frustrating as I found texting, I was taken aback by the consistent attention he gave me. *Is this going to fade into nothing once he gets me?* Over-analyzing Veronica started to take over again.

Finally, with very hesitant thumbs, I sent him the text message that would change my life.

> Do you still think that you are strong enough to catch me if I came down from the safety of my wall?

> Strong enough to never let your feet touch the ground. I will keep you safe always.

> Then I'd like to come down now.

> YAHOO! To celebrate, I would like to make you dinner on Thursday. Will you do me that honor?

Make me dinner? Wow. No man had ever done anything like that before. Well, that's not totally true; Phil made his famous bachelor chicken dish for me once, but it's not like it was a date or anything. Okay. Technically, dinner had been prepared for me by a man before, but for some reason, I couldn't put those instances into this category of dinner-making. Let's be really honest… I was totally gaga for this guy, so he could basically do no wrong.

That night, Greg and I spent a few hours on the phone and I told him about the school that Daniella had chosen and how I now needed to find a rental home in that area. That school happened to be just a few blocks from his house. I was starting to think more and more that this was meant to be. Everything that had occurred since coming for my look-see the previous December had just been leading me closer to him.

CHAPTER 24
CLARITY

Since I decided to come down from my perch, I needed to be honest with Stefan. As we hadn't seen each other in a couple of weeks, and I'd barely heard a thing from him, I felt an email to end it would suffice. My heart was torn up about him because, really, he was a truly wonderful man. I sat at my office and wrote a very long and heartfelt email to him. I thanked him for helping me take one step closer to finding the real Veronica. I didn't tell him that he helped me add a few things to my *but* list, but I did say what a huge difference he'd made in my life. I felt very conflicted as I clicked the send button.

I sent Greg a text telling him what I had done, and he immediately called me. I took the phone call to a private office and I cried. I was scared. Yet, here I was, on the phone with my new love interest, and he was gently consoling me for breaking up with a past beau.

Who does that? Who is this man? Is he really this amazing, or just too good to be true?

After work that day, I was to do a couple drive-bys of rental houses on my way home, so I sent Greg a text that said, Would you like a kiss?

> X's and O's or a real kiss?
> A real kiss.

Although he couldn't see it, I was grinning from ear to ear.

He sent me his address which sent me into a momentary state of shock. He lived on Ruth Avenue.

Ruth?

Ruth?

Was this a sign? I duly punched the address into the temperamental GPS. My stomach was doing flip-flops the entire way there, and the fifty minutes it took to arrive felt like hours.

All day, Greg had been the only thing on my mind (especially after he consoled me on the phone). I realized that when I was with him, I felt clarity and peace. For the first time in years, and I mean *years*, my mind was not on any other man. While I was married to HV 2.0, I'd see other men and think, *Why can't he be my husband? Why can't I have that?*

I no longer felt restless or curious about who might be on the dating site. I also didn't feel the need to check when Greg had last logged on. As it happens, after I made the request to come down from my perch, he deleted his profile. *Deleted* it.

I pulled up to a modest but well-landscaped home, and he greeted me at the door with a warm kiss and a very loving hug. We sat on his living room sofa and talked and talked and talked. Although our previous two dates had been filled with extreme passion, just sitting there talking to him felt more passionate and gratifying than any intimate encounter I had ever had in my lifetime.

Greg told me of the path he had taken to find me. He'd attended a spiritual gathering with a friend of his and when he was asked why he was there, he said, "To find true love. Because when you have true love, you have everything."

Each person there was tasked with making a list outlining what they wanted—whether it was a new job or changing something about themselves or finding true love. They were instructed to list the negative aspects of their current situation in a column and then in a second column, list the positive results or changes they wanted for each corresponding item.

Greg showed me his list; it was four pages long and complete with the most specific and random traits of the woman he wanted to share his life with. There was not a single thing on that list that was not 100% me. It wasn't that I was reading between the lines to feel as though I was his match—no—it was completely me.

The second task the class was given was to write down nine things they wanted in their life. They were then told to read those nine things every morning before they got out of bed, and every night before they retired—for forty-nine days. On the forty-ninth day, they were to take that piece of paper and set it to a flowing body of water so that their wishes and desires could be released into the universe. As fate would have it, Greg attended that course while I was in his city looking at houses; then he "set me to water" exactly three months—to the day—before we met face to face.

Greg confessed to me, "When I'm with you, or when I think about you, I feel a certain… a certain… clarity. A peace in my heart."

Oh my gawd. What did he just say?

He said the same two words that I had thought earlier that day to describe how he made me feel—*clarity* and *peace.*

Clarity was a word I *never* would have used in reference to my life, so for something like this to happen was just overwhelming. I confessed to having used those exact words earlier that day, and we held each other and sobbed for what seemed like an eternity. Leaving his arms that afternoon was one of the hardest things I'd ever done. Had I found the one? Was this really happening or was this just the old "ten fingers, ten toes, okay I'll marry you" Veronica coming to the surface again?

The next afternoon I drove nervously to his home for our dinner date. As I pulled into the driveway, I could see him standing at his barbeque waiting for me. He greeted me with a kiss that I felt right down into my toes. The minute he touched my face, I was a goner. Putty in his hands.

He led me inside the house and, from behind his breakfast bar, presented me with a silk rose and card. I went over and sat on his couch to read the card, as he stood a few feet away watching me. This was all very overwhelming, and to have him *watch* me read the card just made me feel more nervous. The card said:

> ***Veronica, Will you accept this Rose?***
>
> ***I sought, and thought real would not last...***
>
> ***This rose is real as I, and is the memory that will continue forever.***
>
> ***The scent that it bares is the scent that I wear this night.***
>
> ***The scent will wear—returning, I will give you the sense my presence will never leave your life.***
>
> ***A rose doesn't grow overnight, and for us coming together is only the beginning of growth that will bring a blossom of beauty for all to witness.***

Thank you for the blessing of touching the earth... my hand will hold comfort and walk beside. You are an angel of unimaginable proportions to me.

If your days or nights are cold, I would bring warmth. If desire burns, I will pleasure and console your needs.

If sorrow and sadness dismay, I will comfort and reassure. Cry on my shoulders, embrace my body, mind and soul, for only an angel could do more. I have been called to you, and you blessed unto me.

As the angels cast their flaming arrows, arched into our hearts, not for a day but to last an eternity.

Always yours. Greg

I read his card again a few days later, and could see the true beauty and sentiment that came from it; but with him standing there that night, I did not fully receive the message as it was intended. Regardless, it was filled with words that no man had ever uttered in my direction. Never mind the fact that he was uttering them to me only four days after our first date. How could he be so sure?

Then Greg pulled out a pair of martini glasses from behind the bar—my first martini. It was looking as though I would be experiencing many firsts with this man. We sat at his bar talking for ages, sipping our drinks and talking and kissing and giggling.

Finally we sat down at his kitchen table for the *pièce de résistance*—a gourmet meal à la Greg. He'd made a fresh salad with homemade vinaigrette dressing, and then piled a dinner-sized plate with a mountain of rice, a side of vegetables, and a full breast of chicken. Not a half breast of chicken... a *full* breast of chicken.

Does he think I'm a lumberjack? How am I ever going to get through this meal?

The task ahead of me was daunting. As we ate and talked, the room filled with an aura that made everything feel so calm, almost as if we were in slow motion. I listened to his words and was mesmerized by his presence. Despite my emotional euphoria, I was starting to get full and needed a break from all the food, so quickly and ingeniously, I went over to him and straddled his lap. We sat that way for about an hour, talking, crying, and kissing.

Being the gentleman that he is, he paid no mind to the fact that his food was becoming ice-cold; he just enveloped me with his passion and dedication towards getting to know me. I finally sat back down and continued with my lumberjack feast. What originally started as a ploy to digest turned out to be an hour that would bring our relationship to a new level (if that was possible for something that was still so new). As we sat together on his chair, I focused on listening—something I've never been very good at.

Many, many years before, I heard the story of a very spiritual man who counselled a woman I knew on how to find her perfect man. He told her to write down every single thing she wanted in a man, and to pray about it every night. Her list was over two hundred items long and even included obscure things like "must love sushi" and "must love old Western movies." That woman did meet her soul mate, and he was everything and more.

Although I was still married to HV 1.0 at the time she told me the story, I did it too. When I created my list, I very quickly realized that not only did HV 1.0 fall short of that list, he didn't make a single part of it. I still stayed committed to the marriage, but that list's creation had left a huge void in my heart. When I met HV 2.0, I knew that he fell dismally short of the list as well, so I threw it away and accepted the *buts*.

The list that had haunted me years before was a huge part of my list of requirements during the various phases of my online dating experience. As I sat there listening to Greg talk, my mind wandered; I began to recap everything that I experienced about him up to that fifth date, and as he spoke, I started going through the list in my head.

Check.

Check.

Check.

With each item I checked off my mental list, I became increasingly gaga for this man.

After dinner, we snuggled up on the couch and enjoyed a delicious bowl of fresh fruit for dessert. This had to be the most amazing night of my life. The best part of it was that my usually sexually insatiable-self had not reared its horny head. Being with him was sincerely enough.

It was at that moment that I realized that my years of insatiable sexual desires had just been compensation for the fact that there was practically nothing else of value in those relationships. Two, three times a day—I could never get enough. But although I was extremely aroused by Greg, I was satisfied to just sit beside him and talk (and cuddle… and nuzzle… and giggle). Totally satisfied.

He took me on a quick tour of his home which ended at his bedroom (how convenient, right?). He stood me in the doorway and said, "Look straight ahead." As I stared at the bright orange wall that donned a stencil of a large sun, he flipped on the lights to reveal the words that he lived by, written in a glimmering gold paint:

LIFE is short

LOVE truly

KISS slowly

FORGIVE quickly

SMILE from the HEART

It was completely obvious to me that he was truly a man of passion and heart. What blew me away more, though, was that his closet (which did not have a door on it at the time) was immaculately organized in order of color.

"I think I just had a mini-orgasm," came tumbling from my lips—it was a Type-A personality's dream come true.

The sound of Greg's true and sincere laugh at my spontaneous comment and his response of, "You are just adorable," made the heat in my face dissipate. I really could be me when I was with him.

Next thing I knew we were falling down onto the bed together.

What happened next shocked me to my core.

We began to kiss with a passion that I had never felt in my life and, after what felt like a split second, I had removed my clothes and was making love to him. We weren't having sex. We were making love. It felt so natural and so right that I didn't have a single moment to feel any guilt or hesitation. I was making love for the first time in my life.

As we lay together, he held me in a way that I'd never felt before either. I couldn't seem to get close enough to him; I just wanted to melt into his skin and become a part of him. One thing I've always hated is being spooned in bed, but it was like our bodies were made to be together. We fit so perfectly together.

"Let me know when you want me to get out of your hair," was my awkward little statement as we lay in our sexual fog.

"You can stay as long as you like," he said, pulling me closer and nuzzling the nape of my neck.

"Well," I stammered, "did you want me to leave tonight, or tomorrow?"

There was silence from behind me and it made me extremely nervous. *Words come back! Words come back! Now he's going to think that you're one of those clingy and obsessive women!* Greg pulled away from me and abruptly turned me to face him.

"What did you say?" he asked incredulously.

"Um… I said, 'do you want me to leave tonight or tomorrow?'" I was becoming increasingly unsettled by his reaction.

"You can spend the *night*?" was his excited reply. "WAHOO! You just made my year! You are a woman after my own heart! Of *course* I want you to spend the night!" He pulled me back close to him and kissed me with so much passion that I could feel myself ready for round two. *Easy girl! Let's not scare him away this early on.*

I rolled over and we fell asleep in each other's arms with our legs intertwined, and it was the first good night's sleep I'd had in years. I slept deeply and peacefully and felt as though I was finally home.

When we woke up, he made me a light breakfast and delicious cup of hazelnut coffee while I got ready for work. It was so hard to leave him that morning. As I gathered my things, he kissed me gently on the back of the neck—my Achilles' heel. That kiss sent shivers and shock waves through my entire body and I spun around, pushed him against the wall, and kissed him with a passion I'd only ever seen in movies and definitely never felt before. That kiss very quickly got out of control, and I had my way with him one more time before heading out the door to float through my day. Needless to say, I was late for work. The first time ever—but so worth it.

CHAPTER 25
CLOUD 10?

That day at work was torture. I could barely function. All I could think about was Greg. The worst part was that he had his boys that weekend, so I wouldn't see him again until Sunday evening. Wow. That sure sounded greedy. I cannot possibly be faulted for having such selfish feelings in the beginning of a new relationship, can I?

At least that Friday morning—six days after laying eyes on that incredible man—I got to start my day by waking up beside him and experiencing what it felt like to be sent off to work with a loving goodbye.

If there was such a thing as Cloud Ten, I was definitely floating on it. I beamed the entire day at work, and with each text message Greg sent me, my already questionable level of focus was reduced even further. My elation was so obvious that a co-worker walking past my desk stopped dead in his tracks and abruptly blurted out "Oh my god! You're effing glowing!" This particular young man was a "man's man," so the fact that he'd seen right through me made me realize that I couldn't hide what I was feeling from anyone. Needless to say, his comment made me giggle like a schoolgirl, and I could feel my face and ears begin to burn.

The following day, my roomie Patricia gave me a card that she said made her think of my situation, and she thought I might like to give it to Greg. It said:

> ***"We haven't been together very long, and yet you're already becoming a very important part of my life.***
>
> ***In the mornings, I often wake up thinking about you, feeling happy and excited when I know we'll be seeing each other during the day.***

You're in my thoughts so often all day long as I remember things you've said and special moments we've shared.

And when we're apart, I find myself thinking about what I want to tell you next time we're together.

You've brought a new energy, a new focus to my life.

And I want you to know how happy you make me and how much you mean to me."

It was written by Eva Allen. *Who is this woman and how does she know exactly what is in my heart?*

I gratefully accepted the card and added a little piece of me as well.

Greg,

Imagine my surprise to find a card that expresses how you have affected me in this very unexpected coupling of souls. The surprise is more so a relief in knowing that, if someone else has felt these feelings enough to write them down for the world to share, then maybe this isn't too good to be true.

Maybe I need not be worried.

Maybe I can stop waiting for the "catch."

Maybe I can stop waiting for the bottom to fall out.

Maybe I can just enjoy the warmth of your heart, the twinkle in your eyes, your gentle touch, your positive words, your pure soul, and your passionate kisses.

Maybe, for the first time in my life, I can just enjoy.

No more worries, just enjoyment of every blessed moment knowing you. Never taking a moment for granted.

Each time I kiss you good-bye, if it is, God forbid, the last time that we are to be together, I hope that we part with you knowing how much you have blessed me. How much you have touched my soul.

I never imagined I could be so deserving of knowing such an amazing man.

Veronica xoxo

I cried as I wrote those words—my heart was overflowing. As my pen touched the paper, a loving warmth washed over me and made me realize something so very scary: I was in love with him. I wasn't in love with the *idea* of him, like I had been so many times before with any man that had a pulse; I was totally and absolutely head over heels in love with this man. I couldn't tell him, though… it was too soon. If I told him something like that, I might risk scaring him away.

I drove feverishly to his house to deliver the card but, because his children didn't know about me, I had to do it while they were out. He was at the park with them, and we were texting back and forth, so I knew exactly where he was. As I drove there, he said they were heading home.

Yikes! I'm not there yet!

As I pulled around the corner onto his street, I saw a man and two children riding on their bikes towards me. My stomach lurched as I thought it might be them, but no, the coast was clear. I ran down his driveway, dropped the card in his mailbox, and tore off down the street. Actually, I ran down his driveway, dropped the card in his mailbox, and drove slowly and watchfully down the residential street in order to ensure that all children playing outside were safe. As any responsible and caring mother would do while behind the wheel of a moving vehicle.

Phew! My hands were shaking and my heart was racing. I hoped none of the neighbors had seen me and thought I was some lunatic stalking Greg.

I sent him a text later that night asking if he had looked in his mailbox. A few moments later, my phone rang and he was giddy—and emotional—at the fact that I had driven all the way out there just to deliver the card to his home. He put his children to bed and we talked for hours.

The next day, Sunday, I was to go to his house and spend the night after his boys went back to their mother's. He made sure that I wasn't lonely and sent me multiple text messages and photos of him throughout the day. My tummy would do flip-flops whenever I looked at his face. Greg had told me that the boys return to their mother's at eight on Sunday nights, but then sent me a message saying they'd gone back early and I could come over whenever I wanted. I would have been out the door before even finishing reading the message, but I was busy doing something for him.

In a previous conversation, I'd told him that I have naturally curly hair. He went nuts when he found that out, and said that he'd always wanted to be with a woman with naturally curly hair; it was a huge turn-on for him. I hated my curly hair and told him that he'd have to live with the fact that I'd never wear it that way. In the brief time that I'd known him, though, doing things to bring him happiness were becoming a priority for me. So there I was at home, struggling with my curls, when his message came in.

When I got to his house, he was sitting on his veranda, and when he saw me he shouted, "I knew it! I *knew* you were doing that for me."

He had martinis prepared for us again and we sat together on his veranda catching up on the fifty-nine hours that we'd been apart. Then he asked, "Do you mind if we go somewhere?" I was game for anything with him.

Greg took us to a location close to where we'd first met. He led me down to a rocky area on the water and sat me down near a lift bridge in amongst the squawking seagulls whose overhead circling made me wish I had brought an umbrella. He told me that he always knew that one day he would sit and watch the sunset with the woman of his dreams. He said that every time he drove over the bridge above us, he'd say that to himself. He had been praying for me to come into his life for so long.

As the sun set, he turned to me and said, "I know that, by society's standards, this is far too soon, but I know that we are meant to be together, and I would like you and Daniella to come and live with me."

I was speechless. What man *does* that? What man puts his heart out on his sleeve like that? He was a faster mover than I was. An unbidden thought popped into my head.

Is this typical for him? One kiss, one romp in the hay, and then he's ready to commit?

Despite my knee-jerk reaction, my heart knew that he was genuine, and the little girl in me wanted to say *Yes, yes, yes!* But I couldn't say it. How could I make such a decision after knowing a man for such a short period of time? How could I do that when we both had children to think about? I had only ever lived with husbands before, and, although I was no virgin angel, living with someone out of wedlock was a *huge* moral issue for me.

I didn't give him an answer right then, but I knew what my heart wanted. We went back to his house again and made love so passionately that I wanted to accept his offer even more. I never wanted to leave his side. I wanted to wake up next to him every day for the rest of my life.

Then it happened. The thing I was working so hard to keep under control. My heart was now wide open because of what he'd asked me, and I blurted out, "Greg, I think I'm falling in love with you."

Words come back. Words come back!

The stunned look on his face made me want to curl up and hide. He didn't say a word, just smiled and kissed me passionately once more. *Damn it. Damn it. Damn it! Why do I always do things like this?*

The next morning, though, as I hesitantly peeled myself out of his arms to go to work, he gifted me with a key to his house. I was stunned. It was all happening so fast. He didn't reciprocate with the three words I hoped to hear; but the words in his card, the talks we had, the move-in request, and now the key all made me believe that he felt the same way as I did.

The following few days were torture because I could not control myself and told him daily that I loved him. My words were received with a look that felt like the equivalent of a pat on the back from your baseball buddy. *Ugh. What have I done?*

Greg then put me on the fast track to meet his family. The very next day, only eight days after our first meeting, I met his boys. Greg changed in their presence, though; he became impatient and gruff. I watched his interaction with them and was concerned that maybe I'd found a deal breaker.

The next day, I expressed to him that I did not like who he became when he was with his boys, and admitted that I did not want someone like him around my daughter. Daniella had been through enough and I was not going to make her share her life with another emotionally abusive father figure.

Greg broke down (literally) and admitted to me that, because of how volatile his marriage had been, he did not get any pleasure from being around his own children. The poison that was fed to them by their mother and the levels of manipulation she had used to try to make them hate their father as much as she hated him had destroyed his relationship with them. He had never known the joys of being a father—he only knew it as a chore that he would rather do without.

Greg then asked me if I would help him learn to be a good father. I was overwhelmed by the fact that he was able to tuck his tail between his legs, admit to a weakness, and ask for help to become stronger. I fell in love with him a little bit more that day. We had a long, painful road ahead of us, but I was willing to stand firm beside him and grow with him.

I think I passed the test of meeting his children, so now I was going to be presented to his brother and sister-in-law. We went over to his brother's house and chatted while we sat and watched TV. Again, I saw another side of Greg that I didn't particularly care for. It was the way he was demanding of his sister-in-law to make and serve him tea.

Was he just playing *the man*, or was he another arrogant male hiding his true self while he won me over? I had dealt with this kind of behavior with HV 1.0 and was not going to be someone's slave ever again. I wanted a partnership, so I made my disdain clear to him that night.

Again, he agreed that his behavior was heavily doused with testosterone (as well as old European tradition), but argued that his sister-in-law had always been a server to everyone—it was in her nature. I explained to him that, regardless of her serving nature, he could stand to drop the arrogantly expectant tone. Rather than argue with me, he put his hand on my cheek, looked lovingly into my eyes, and said, "I love you so much. I know that you are going to help guide me to being a better man. A true man."

He said that he loved me! I fell into his arms and refused to come up for air. I had found the man of my dreams and he was in love with me!

The next night, he came over to our house to pick me up and *officially* meet Daniella. What happened next is something that no one has ever believed when we tell this story.

Greg walked in the door, and Daniella was sitting watching TV with Leopold. As I said before, Leo has never really liked men and especially hated HV 2.0., who used to literally kick him across the room when he was upset with him. Leo would, in turn, pee on his clothes and crap in the boxes of his junk and computer parts. Looking back now, I should have given that cat an award for his behavior.

Before I continue with our present story, I *must* share the action that, in my mind, launched my neurotic pet into legendary status.

One Saturday morning I was lying in bed reading and Leopold was lounging at my feet. HV 2.0 had just finished his shower and was standing in our bedroom towelling off. Leo suddenly hopped off the bed and crouched down on the floor like he was stalking a bird. I was so focused on watching him prowling that I didn't bother following his gaze to see what his target was. Just as he was about to pounce, I raised my eyes and saw what was in his crosshairs. HV 2.0 had his back to the cat and was bent over and towelling his legs off with vigour. So much so, that his brass jangles were swinging and bouncing about—much to Leo's delight. Before I could utter a word, the stealth feline launched across the room and took an enthusiastic swipe at the dancing danglies. The blood-curdling scream that came from HV 2.0 was like nothing I'd heard before, and he spun around, kicked Leo across the room, and retreated to the bathroom to put pressure on his hemorrhaging scrotum. I did not laugh nearly as much then as I am right now reliving the visual. Boy, oh boy, do I love that cat. Such a good boy.

Leo didn't like Phil much either. He wasn't rude to him, but meowed at him in a very cautious and judgmental way. You see, although Leopold looked like an orange tabby, he was part Siamese and had all the neuroses of such, as well as multiple types of vocal tones. You always knew what he was saying to you, and he *never* shut up.

I had already been shocked by Leo's behavior the first day he met Greg. To hop up on his lap in that way was completely unheard of. Well, when Greg entered the house this time around, Leo hopped down from Daniella's lap and walked across the room towards him, chatting the whole way. Then he stood at Greg's feet, looked right up at him and said, in a voice that was clear to any human ear, "Grehhhg." The three of us stood in silent shock, and I turned to Daniella and said, "So *that's* what he's been saying all these years!"

Leopold used to say that particular meow all the time back when I was married to HV 2.0. How was I to know that he knew what was in store for us? That was the last time Leo ever made that sound, but his point was made. As unbelievable as it may sound, I swear on my daughter's life that it's true.

At that moment, we also remembered the day that HV 2.0 introduced us to *Greg's Spicy Horseradish Dijon.* For years, so many of our meals were enhanced by that condiment. Little did we know that it was just another path leading us to the real Greg.

Greg never disclosed to his family how briefly we had known each other, but after only three weeks I was meeting them all at his eldest son's birthday party. I've never been very good with crowds, so entering into the arena of judgement by both family and friends was a killer. I held my head high and did my best not to be my usual introverted self. It helped that Daniella was with me—at least I had an ally.

The day went well (other than the birthday boy coercing his younger brother to tell me that he thinks I'm ugly) and I think his family and friends thought I was an okay addition to the mix.

Although Greg's offer of cohabitation was still on the table, I continued to look for a place to rent. One night, while driving home from work, I received a call from one of the inquiries I had made the day before. The man had four properties, and three of them were available to rent within the next month. I asked him to confirm the addresses so that I could establish if they were in the neighborhood of Daniella's new school. When he gave me the addresses for two of the locations, I was speechless. In the end, the prices were out of my range, but they were both on the same street—two blocks away from each other—on *Ruth*. Not only were they on the same street as Greg's house, they were within walking distance.

Is this a sign?

Is this another sign?

CHAPTER 26
COLORS

One of my biggest pieces of baggage was my trust issue. As I explained before, HV 2.0's four-year-long habit with my lingerie catalogues was the main reason for the demise of our marriage (the financial ruin was a cake-walk compared to that one). That one thing had scarred me deeply and taken a long time to get over, and my ability to trust was never quite the same.

Shortly after Greg and I met, he asked me if I'd help him purge and organize his home. I agreed and was excited about helping him get over his hoarding hurdle. Before getting started, I informed him that I would be going through every drawer, cabinet, nook, and cranny in the house and recommended he remove anything he didn't want me to stumble across. He told me that he had nothing to hide and that I should go for it. I did so hesitantly because I could feel my trust wounds opening again.

One night, I decided to surprise him and show up at his house unannounced. We were talking on the phone, but what he didn't know was that I was actually driving to his house as we spoke. When I arrived, my hands began to shake uncontrollably.

What if he's doing something I don't want to know about?

I crept through his basement door and snuck my way upstairs towards the one light that was on—his bedroom. My entire body was trembling now. When I walked through his bedroom doorway he just about jumped out of his skin. Not because I'd walked in on something private or inappropriate, but because I'd startled him. He just was sitting on his bed talking to me. Nothing else. I was so afraid that he'd be upset with me for doing that, but he flashed me the biggest smile and said that I was a blessing and it was an amazing surprise.

I did that to him on one other occasion too—I guess I'm just a glutton for emotional punishment. Again, my hands were shaking uncontrollably as I pulled up to his house because I could see his office light on. All I could think about was what HV 2.0 used to do in his office when I wasn't around. I felt my heart lurch into my throat and my stomach drop into my bowels as I approached the open doorway of Greg's office. There he was, at his computer, with his feet on the desk… on the Internet… on a *recipe* site! Again, I scared the buhjeezus out of him, but again, he loved the surprise. And again, my paranoid distrust was unfounded.

Can I really trust this man? Is he really pure of heart and soul?

When I first embarked on a new relationship with someone I met online, I'd usually make the mistake of telling the guy about all of my phobias and fears. I didn't realize at the time that revealing those things would make my efforts to heal and change very difficult. Phil, Mick, and Branden were the ones I had become close enough to confide in, and they used to consciously and subconsciously make me very aware of my issues (and even mock and taunt me because of them). To be fair, Phil never mocked or taunted me, but he coddled and protected me too much, which I found very patronizing. He had wonderful intentions, but I didn't realize how detrimental it would be for my efforts to grow and change.

Phobias, panic attacks, severe depression, and suicide attempts no longer had a place in my life; it was time for me to shed my damaged skin.

About three weeks into our relationship, I told Greg, "I've struggled with a lot of phobias over the years. In the past, I've shared them with people and it's made things worse because they focused on them more. So instead, since I'm doing my best to be the anti-Veronica, I'm only going to tell you about them once I've conquered them."

Greg wrapped his gorgeous, strong arms around me and told me that I had "no worries" with him and that he would be there right beside me as I conquered my demons. Over time, he proved to be true to his word; he stood strong no matter what. On the days that my outrageous behavior justified me being kicked to the curb, he just looked past it.

Little did he know that a huge one was coming.

He told me there was a barbeque party that a friend of his held every year for all of his clients, employees, and friends; and he wanted me to go with him. I spent the three weeks leading up to it in an absolute tailspin. Daniella got to witness me coming apart at the seams at the prospect of facing three of my fears: 1) Crowds; 2) Dressing in casual clothing (seriously, it's a big panic for me, I've never known how to do it); and 3) Public Displays of Movement (PDMs)—a.k.a. dancing.

The day of the party arrived, and as we approached the venue, I felt ready to burst into tears; but I held my head up high and then proceeded to get completely and utterly polluted. I am someone who barely drinks, but I downed three girly cocktails, Greg's gin and tonic, and a few shots of tequila. I learned a very valuable lesson that night: Veronica mixing alcohol and tomato-based sauces is not a good idea. Being a pro at the upheaval of unwanted things in my system, I worked those port-o-potties like they had never been worked before.

We danced all night long and Greg said he could tell I had an amazing time because, apparently, I was beaming the entire night. He told me he fell so much deeper in love with me because of it. I remember almost everything about the evening, but I mainly remember asking him repeatedly if I was behaving okay; if I was talking too loud; if I was embarrassing him; if my boobs were okay (I chose to wear a very low-cut halter top that night). Each time, he'd laugh and say, "You're adorable. You have no worries."

Around the one-month mark of our relationship, Greg asked me if I would do him a favour and review some letters he'd received from the child support enforcement department. The letters showed a breakdown of all the monies he owed to his ex-wife (over $10,000) and went on to threaten to garnish his wages and take away his driver's license, car, house, etc.

"Greg, what have you done?"

He explained that he hadn't responded to the letters because he didn't think he'd done anything wrong and thought his ex-wife was just being stupid. He sincerely did not realize the gravity of not responding to this agency. In layman's terms, I explained to him how serious the situation was and told him that he must take immediate action. Greg immediately welled up with tears and said, "I just want peace. I don't want to deal with any of this." At that moment, I realized how overwhelmed he felt and promised I would help him get through it.

The next weekend, I spent two full days going through every single piece of paper he had in his house. I sorted more than ten years' worth of papers and receipts, in addition to reviewing his separation agreement with a fine-toothed comb. Although it was a daunting task, it gave me a window into who he was before I met him. I discovered that no matter what the circumstances were at the time, he always paid his bills on time, and practically the only thing he ever spent money on was food. Despite the negative reason for my audit of his documents, knowing that he was fiscally responsible gave me a peace in my heart. I presented the results of my research to him and explained that the summary of costs owing to his ex was falsified; he maybe only owed her six hundred dollars. I would still have to go through things more thoroughly, but he had all of the cancelled cheques for the payments he'd made (which she claimed he had not). I also pointed out all the things she was in breach of in their separation agreement. So much so, that he could take legal action against *her*. He was close to tears when I made him realize what a strong case he had.

The following day he signed a third-party authorization form for his case with the child support authorities, and I immediately contacted them. They agreed to delay action against him, but said that he must write them a letter explaining the situation. After that, they could not make a change to anything until they received a legal document from the courts.

I should back up a bit here to explain why Greg's ex-wife was trying to get extra money from him.

When they separated, the lawyers did a rough calculation of his earnings (including overtime) and he agreed to pay child support based on a certain amount. Soon after the agreement was signed, he lost his job. When he found a new job, it paid the same hourly wage, but they did not allow the employees to work overtime, so it knocked his income down by about forty thousand dollars. He drew up an amendment to their separation agreement for the adjustment in income and support payments, but she refused to sign it. After a few months of continuing to pay her four hundred dollars more per month than he was expected to, based on his actual income, he attempted to appeal to her kind side and explained that he just couldn't afford to keep paying that much. She told him that she didn't care and it was the money that he owed her. What he did next is what caused the problems.

He calculated what he should be paying her based on his actual income and gave her a cheque for that amount each month. She cashed the cheques every month without any further argument, so he assumed that she was in acceptance of the lesser amount. I guess someone told her that she had rights, and that was when she went to a lawyer (about a month before Greg and I met).

He was forced to honor the separation agreement *and* pay an additional two hundred dollars a month as a good faith effort to repay what he "owed" her. He would have to continue to pay that until he could prove he owed otherwise. So, he was now paying six hundred dollars more per month than he should have been.

After I enlightened Greg with my findings and pacified the government, he tried to settle with his ex out of court. She finally agreed to an amount two hundred dollars more than he should be paying her, and also agreed to drop the case for monies owing. Although I didn't agree with him paying her more than she was due, it was his life and it was also better than having to shell out over ten grand to repay her what she had initially asked for. Greg promptly prepared a revised separation agreement, and it went back and forth for a couple of weeks until she finally called him and said she wouldn't settle. Her lawyer had apparently refused to represent her in the future if she settled with Greg. She further stated, "My lawyer is going to ruin you. I am going to make you bleed from the eyes."

Bleed from the eyes? Really?

Those are fighting words, my friend.

For those of us who have had long-term relationships or marriages, it's a given that there is going to be baggage. Had I met Greg when we were teenagers, we would have grown together and experienced all of our firsts together. Unfortunately, though, like so many other things we can't control in life, we were not dealt that hand and were forced to unpack an assortment of emotional baggage together.

I saw enough of who he was to know and love him, and his invitation for moving in was still open, so I met up with Samantha to bounce the idea off her. She reassured me that I was making the right decision, and I gave Greg the good news the next day when he came by my office to take me for lunch. He was over the moon, and we quickly started preparing his house for our arrival.

No one besides the three of us knew of this decision. Not Patricia, not Greg's family, not Phil.

Why the secret from everyone?

Patricia's possessive and controlling behavior had reached quite a few highs during our time together (directing me on cyber-dating etiquette, instructing Daniella on the proper way to wash the dishes, hovering over my shoulder and coaching me as I cooked even though her own repertoire consisted solely of scrambled eggs and toast); and when I'd given her one month's notice that we were moving out (back when I was looking for a place to rent), she'd said, "I hope you aren't planning on moving in with Greg."

End of conversation.

Greg avoided telling his family because he knew what their reaction would be. He was totally right—when he finally did tell them, they said he was making the biggest mistake of his life and warned that I was just out to get my hands on his property. Their pessimistic viewpoint was understandable after everything he'd gone through (and lost) at the hands of his ex, but he held his ground and told them that they didn't know me—that he knew *exactly* who I was.

I actually prepared a cohabitation agreement to protect all of Greg's material trappings, but he adamantly refused to sign it. He told me that he knew me and loved me, and knew that I would never—could never—rob him of what he had worked so hard to achieve.

As for Phil, he had not responded well to the news of my serious relationship with Greg and had stopped speaking to me again. Like I said before, even though he didn't want me in *that* way, he couldn't handle me being with anyone else. I really missed Phil and hoped that we could one day be friends again. Greg knew the entire truth about Phil and me and, although he wasn't sure how he felt about having him in our life, he couldn't deny how grateful he was for what Phil represented. Phil was our "Ruth," and "Ruth" was the reason that we were together, after all. Only time would tell.

CHAPTER 27
HONORING A PRINCE

It was beyond me that no woman had ever been able to hold on to Greg. He epitomized the perfect mate. Not only was he handy with everything—plumbing, electrical, carpentry, automotive—he was a true partner in every sense of the word. He cooked, he cleaned, he cried, he admitted when he was wrong, he forgave me when I faltered, and he was patient, caring, and *gorgeous*. My silver fox. He gave me the marriage I'd always wanted. Even though we were not actually married, he was more of a husband to me than either HV 1.0 or 2.0 had been, combined.

I first fell in love with Greg twenty years ago. I remember lying in my bed each night picturing my husband walking up the sidewalk towards our house. As he came through our quaint white picket fence (yes… really… I wanted the *Leave it to Beaver* white picket fence life), I would burst out of the house, run down the front steps, and jump into his arms. Our two children would be fast on my heels, and the four of us would stand and hug like this every evening when he came home from work. I could never see his face, but it was a vision that I always held clearly in my mind and tightly to my heart, even throughout my two marriages.

When the sales position Greg had tried didn't work out, he took a job back making custom store fixtures at a location that was halfway to my office. Every morning we drove hand in hand as we carpooled to his job and then I continued on to mine. Although our shifts finished at the same time, I usually ended up waiting in the car for at least half an hour while he finished up. It didn't bother me, though, because I enjoyed sitting and watching him work through the open bay doors.

Greg was a real man in my eyes. He was sensitive, but so capable. I told him that he was my *Flashdance*. Do you remember that movie? She was a welder by day and a dancer by night. Well, each time I watched him weld, I fell more and more in love with him. He'd do that thing where he flipped his welding mask down with a quick nod of his head and then spark his flame.

Every time I saw that, it sparked *my* flame. Yum! So sexy! Then he'd come out to the perimeter of the shop and from underneath that grimy face would flash me that gorgeous smile. I felt butterflies in my stomach each and every time.

I'm not sure when it was or how it happened, but one day as Greg left the shop, I burst out of the car and ran and jumped into his arms. I had never done that before in my life and it made me feel completely free and liberated. I felt like a teenager. I honestly think that Greg loved me doing it even more than I did. That became our ritual at the end of the day, or after we had been apart for more than a couple of hours. I know that I could have *never* done that with any other man. Well, I was taller than both of my ex-husbands and probably would have knocked them over… but I had never trusted anyone enough to open up my heart that way.

Being a hopeless romantic has always been a downfall of mine, and I never thought that any man could live with me in my fantasy world. Greg is not romantic in my sense of the word, but he is definitely my muse. Almost daily, my mind is flooded with ideas of how to honor him, spoil him, or just make him smile.

We had only been together two short months when I began to spin a tale of lies to create a memorable gift for his 39th birthday. It all started when I was cleaning out his basement before I moved in. I came across a portfolio of photos of him; they were from eighteen years before, when he'd tried his hand at modelling in Brazil. When I showed it to him, he was ecstatic because he thought his ex had thrown it away. It was obviously a time in his life that he remembered fondly and was proud of. I knew I needed to honor him with those photos somehow.

One thing about me is that I make decisions based on emotion; if it doesn't flow emotionally, then I won't force it. The times that I have forced something (like two previous marriages), it just never worked out. I thought of making a poster or a calendar out of the photos, but I was struggling with those ideas and they somehow didn't feel right. I turned to my sister, a graphic artist, for advice. She suggested that I make him a book and pointed me to a site that had free downloadable software. That was it! That was the gift. The ideas for the structure of the book then started to pour out of my heart.

The book that I made for him was a black and white coffee table book entitled "Clarity—A collection to celebrate the life of a man who embodies true integrity."

First I made a list of all the personality traits and characteristics that I felt best described Greg; then I researched the flower that represented each word's meaning and found a photo of each flower; then I found multiple inspirational quotes about each personality trait. On the facing page of each trait page I put a full-page photo of Greg. I did my best to choose photos that complemented whatever trait I chose.

What words embodied this incredible man? They were: balance, clarity, compassion, courage, dignity, faith, fidelity, gratefulness, happiness, hope, humility, integrity, kindness, loyalty, modesty, passion, patience, peace, perseverance, reflection, respect, sensitivity, strength, success, truth, and wisdom.

Although I had not known him very long, I was confident that he had never been truly honored in his life and wanted to bless him in any way I could. In the beginning of the book I wrote:

> ***This book is dedicated to a man whose physical appearance cannot compare to his breathtaking inner beauty.***
>
> ***A man whose strong hands seem weak in the presence of the strength of his pure and moral heart.***
>
> ***A man who has chosen to live a life of balance, open-hearted love, sincere friendship and never-ending compassion.***
>
> ***A man who lives each day with passion and has found clarity and peace.***
>
> ***To be blessed with the love of such a man can only be viewed as the greatest gift a woman could ever receive.***

Greg and I were inseparable, so I knew that the only way I could get the gift done was to do it at my office. I then began to weave my first web of lies. I told him that I would have to work an entire weekend doing translations from Spanish for all of the legal documents for a $6.8 billion proposal for my company. I explained that the legal secretary in our Santiago office, who was meant to do the translations, had been hospitalized, and they needed me to fill in. They didn't know what was wrong with her or when she would return, and the proposal had to go out the following week. I further explained that although I was fluent in Spanish, I didn't speak technical or legal Spanish, so I would translate into English and then our local legal department would convert it into the required industry legalese.

The hardest part of all this was the lying. While I worked away on his gift at the office one night, he went for dinner with his boys at his parents' house, and proceeded to totally sell me to his mother and father. He told them how I'd unselfishly stepped up to the plate to help out the sick woman in Santiago and to make sure that our company's proposal did not falter. He put me on such an elevated pedestal that my betrayal (albeit minor) made me feel like a horrible person. Lying to him was so hard because I felt as though I was making a fool of him, and I would never want anyone to make a fool of me. I consoled myself with the fact that the gift would make it all worth it in the end.

When the book was finished and I was awaiting its publication and delivery, I had to keep up with the lie, as Greg asked me for updates on our poor fallen employee. I sent him a text message one day telling him that she had kidney failure and needed a donor. I also told him that my company was so amazing that they had sent out a plea to all ten thousand employees globally asking that they volunteer to be tested for a possible match. His reply made me literally sob at my desk.

You should tell your company to send out an email asking everyone to pray for her because group prayer is so much stronger than any individual prayer to God's ears.

Once I collected myself and could see my phone's screen again, I informed him that they had also requested our prayers in the email. I fell in love with him a little bit more that day.

Two more weeks went by and I came home and excitedly told him that an engineer in one of our Canadian offices was a match, and the company was flying both him and the fallen employee to a renowned hospital in the U.S. for the transplant. The company was going to pay for both of the surgeries and anything related to their recoveries. Greg was flabbergasted at the company's generosity and expressed what a blessing it was for me to work for people of such integrity. I died a little inside at the evolution of my lies.

His birthday finally arrived, and we planned to have dinner at the restaurant that overlooked the place that we first met. Ironically, though, I had caused an argument over text message that morning and received,

Thanks. Thanks for ruining my birthday. I'm sure most would wonder what I could have possibly done to cause such a reaction over text, well, here goes:

Daniella and Hailey were getting ready for school and found a tube of prescription cream in Greg's name at the back of the cupboard in the basement bathroom (the bathroom I never went into). They presented it to me and asked what it was for. Seeing as I'd never heard of the medication term before, I asked my friend, Mr. Google, and he told me it was used to cure scabies. Most people from my generation are only familiar with the term "scabies" as a term we used to mock the boys in grade school—"Ewwww! Marcus has scabies!" or also referred to as "cooties." As kids, we didn't know what it really meant, but as an adult, I knew it was commonly contracted sexually (or skin-to-skin contact). Needless to say, I flipped out. I was embarrassed that the girls found it, and wondered what kind of dirty whores Greg had been with—and also if he had potentially exposed me to it. So I confronted him over text. Greg explained that he contracted it while he was not in any relationship; it was only on the back of his calves and he suspected it came from tanning himself on a particular fabric lounge chair he bought at a garage sale. His doctor informed him that people can even contract it from trying on clothes; so his assumption that it was from a cooty-infested lounge chair was probably spot on.

I felt sick to my stomach for what I had done and wondered if he'd even want to go to dinner with me anymore. In addition to the balloons that he found tied to his car after work that day, he was greeted by a giant banner across the front of the house when he came home. It softened his heart towards me a little, but things were still strained between us as we got ready to go out. I did my very best to apologize for my inconsiderate behavior, but although he assured me that I was forgiven, things still felt prickly.

On my way home from work that night, I had stopped at the restaurant and dropped off his gift. I asked that they guard it with their lives and place it on the table that was reserved for us upon our arrival. Greg was taken aback as we approached our table and he saw his gift bag proudly displayed as the centerpiece, but he wouldn't open it right away and tucked it under the table. Finally, after dessert, he agreed to open it. He was literally speechless and I could see him welling up with emotion. He kept himself composed, but after we returned to the car, we sat and cried in each other's arms and exchanged so many words of love and devotion. I knew that making such a gift for any other man would have never been successful and would have been a forced attempt at making something of a relationship that didn't actually exist. My passion was reserved for him all these years.

A couple of weeks after his birthday, though, I suddenly went into a panicked tailspin.

What the hell am I going to possibly do to top that gift for his fortieth birthday? Why didn't I save it for his next birthday? The "milestone" birthday. What was I thinking?

I began to rack my brain for ideas.

When we first met, Greg told me that he'd always planned to go to Vegas for his fortieth, but during random conversations since, he expressed a waning desire to do so. After the success of the book-giving, I asked him if he felt comfortable giving me *carte blanche* to take him somewhere for his next birthday. Being the incredible man that he is, he accepted the request with enthusiasm. I asked if there was any special activity that he really wanted to do to celebrate, and he said he would love to play golf. Golf. Ugh… oh well, I guess I could tolerate being his caddy for the forty-five hours it takes to play one round of the damn game. I agreed and began my planning.

Soon after I started, my emotions took hold and it became totally clear that the only place the trip could be was Montreal. I don't know why, but I was suddenly filled with an incredible feeling thinking about walking through the cobblestone streets of Old Montreal with him. I began my planning and research for the event, but it just didn't feel like enough. There had to be something more. Even with the surprise party I was going to throw two weeks after his birthday, my plans for the trip felt as though they fell short. Then it came to me.

During the summer (a couple of months before his thirty-ninth birthday), I went to a driving range with him for the first time in my life. Even though I only went as his caddy, it was *not* a positive experience. I agreed to try to swing at those annoying little orbs, and at one point, a ball bounced up and hit me in the nose. It was obvious that my career in golf would end that day. Despite my negativity, Greg told me that his dream was to one day golf with me by his side. That conversation suddenly hit me square in the face, and I knew: the only thing that would make his birthday complete was if I were to golf *with* him.

Lord help me with this next chapter of my life.

CHAPTER 28
MEETING THE FRIENDS

I'd survived meeting his family; now it was time to meet his closest friends. Greg asked me if I would attend a two-day motivational seminar with him that was taking place at a large conference center downtown. It was free for me to attend, we'd get to have a nice weekend away, and I would get to meet two of his closest friends—Jeannette and Tiffany. Although I was not keen on attending a motivational seminar, I was keen to become a part of every aspect of his life. Greg had started on a path of personal change and growth before we met, so I was honored that he would want me there with him.

When Greg's marriage dissolved, he started going out dancing again. He loved to dance and just wanted to get out there and enjoy himself for the first time in a decade. Although his intention was not solely to meet women, he met a few and had a few dates. During that same time, he also met Jeannette, who was about ten years older than him; he had no romantic interest in her but found her to be a fun friend. Greg would meet up at various clubs with Jeannette and her friends and have a great time. They adored Greg (but really, who wouldn't?) and I know he was thrilled to be laughing and dancing again; but most importantly, he was being treated with the love and respect that he deserved… that he longed for. During those dancing days, he eventually met Jeannette's friend Tiffany, who was a little closer to Greg's age but was again just another fun friend to have.

Greg told me he thought Tiffany would be a great match for Phil. He showed me a photo of her and I sent it to Phil for his comments. He very much liked what he saw and agreed to contact her. About a week before our motivational weekend away, Phil and Tiffany had their dinner date, and he was quite smitten with her. She was beautiful and intelligent and he could see that there might be something there for the two of them to investigate. Although they had tentatively planned to meet again, Phil knew that we were going to be with Tiffany the following weekend, so he asked me to subtly pry and find out how she felt.

The day finally arrived when I was to meet these two women I'd heard so much about. Normally, the insecure Veronica would have been nervous and jealous of the two women who were so close to his heart, but I knew I could trust Greg, and I was excited to have two new female friends in my life.

We picked up Tiffany first. She stood about 5'2" tall and had bleached blond hair cut in a bob, a pretty face, breasts supported by a *very* good push-up bra, and lips that looked as though she had lost a battle with a swarm of bees. I wish I could say that I was jealous of the size of her breasts, but I was more concerned that she might topple over because of them. The lips. Well, my daughter was blessed with gorgeous, full, bee-stung lips—and is the envy of most women that meet her—but Tiffany was not so lucky. Tiffany's mouth had received a lot of help to look that way—a little too much help, in my opinion.

Jeannette was a petite brunette with braces. I silently respected her for having the guts to get braces at her age. Her face was a little wrinkled (mostly laugh lines, which are a good thing in my books) but she looked great for a woman her age. She was sort of pretty, but had an odd look to her. I swear I'm not being catty; there was just something strange about her face. I'm sure she could put herself together really well when necessary.

The hour-long drive to the event was sheer hell. I felt as though I was babysitting my teenage daughter and a giggly friend (except that Daniella has never acted that immature). Tiffany and Jeannette spent the majority of the drive talking about Botox. They told Greg that he should get it done to eliminate the wrinkles on his brow. I interjected and said that I loved the creases in his brow; he agreed and said that he'd never do something like that. With Greg having cut them off at the pass, they decided that I was their next target of Botox advice. My comment of "I'll never do something like that" was received with, "Never say never. Just wait. You'll have it done!"

Calgon, take me away!

I learned a lot about Greg that weekend, and I learned *too much* about the two cheerleaders. Tiffany drove me to distraction as she jiggled and bounced around like a fifteen-year-old and repeatedly slathered lip gloss on her two newly enhanced facial appendages. Her lips and breasts were so extreme that I found myself staring at both sets for the entire weekend. Even though Jeannette was more subdued and down to earth, the two women together made damn sure that our weekend felt like an excerpt out of high school—I was the nerdy math geek and they were the bitchy cheerleaders. They spent the entire weekend referring to Greg as "our Greg" and did their very best to imply that they knew him super well and I had no idea who he was. Greg finally interjected and told them point blank that I knew him *very* well—better than anyone, actually. Score one for the nerdy math geek!

At one point during our weekend, though, Greg made a very strong comment to me about not getting between him and his time with those two women. I immediately pictured myself standing at the front door of his house and waving goodbye to him, as he drove off to spend the night out dancing without me. I was very hurt at his comment and told him so. I explained to him that I would never get in the way of his friends, but didn't appreciate being treated so rudely about it. My response made him realize that he was having a knee-jerk reaction based on how controlling his ex had always been.

I didn't tell him that I couldn't stand those two women, but for the life of me, I couldn't understand why he surrounded himself with such shallow people. Although I tried not to let my feelings show, it was very clear to me that neither of them were fans of mine either—I was getting between them and *their* Greg. Their behavior was that of scorned lovers, and was so extreme that I did gently approach him with the question of whether or not he had been involved with one or both of them romantically. He emphatically denied it and seemed repulsed by the thought.

During our weekend, I was able to query Tiffany about her date with Phil. She said she thought he was a really nice guy but wasn't her type. The conversation then took a bizarre turn. All weekend long she had kept mentioning her married friend Michael, the architect. She had talked about him so much that I finally asked her if they had been involved at some point. She laughed and said, "Are you kidding? I'm his mistress. Didn't you get that?" I can sincerely say that I was completely speechless. I could not even dig down deep to find one of my usual smart-aleck responses to break the awkward silence. For the rest of the weekend, she talked incessantly about her decade-long affair with this man.

I was livid with Greg. "Why the hell would you set up Phil with that whore? Phil may date a lot but he cannot stand lies or that kind of behavior. I can't believe you set him up with her!" Greg swore to me that he'd had a feeling something was up but didn't know outright about her affair. Needless to say, I had a talk with Phil and told him everything.

In the next few weeks, Tiffany began to show her true colors, and Greg was sincerely hurt by her behavior towards him. I finally asked him why he spent his time with someone so shallow and plastic since he was the purest, truest, and deepest man I'd ever met. He explained that she was just easy to be around; shits and giggles were all that Tiffany was about.

Although my exposure to Jeannette was limited, I soon came to believe that she was sincerely a good person and that her association with Tiffany is what made her behave that way. But I was still very confident that she was secretly in love with *my* Greg.

Now that I had survived the cheerleader weekend, it was time for me to meet Greg's best friend, Dwight, and his wife, Naomi. Greg had known Dwight since grade school and I was so excited to finally get to meet him and have "couple" friends with Greg.

Dwight and Naomi invited us over for a small dinner gathering at their house, where I would meet not only them, but two other couples that were close in the group of friends. I was really nervous this time. I've always felt so awkward in group social events and didn't want to embarrass Greg by being my usual introverted self; this was going to take a lot of faking on my part.

We drove up to a newly built home with unfinished landscaping. They had apparently only finished building a few months earlier and were holding off on the landscaping until their pockets were lined with more cash. When we walked into the house, which was shiny and new, the coldest feeling greeted me. We can't all have the same taste, so I surely didn't judge Dwight and Naomi on the fact that I didn't care for the emotion that their home conveyed to me. The wonderful warmth they greeted us with did much to dissipate my fears, and I looked forward to a nice evening with them.

The night was a disaster and I wanted to go home after an hour.

Dwight stands about 6'6" tall and is skinny as a rail; he has dirty blond hair and green eyes and leans closer to creepy-looking than good-looking. Naomi, on the other hand, could be pretty (if she was a little better put together). She is a fellow redhead, a bit taller than me, and quite plump. Her shape was obviously a result of bringing four children into the world. Within that shape, one part stood out as her clear favorite: her enormous breasts. Her enormous I've-fed-my-litter-with-these-feed-bags breasts. They were not attractive at all and were spilling out of her very, very, *very* low-cut dress. I was sincerely in awe, though, at how they didn't jump right out of their minimal-coverage push-up bra. I think it would be safe to say that it was the eighth wonder of the world.

Dennis and Jean were an older couple and very sweet. I didn't get much of a chance to talk with them, but they seemed like great people. The other two, though, were a perfect friend-match for Dwight and Naomi. Ryan and

Irene were around our age, and it was very obvious who wore the pants in that household. Irene was so overbearing and brash to Ryan that I understood why he was already half-in-the-bag by the time we got there. Poor guy. Finding the bottom of a bottle was obviously his favorite pastime being married to that gem.

The meal they prepared was visually elegant but tasted disgusting. I can't find another word to describe it. Salmon was the main course and I choked back as much of it as I could, but it was horrible. I don't like salmon to begin with, so I was really having to fight my gag reflex during the entire meal. Had I been throwing a dinner party for a new guest, I would have surely had the good etiquette to query if there was something they didn't like or had allergies to. I didn't fault them on that, though, because I tend to be far too considerate when it comes to things like that. In any case, the meal was the least of my worries.

My humour can be sarcastic and, when I feel cornered, it can be perceived as offensive to some; so I made sure to dial it back (even though I felt like I was in front of the firing squad) and did my very best to blend in with our hosts' sarcastic (and rude) banter. I was treated like… well… I was treated like crap. At one point, Irene said to Naomi, "You should watch what you say, Naomi; Veronica doesn't know us well enough yet, and you may blow her out."

Naomi's response? "Well, if Veronica doesn't like it, that's her fucking problem!"

I was blown away. Then I was further blown away when Ryan started watching a porn movie on his hand-held device and showing it to everyone. I was done. I was humiliated and done.

So, to summarize: the meal, their house, and their behavior was pretentious and cold and left a bad taste in my mouth—both literally and figuratively. I would go so far as to say that the vibe I got from Greg's best friend was that of a pervert, and I couldn't stand being near him (nor would I even dream of including my teenage daughter in one of these get-togethers). Again, I kept my feelings to myself, and again, I asked myself why Greg would associate with such shallow people.

In the months to come, this group of friends, just like the cheerleaders, acted like jealous lovers of sorts, and didn't seem to want me near *their* Greg. One of their biggest bones of contention with me was my cooking; every dish that I brought to an event was raved about by all the attendees, while theirs got lost in the fanfare of my culinary excellence. Greg was very proud of my contributions, and there was no way I would ever dishonor him by bringing a less-than-amazing dish to any social function. Apart from protecting my own culinary ego, I didn't want people whispering behind Greg's back about what a crappy cook his tart-of-the-day was (like I am doing right now about Dwight and Naomi's culinary disasters).

At Phil's office, the guys referred to a man's flavour of the day as a *skank-du-jour.* That's exactly how this group of friends made me feel. I felt like I was being treated like some insignificant piece of ass that would get tossed to the curb as soon as Greg had his fill. Although Greg hadn't dated many women before he met me, I was the first girlfriend he'd ever introduced them to, and they were still nasty as hell to me. You would think that a true friend would appreciate the significance of that gesture; but not this group.

I met some nice people at those parties, and some not-so-nice people. One gross old man in particular fawned all over me one night, and out of politeness to Greg, I let him. We had brought our bathing suits with us that time to take a dip in our hosts' hot tub, but Greg pulled me aside and said, "You are NOT getting into that hot tub!" I didn't argue, but was perplexed by his behavior; he was definitely not a jealous or insecure man. It wasn't until a couple of days later that he confessed to being bothered by drunken old Father Time hanging all over me.

At each party we went to, Naomi, Dwight, and Irene found ways to make digs at me or insult me to my face. On the night that Naomi told me outright to "fuck off," Greg finally took notice. A bunch of us were sitting around their kitchen island chatting and having drinks, and I had just finished reading the ingredients of a drink can that Greg had added to his cocktail. Naomi asked to see it as well. She strained to read the small print, so I offered to read it to her, but she snapped at me that she was fine and pulled out her glasses. When she was still having trouble seeing it with her glasses on, I said, "Oh dear" in a truly gentle way. That's when she said, "You know, Veronica, I've never said this to you before, but fuck off!" I laughed uncomfortably, but Greg just sat there staring at her incredulously. He, too, must have been in shock at the completely unjustified remark.

One night, Dwight, Greg, and I were sitting at their kitchen table, and the two men were talking about Dwight's sister and her recent marital disaster with a gigolo she'd met and brought back from Cuba. Dwight went into the most detail about how ugly she is (including a comment about her moustache) and I just sat and listened with only the odd "oh my" or "oh my goodness" comments. Then Dwight turned to me and said, "Well you have frizzy hair!" and got up and walked away.

Did that just happen? What on earth did I say or do to deserve that?

I literally sat with my mouth agape and noticed that Greg was also in a state of shock. I spent the rest of the evening feeling humiliated at how awful I must look and how ashamed Greg must feel having to be with someone who looks so bad that someone would outwardly comment on it.

I still kept my mouth shut, until one day, I couldn't take it anymore.

On one occasion, Dwight cornered me and decided to offer me a window into Greg's past. Dwight had been the best man at Greg's wedding and went on *ad infinitum* about how it was the most romantic wedding he had ever been to and how he had never seen a man more in love than the groom that day. I was stunned that someone would do something like that, but not the least bit surprised to discover yet another moral shortcoming of Dwight's. I let that brew inside of me for a few weeks and then approached Greg with it one day in a roundabout way.

"Greg, could I ask your opinion on something?"

"Sure sweetheart, what's up?"

"Pretend that you had a friend that you'd known for years and you had even been the best man at his wedding. Well, let's say that your friend's marriage dissolved and he was now with a new woman and made it very clear to you how much he loved her. As you got to know that woman, would you ever talk to her about your friend's ex-wife?"

"Well, I'm not sure. It would really depend on the context. Like, if the new girlfriend asked me something about his ex, I'd probably give her an answer. Unless I thought that the answer would hurt her or cause some kind of conflict between her and my friend. Do you mean something specific?"

I stammered a bit because I really didn't know how to fish for an answer in an eloquent way. So I just went for it. "Specifically, would you, without her initiating the conversation, approach her about your friend's wedding day to his ex-wife? Would you tell her that it was the most beautiful wedding you'd ever been to and that you'd never seen a groom more in love with his bride?"

"*What*? Are you kidding me? Of course I wouldn't! That's just rude and uncalled for."

I was quite surprised at his fierce reaction to my question, but said only, "Oh, okay. Thanks," and wandered off down the hall to continue what I was doing.

Greg shouted after me as I walked away, "Veronica... come back, please." When I returned to the room, he continued, "Did something happen? Why are you asking this?"

"No reason. I was just wondering how you would handle a situation like that."

"You're lying to me. What happened? Did someone say something like that to you about me? About my wedding?"

My eyes began to well up with tears, so I could no longer fake my blasé attitude.

"Who said this to you? Did my mother say something? My brother? Who?"

When I told him it was Dwight, he completely blew up. "I knew they had been acting like assholes towards you, but I thought they'd grow up at some point. They *hated* my ex and she hated them, so I can't believe that he'd sink so low as to say something like that. That's it. I've had enough of how they're treating you."

As much as I loathed his friends, I still defended them and argued that maybe they just needed more time or were being protective of him to ensure that he didn't make another mistake like he had with his ex. I did, however, ask him to come to my defence in the future if he was witness to any further mistreatment. I was relieved that his eyes were actually open and that I wasn't just being hysterical, paranoid, and insecure.

CHAPTER 29
BAGGAGE

Even though I saw enough of the man Greg was in order to be comfortable moving in with him, we still had a lot to learn about each other as we settled in. What made it more difficult was the fact that I was moving into his matrimonial home, sleeping in his matrimonial bed, surrounded by their matrimonial furniture, and sweeping up their matrimonial dust bunnies from every corner of the house. Not only was I sleeping in their bed, I was sleeping on *her* side. Not just her side, the side that she was laying on when her water broke with their first child. I thought of this each time I changed the linens. While I did my best to bury my feelings of resentment (and general disgust), it didn't help that everyone who found out about my living situation (including men) made the common statement of "I could never live in someone else's matrimonial home. How can you handle that?" I lied to those people and told them that it didn't bother me because my love for Greg was unconditional. Boy, oh boy did it ever bother me.

Shortly after I moved in with him, Samantha and I met up for one of our gabfest lunches. It was so good to see her again; I only wished that we didn't live four hours apart. She was not dating anymore because she'd discovered she was still completely in love with her ex-husband. We talked about it at length and she decided to confront him with her feelings. After we wrapped up her challenges with a bow, I spilled my guts about my issues with living in Greg's matrimonial home. She, like so many others, told me that I should talk to him about it. Hashing it out with her made it all sound so logical, but in the end, I couldn't confront him with it. I opted to add it to my baggage.

I put Greg through a lot of trials and tribulations over the coming months, and he rose above most of them without even flinching. Remember that "cute little carry-on" I spoke of in my dating profile? My "whatever it is"? At the time I created that profile, I didn't realize that during the two years it was buried deep inside of me, it had grown into a full-sized steamer trunk busting at the seams. All the things I thought I had conquered were just lying in wait, like a dormant volcano. My jealousies, fears, insecurities, and now, loathing of the matrimonial home were making me near ready to explode. What made it worse was alcohol.

I stopped drinking when I was twenty-one because I had been fuelling a four-year habit that had morphed into something I felt I could no longer control. I drank more than I ate and I craved that escape every day. So, after a night of binge drinking that led to me witnessing what my insides looked like coming out of me at four in the morning, I took a long, hard look in the mirror and decided to grow up. I never really drank again until after my separation from HV 2.0—fifteen years later.

Now Greg was in my life and he introduced me to the grown-up world of alcohol. He would surprise me with a special martini once in a while, or have some wine waiting for us to enjoy with our dinner. Was I going to be able to control the bad habits I had established before? Was I going to be able to enjoy the occasional drink as a nice enhancement to a meal? Or was I going to be hiding in a corner with a long straw and a mickey? I guess only time would tell how the new Veronica handled moderation.

Before I had any contact with Greg's ex, he told me a few things about her and their past. I took everything he said with a grain of salt because we all have hurt feelings when a relationship fails, and most people tend to embellish things a little when they share their "ex" stories. What I didn't realize was that Greg was actually downplaying his stories about her behavior. I soon came to experience someone so vile and disgusting that I actually started to question who *Greg* really was. He couldn't possibly be the sweet person he claimed to be if he lived for a decade with *that* woman. He must be hiding something. It took a long time for me to trust him unconditionally because I kept waiting for *that* man to show his face.

Her episodes were unbelievable. I use the term "unbelievable" because if I described them here, you wouldn't believe that I was telling the truth. Her behavior was something you would only think happens in a movie. At one point, when she was in rare form, Daniella turned to me and said, "If he was anyone other than Greg, would you still be here?" I couldn't give a complete answer at that moment, but in my heart, I knew that I would never have stayed with any other man had I been faced with what she was serving up on a daily (and sometimes hourly) basis. She did everything in her power to put a wedge in our relationship and make us miserable. Instead, her behavior actually led to a nightly ritual between us where we would express our gratitude for each other. Despite Greg's guilt over the trauma she caused to Daniella and me, his ex's psychotic episodes made us closer and our love for each other stronger. One day, maybe I'll thank her.

Once I began to experience her behavior firsthand, Greg told me everything. Every disgusting detail of his decade with her. He even let me listen to the voicemails she left and read all of the text messages. This was not a case of "he said, she said," this was real. He told me things she had said and done that made me want to vomit. *How could any human being live like that? How could he hate himself so much that he would allow someone to treat him like a dog?* Although I asked myself those questions, I knew firsthand how easy it was to stay in an abusive situation. Like they say, "Better the devil you know than the devil you don't know."

How did he find this gem of a woman?

It was in Brazil that Greg met his soon-to-be spouse at a club one night. After a brief courtship, they married and he moved back to Canada with his new bride in tow to begin his life of hell at the hands of a completely imbalanced woman.

In a desperate attempt to try to find the good in his ex, I said to Greg one day, "Surely you had to have been in love with her when you married her. Can't you draw on those memories to find the good in her and try to bury all of this hatred?" Greg informed me that he wasn't actually in love with her when they married, but thought that she would change once she was away from the influence of her family. He said that he was sure that he felt as though he was in love with her at one point, but really couldn't remember when, why, or for how long. He just waited patiently for her to change.

After their separation (long before my existence in Greg's life, but ironically at almost the same time I separated from HV 2.0), she began her tirade of emotional manipulation on their children to the point where they didn't even want to go to his house anymore. She would call and leave a handful of voicemails every day, along with five, ten, twenty daily text messages. Once she found out about me, this continued and ramped up considerably, to the point that, during the course of one supermarket trip, she called him *eight* times. She never stopped. She was such a miserable person that I'm sure she couldn't stand the thought of Greg being happy.

Greg has two boys, Colin and David. The first time I ever saw their photos I remarked that Colin looked very sensitive and David was probably a little shit. Greg laughed and told me that I hit the nail on the head for both of them.

Colin was almost nine and quite overweight. He reminded me of the big, dumb sidekick character in a movie. I soon discovered that the combination of his mother's psychological stronghold and his developmental shortcomings made him a cookie-cutter kid with issues. He was a tortured soul and it infuriated me that Greg's ex was allowed to be a parent.

David was a wiry six-year-old who sucked his thumb like it was his main food source. It was obviously emotional thumb-sucking. He was a good little guy and soon became my shadow, but the contempt he had toward his mother was apparent and he had no problem voicing it. Another child damaged by that imbalanced woman.

I was getting so sick and tired of the behavior between Greg and his ex that I asked him to request a meeting with all of us present. I thought about how I would feel if my children were going and living with some strange woman, and I felt that I owed it to her to get to know me so she could feel comfortable knowing that her children were safe.

Greg sent her a message and informed her that we wanted to meet with her and her boyfriend when we returned the boys to her house that coming Sunday evening. She agreed.

We arrived there and I was immediately intimidated by her beauty; she was a tall Brazilian with long, perfect blond hair, piercing blue eyes and a beautiful face. I started to wonder why Greg would settle on someone who looked like me when he could attract women who looked like that.

Maybe he's opting for "dowdy" because he's already experienced how psycho "beautiful" can be.

We had a nice talk (or so I thought), and I explained to her that the reason he doesn't answer her calls is because of how disruptive it is when she calls one phone, and then the other, and then back to the other, and then the other—never leaving a message. I asked her to please stop that behavior and just call once, and if he doesn't answer, leave a message asking that he return her call. I assured her that if she stopped the obsessive calling, I would ensure that he returned her calls promptly. She agreed. I further informed her (in front of the children) that we have no secrets in our home, and that they can tell her anything that is said or done while they are with us. My closing remarks were that, despite the feelings of anger she and Greg have for each other, we all needed to focus on being positive for the kids.

At the end of the talk (which I did most of), she shook my hand and called me "friend." I left her house feeling optimistic that we could make the best of this situation.

The following day, however, she called Greg and, screaming, asked him "who the fuck" I thought I was talking to her like that. She called me every name in the book and asked him if I "knew" who she was. Greg explained to me later that she and her family believe they are the mafia and threaten everyone that way. Sigh… back to square one… or square *minus* one.

Things did change slightly, though, and I patiently did my best to deal with her. She called me one day and said that I must be a very nice lady for washing and folding the boys' clothes, because Greg always sent them back dirty. Those feelings were short lived; Greg soon did something that pissed her off, and she told Colin to tell me not to wash the clothes anymore because I don't fold them right. Double sigh… whatever. One less thing for me to do on Sundays.

Then there was the call where she informed me that if I wanted Colin to like me (he had been giving me a lot of grief), I had to buy him things and take him places. I informed her that I was not that kind of mom, and he would have to learn to accept that. I think that was the last civil discussion we ever had, and her tirades went full steam ahead shortly after that.

Her text messages to Greg were vile, crude, and sick. We would also hear her shouting obscenities about Greg in the background as he spoke to his boys on the phone. She made me feel ashamed of my part-Brazilian heritage and I began to hate everything Brazilian. I wasn't alone: the husband in one sweet Brazilian couple that I had gotten to know through Greg once told me that he felt absolute shame to call himself Brazilian because of how disgustingly she behaved in their community. I was also told she'd been banned from one of the local supermarkets because of her outlandish and disrespectful behavior toward the employees. That one still makes me smile.

One day, Greg sent me a text message with his usual gushing, loving words. My reply to him was, **Greg, my life with you is like a fairy tale… complete with the evil villain.**

What is that villain's name?

I don't know where it came from, but what immediately came to mind, was **C— Dracula.** Needless to say, I received a ROTFLMAO!! response from Greg and we proceeded to refer to her by that name or "CD" for short when the kids were around.

Shortly after our naming ceremony for his ex, Greg approached me about it. He and I are firm believers of the power of the spoken word, and he felt we were empowering her with the nickname we had so fondly bestowed. So we changed it to something simpler—*Stupid.* In the coming months, to our joy and amusement, she would live up to her name a thousand times over.

CHAPTER 30
STUPID IS AS STUPID DOES

Each day was a blending process when it came to our little family, and some days were downright exhausting. Six months into our relationship, amidst all of the turmoil with his kids and his ex, and the regular adjustments of a blended family, we brought in a foster daughter—Hailey. Hailey was Daniella's friend from our old hometown and came from a very imbalanced home and bleak situation. Greg, being the incredible human being that he is, opened his home to yet another stranger. His act of generosity and heart made me realize even more what an absolute blessing he was. I fell in love with him a little bit more that day.

The emotional roller coaster that I was on was not an easy one. I was spread thin by being a mom, a stepmom, a foster mom, the other half of a new relationship, executive assistant at a new company, and part-time unofficial lawyer over Greg's legal battles. I was frustrated and didn't feel like I was being effective in any area of my life. I decided to take advantage of the free counselling that was offered through my company's benefits program. I would have four hour-long sessions over the phone, and then we would evaluate what form of assistance, if any, I may need after that.

During that first session, I outlined my situation and told the counsellor that I felt ineffective towards everyone in my life. I asked for her advice on one particular thing as well. I told her about how horrible Greg's ex behaved and explained that I made sure nothing negative was ever said about her in our home in front of the boys. My question to her was how I should react to certain things that the boys tell me. For example, I was making dinner one day and stirring the pot with a wooden spoon. Six-year-old David came into the kitchen and said, "My mom has one of those." I replied, "Yes, lots of people use these for stirring food." He responded with, "No. That's what my mom uses to hit me." I explained to the counsellor that I didn't know how to respond to that comment, and felt feeble for simply changing the subject with him.

At the end of our discussion, the counsellor said, "Veronica, before you go, I must ask you if you remember me telling you at the beginning of our conversation that if anything is said that makes me feel as though children are at risk or in danger, I would be obliged to take action?"

"Sure. Yes. I remember you saying that. Why?"

"Well, the story you told me about David and the wooden spoon makes me concerned for his safety, and I will need to contact child services. I can either contact them on my own, or you can be on the line with me when I call."

What? Oh my gawd! What have I done?

I sputtered and stammered and asked that she not call child services until I spoke to Greg. I could not—would not—betray him in this way. She agreed and I immediately called Greg to explain what had happened. He wasn't upset with me, but explained that he didn't feel that the boys were in danger, and said to tell her that it was not necessary to call the authorities.

I called her back, thanked her for her offer, and said that Greg did not feel it necessary to take action against the boys' mother.

"You don't understand, Veronica. Calling child services is not up for negotiation. The only choices you have are that either I call them on my own, or you call with me."

My heart sunk and I sincerely felt that this would be the end of my relationship with Greg. I agreed to be on the line with her, and we both spoke to the agency. I stressed to the case worker that Greg did not feel that the boys were in any danger and did my best to circumvent the situation. Nothing I said worked, and they informed me that they would be paying his ex a visit. I called Greg again, sobbing. Again, he was not upset with me, and said, "What's done is done. We'll just have to deal with it."

Sure enough, child services paid her a visit and she was the best actress on the planet. She portrayed herself as an amazing mother and neither of the boys said anything to oppose that. David also lied and said that she never hits them. The social workers left her alone, and, needless to say, the barrage of verbal abuse from her amped up to epic levels.

Even before the child services incident, every time Greg went to pick up or drop off the boys, she would spew insults and try to argue with him in front of them. One day, I was with him when he went to get them and when she saw me in the car, she did not utter a word to him. On another occasion, she came flying out her front door in an obvious fury, about to launch into a verbal attack on Greg, and when she saw me, she spun on her heel and retreated back into her house. We began to recognize the pattern. Whenever I was with him, she would either tuck tail and go back into the house, or not come out at all and hide behind the front door. Once we realized this, Greg insisted that I accompany him each and every time. I was now the force field; I was the reason that the children didn't have to be subjected to her verbal abuse towards their father. Oh well, I guess I can wear one more hat—"protector from the dark forces."

One good day for me, as an insecure woman, was the morning that we went to pick up the boys and Stupid came chasing after David in her pyjamas to zip up his coat. She saw me and quickly turned her back to us, but it was too late: I'd seen what she looked like bra-less in her thin pajama top, with messy hair and no makeup. I smiled inside. The minute it happened, Greg groaned and said, "That was horrible. I'm so sorry you had to see that."

"Actually," I admitted, "it kinda made my day." That beautiful woman I was intimidated by upon our first meeting was actually rather hideous *au naturel.*

Our first Christmas together was going to be one to remember. The boys came with us to Greg's parents' house for their usual holiday festivities. Once the meal was over, he returned them to their mother's for her family's celebration. Just as we snuggled down on the couch to watch some TV, Stupid called. She screamed at Greg about how Daniella had stolen Colin's MP3 player that cost her five hundred dollars. I went and questioned Daniella and she denied it and said that she and Hailey last saw it on Greg's mother's dining room table. This drama went on for about an hour until Greg went back over to his mother's and found it between the couch cushions in her basement where Colin had been playing with his cousins. Merry Christmas, everyone!

A few days later, David came over to play in the snow with Daniella and Hailey, but Colin wanted to stay with his mother. Before that, Stupid had said the boys must always stay together, so she forced him to come over and he came into the house crying hysterically and ran straight to his room. Greg called Stupid and explained that Colin did not want to be with us and told her not to force him just because she doesn't want Colin and David to be apart. Greg had the phone on speaker, and I heard Colin go silent in the other room and knew he was listening in. Greg always spoke to Stupid on speakerphone because she had previously made unfounded claims about things he had said to her, so he always made sure that I was witness to their conversations. Now Colin was within earshot of the profanity she was using towards Greg. I didn't know what to do, so I asked Colin how he felt when he heard what she was saying. He said, "Not good." I asked him if he felt that it was right to talk to people that way, and he said no. I was trying to use the bad situation as a learning tool to make the best out of something that he never should have heard. Stupid finally came and took Colin back to her house, but then called Greg yet again. She was even more livid than before and demanded to speak to me.

Before I continue, I must explain that Colin and David were accustomed to lying a lot. Not a little… *a lot.* We had caught them both in many lies, and we had also had to deal with lies that Colin told his mother about me in an attempt to get me out of his life. In true Colin form, he lied to his mother about what I said to him after that conversation, and she went completely off the rails. She went up one side of me and down the other. Never in my life had anyone spoken to me in such a disgusting and disrespectful way. So, during one of my lowest moments, I thought I'd try fighting fire with fire because a civil tongue had not worked with her up to that point. I called her an effing bitch. And I repeated it a couple more times as well for effect. Greg took the phone away from me and told her that this had gone far enough and to stop the behavior. She screamed, "Does she know who I am? You tell that bitch to watch her back because she'll never know when I am coming. I'm going to make that bitch pay!"

She then proceeded to tell him that she was on her way over and would show me *exactly* who she was. Greg told her that he'd have the video camera ready and welcomed her to come over. I had had enough by that point and called the police. No one should have to live like this, and there was no getting through to this woman; so, unfortunately, I was going to have to have the police intervene.

We explained everything to them and they paid her a visit. She, of course, lied, and the police called me back afterwards and told me they could tell she was lying through her teeth. Because a child was present when they went over there (Colin was at her side), they were obligated to call child services. Here we go again. Although child services contacted Greg to speak to him about the situation, we never did hear back from them about how their interview with her went. But now she had two incidents on record with them, and one with the police.

On top of all this, we were starting to get a bad feeling from Hailey. Her influence on Daniella was a negative one; Daniella was becoming very self-absorbed and disrespectful and was no longer making an effort in school.

Although I had many heartfelt talks with Hailey, she was lying to us at every turn. Daniella was becoming more and more miserable too, and she finally confided in me that her "friend" was spreading rumours about her at school and now everyone hated her and was calling her a slut. I'd had enough and made the decision to send her back. Before doing so, I called her mother and had a long talk with her about her past. Apparently, Hailey had spun an intricate web of lies in order to come and live with us. Her life really wasn't that bad at all, and I found out through speaking with a mutual friend that her mother was actually a wonderful woman. Although her time with us helped repair the damage between Hailey and her family, we were all glad to close that chapter of our lives eight months after it had begun. I know that everything happens for a reason, and we all learned many things from that experience.

About five months into Greg and my relationship, Phil finally came around. We started speaking again, but he was not ready to meet Greg. One night, though, he came by to pick up some baking on his way through our neighborhood, and I went out to his car. As Greg stood in the doorway inside, Phil waved at him through the dark distance that separated them. Greg mistook his wave for a signal to come out and Phil just about had a meltdown. "I'm not ready for this, I'm not ready for this," he muttered under his breath to me as Greg approached. The two most important men in my life were finally going to meet.

Phil later admitted that he fell in love with Greg a little that night. Well, not in love per se (take note of the spelling, Greg)... but he said that he could tell what a stand-up guy he was and said he was sincerely happy that I found him.

Phil was the least of our worries during the blending period, though, because a lot of healing still needed to occur with Greg's children.

Every day, Greg and I worked on creating a peaceful and loving home for our children. We knew that if we just stayed consistent, one day we would have the peace we both desired. Through it all, we just held onto each other tight and never lost sight of our love and devotion for one another. I don't think a single day went by that I didn't tell him how much I loved him. I was determined to never let him have a single doubt about how I felt about him. Every time I told him he was perfect, he'd say, "Nobody's perfect." So instead, I changed my words to "You're perfect… for me." He was okay with that one.

I have always told couples to never lose sight of why they first fell in love. Although I am twice divorced, and it may seem hypocritical for me to say, I know the importance of a couple keeping those memories in the forefront of their minds so that they never lose sight of their love for one another.

Shortly after we moved in together, I asked that Greg and I start a nightly ritual. Each night we had to sit up in bed, facing each other and holding hands, and take turns saying one of two things to the other: "I am grateful for you because…" or "I fell in love with you a little bit more today because…" Most nights, one or both of our devotions would cause us to break down into tears, which would then lead into an hour of crying and talking and falling in love even more. Every day I looked forward to going to bed because of that ritual, but on the same token, I dreaded every bedtime because it meant that I had to go to sleep and wouldn't get to look at him until the next day.

We never lost sight of the fact that neither of us had ever felt a peace like this before, a peace that was so obvious that when Daniella observed us doing something as simple as cooking together one night, she said, "You know, when you two are together you just… you just… flow." If she could see that, and declare it in front of both of us, we knew that we had a winning combination.

Although Daniella claimed to have issues with Greg (mainly because of his expectation for her to discontinue her well-honed skills as the town slob), I could see a change and a peace in her too, that was undeniable. Daniella always freely shared *everything* with me, and as she got older, I longed for the purple dinosaur and fluffy kitten conversations we used to have. Although her topics would sometimes make me cringe, I wouldn't trade that for the usual teenage angst, silence, and disrespect for any amount of money in the world. The amazing thing was that she also had no problem sharing in front of Greg. I saw him cringe a few times, but he just sat quietly and let her speak. She had never, *ever* spoken freely in front of a man before.

When we moved to our new province, we both felt a change within us, but also witnessed a change in one other individual—our cat Leopold. Leo had always been neurotic, but a few months before we moved, he started a ritual of beating up his two siblings every night while we were sleeping. I woke up night after night as he terrorized them, and it was getting out of control. When we decided to move, I didn't feel that we could take the other two with us. They were both very emotionally fragile, and I knew that one of them (the female) would probably die in transit; so I made the very difficult decision to adopt them out together.

We found a wonderful woman to take them and, even though I was wracked with guilt over abandoning my furbabies, it was clear that it was meant to be. Three days after their new furmommy brought them home, her adult daughter passed away unexpectedly. She later told me that she truly believed that our cats were brought to her to help her heal, and said they doted on her daily. Although I still felt extreme guilt over what I had done, my heart felt peace after reading those words.

During the two years between my separation from HV 2.0 and moving to our new home, Leo continued peeing in inappropriate places, but since we moved to our new province, he abandoned those bad habits—or so I thought. Little did I know that he was sneaking into a very cluttered storage area in Patricia's house and peeing on her things. When I discovered it, I quickly cleaned it up and rearranged things in a way that wouldn't give him an opportunity to do it anymore. Fortunately, he didn't ruin anything, because he was just soiling the tops of garbage bags. I monitored that room almost daily after that.

I didn't tell Greg about Leo's bad habits for fear that he would make me get rid of him. I couldn't do that. I could not lose another one of my furbabies. It was bad enough that Greg said he was allergic to cats and didn't want Leo anywhere near him. Little did Greg know that I would secretly start testing his so-called allergy. During the first six months that we were living together, I would love up Leo to get his dander and fluff all over my hands, and then dust off any visible fur and cuddle with Greg. I'd stroke and caress his face, which would have turned into a field of hives and bumps and sneezes if he was allergic. I eventually confessed my sneaky ways to him, and he surprisingly wasn't upset with me at all.

When we moved in with Greg, Leo abandoned his peeing habit completely (I think he had a total of two lapses). He was such a happy and balanced cat that he was almost unrecognizable at times. He loved Greg dearly and we watched Greg slowly fall in love with him too. The two of them would wrestle and fight and play, and it was beautiful. They'd even cuddle and fall asleep together on the couch.

Slowly, at what seemed like a turtle's pace sometimes, our little dysfunctional family was becoming one.

What was the hardest part about all of this blending for me? It wasn't Colin's erratic and unfounded temper tantrums. It wasn't Daniella's "I love

Greg, I hate Greg, I love Greg, I hate Greg" flip-flopping. It wasn't the daily harassment by Stupid. The hardest part of all of this was that I would never be able to look into our children's eyes and see both of our eyes looking back at me. Even though I am confident that I would never have been able to win him over twenty years ago because of all the emotional growing that I needed to do in order to become deserving of a man like him, it still hurt my heart. It didn't help that Greg would often look at me with tears in his eyes and say, "Why couldn't I have met you twenty years ago? Our life would be so perfect."

I knew that it was wrong for me to feel ungrateful, though. God had led an incredible man into my life. How on earth could I be ungrateful?

CHAPTER 31
THREE HUNDRED SIXTY-FIVE DAYS

My continued efforts on Greg's court case were also taking a toll on me. I knew how important its success was, and if we lost, it would all be on my shoulders. What fuelled my stress was not the thought of losing and shelling out money we didn't have; it was the thought of the satisfaction that Stupid would get from bettering us. I couldn't stand the thought of her gloating and mocking us if she won.

On top of all of this stress, Greg fell victim to the "economic downturn" and lost his job (as did all of his coworkers), and I was left to pay all the bills *and* his child support on my own. During the six months of his unemployment, he drove to my office every single day to exercise in our on-site gym and bring me lunch. He cared for the home and was a wonderful househusband. Although it was a financial struggle, we both had an epiphany of sorts. We realized that we could survive on one salary (barely) and that our relationship was only growing stronger. Money troubles are one of the leading causes of the demise of marriages, so the fact that it did not even cause a hiccup in our love for each other made us realize that we had something truly real and special.

Drinking became a big part of my life again, and I was getting drunk on a regular basis. I began to crave that warm, dizzy feeling again… that feeling that made my body feel like warm dough. It was so nice to just melt into the couch and pass out at the end of the evening. Greg fuelled that escape from reality with his readily available homemade wine, but in the end, he was the one that my moods would rear their ugly head at. I was struggling hard with my depression again because of the stress of everything his ex was subjecting us to, and the combination of depression and alcohol was a toxic one.

I began to fly into the most irrational rages at night when we went to bed. I became violent and verbally abusive, and many times, Greg had to physically restrain me because I was completely out of control. There were just as many times when I had absolutely no recollection of what happened the night before, and felt so much shame and remorse the next day that I could barely face him. He, in turn, still loved me completely and openly, which made me hate myself even more. Even during those episodes, though, I couldn't stand the thought of living a day without him.

So why was I doing my best to sabotage this relationship? Was it just a subconscious thing? Was it the old me who felt that I was the common denominator in my failed relationships? Easier to end it now than to drag it out for six, ten, or fifteen years? What was actually the root cause of my behavior?

During the first few months of my relationship with Greg, I was still receiving messages from Stefan every now and again. It was nothing disrespectful; he was just checking to make sure that "Mr. Wonderful," as he referred to Greg, was still treating me well. He informed me in no uncertain terms that he would be waiting with open arms (and an open bed) if ever I chose to go back to him. Each time, I told him that I was completely over the moon with Greg and was very flattered and overwhelmed that I had had such an impact on him.

I could have had a very easy out from my relationship with Greg if I wanted to, so why did I stay? Why did I stay and continue to have my outbursts?

I stayed because I knew, deep down, that he was "the one" and that I could never live a day without him. In the eighth month of our relationship, I received another message from Stefan. He was still waiting. I thanked him once again for his kind words and proceeded to lie to him; I told him that Greg and I were getting married.

I never really had an ex-boyfriend before, so I never had to deal with lingering affections. Lying to Stefan seemed like the easiest way to deal with it. He wrote back to me with sincere congratulations and wished me well. That was the last time I ever heard from him.

That first year was a painful yet crucial phase of our relationship. All of the pain and anguish from both of our pasts came spilling out onto the floor. We cleaned up the mess together and equally traded off the burden of being the strong one through each tough time. I can freely admit, though, that Greg was the biggest key to our success. And so I wrote to him:

THREE HUNDRED SIXTY-FIVE

***THREE HUNDRED SEVENTY-EIGHT** days have passed since you first knocked on my proverbial door.*

***THREE HUNDRED SEVENTY-SEVEN** days have passed since I first thought to cast you aside.*

***THREE HUNDRED SEVENTY-SIX** days have passed since I sat in sorrow over the emptiness in my heart.*

***THREE HUNDRED SEVENTY-FIVE** days have passed since I decided to settle on what I already had.*

***THREE HUNDRED SEVENTY-FOUR** days have passed since you knocked on that door again.*

***THREE HUNDRED SEVENTY-THREE** days have passed since you endeavored to caress me with your words.*

***THREE HUNDRED SEVENTY-TWO** days have passed since I began to falter in getting to know the man behind the words.*

***THREE HUNDRED SEVENTY-ONE** days have passed since I grew more curious about who was behind those words.*

***THREE HUNDRED SEVENTY** days have passed since I wished I was walking by your side.*

***THREE HUNDRED SIXTY-NINE** days have passed since I first laid eyes on the most beautiful man that I had ever seen.*

***THREE HUNDRED SIXTY-EIGHT** days have passed since you first took my hand… kissed my lips.*

***THREE HUNDRED SIXTY-SEVEN** days have passed since I decided that it was only your arms that I wanted to cushion my fall.*

***THREE HUNDRED SIXTY-SIX** days have passed since I was overcome with peace and clarity… since we shed our first tears together.*

THREE HUNDRED SIXTY-FIVE *days have passed since I realized that I was in the presence of the man described on my decade-old list.*

THREE HUNDRED SIXTY-FIVE *days have passed since I sat gazing into your eyes wondering if you were really real.*

THREE HUNDRED SIXTY-FIVE *days have passed since I realized that I was completely in awe of you.*

THREE HUNDRED SIXTY-FIVE *days have passed since I became one with you… body and soul.*

THREE HUNDRED SIXTY-FIVE *days have passed since I realized that I had found the man of my dreams.*

CHAPTER 32
THE LONG ARM OF THE LAW

In the end, I spent a total of ten months preparing and filing *his* case against *her*. My case was not based on a "he said, she said" scenario, or an "I hate your guts" undertone. Mine was based on pure black and white figures and documented information. Greg made one more attempt to settle with her out of court, but her lawyer did not even bother responding.

The day Greg went for his first hearing was the most stressful day of my life. I could not go with him, so he spent the two days leading up reviewing everything I had prepared. I knew that case inside and out, but he didn't, so I was extremely worried that he wouldn't be able to represent himself effectively.

When his docket was called, he entered the courtroom, and the judge immediately said, "I have spoken to the defendant's lawyer and I can tell you that from my sixteen years of experience as a judge, there is no jury that will rule in your favour." The judge set the next court date and that was that. Greg didn't get to say a word.

As he walked out of the courtroom, Stupid stepped in front of him and smugly said, "You better get a lawyer!"

I was livid when Greg told me the story. How the hell was it fair that HER lawyer could talk to the judge privately in advance? We had no way of knowing what was said, but I told Greg, "I hate to admit this, but Stupid is right. You need to get a lawyer."

After that, every time Greg went to pick up the boys by himself, Stupid came out and started chanting "you're going to pay" in front of them, either in English or Portuguese. I was even more determined to win now.

We found a lawyer, and after he reviewed all of the documents I had already prepared, he said that my work was exemplary and thorough and that he would only need to file a couple of amendments. Now we just had to sit and wait until the court date.

The court date finally arrived, and our lawyer discovered that someone had made an error and set the date with the same judge that spoke with Stupid's lawyer the first time around. Our lawyer explained to us that the courts will not allow the same judge to preside over a case twice, in order to avoid any chance of bias. Therefore, yet another date was set.

During one of our discussions with our lawyer, we informed him about the extra child support we had been paying for many months. He instructed us to cease paying *any* child support until the case was settled. He assured us that we would not face any repercussions with the child support services because the case was actively being played out. That was some great news for us for a change.

During the waiting period for our trial, I arranged to take care of a co-worker's pick-up truck while he was out of the country on a project. I selfishly offered to truck-sit because we were doing emergency renovations in our basement (due to a flood and mold issues), and it would help us out a lot for transporting materials. When the boys came over and saw the enormous black truck, they went crazy with excitement and asked Greg if it was his. Greg and I had already agreed that we wouldn't lie to them about it, but that we also wouldn't tell them why it was there, in order to see if Stupid would make an assumption and make a fool of herself. So Greg used his famous line on them: "You don't have to worry about it." And nothing more was said or asked.

About a month after the truck arrived, our lawyer received a letter from Stupid's lawyer stating that, since Greg could afford to purchase a new vehicle, she demanded that he pay the full amount owing to Stupid. I was the one to open the forwarded letter and when I read it I shouted with joy, "She really is stupid! She took the bait! She took the bait!" We had all of the documentation to prove that we were truck-sitting, so now we just had to wait for the court date and hope that Stupid's lawyer would make a fool of herself and bring it up in front of the judge.

On top of all of this, Stupid threatened me multiple times, to the point where I was forced to call the police twice and begin proceedings to file a restraining order against her. Was I afraid of her? Honestly, no. Face to face, she would be no match against me, but I needed to send her a clear message the right way. She needed to understand that this was not how *civilized* people behaved.

Did I vividly imagine grabbing her by her cheap hair extensions and *schooling* her like she'd never been schooled before? You bet.

Although I was not physically afraid of her, when someone repeatedly threatens you and makes statements like, "You better watch your back because you'll never know when I'm coming," a certain concern arises about what I might encounter in a dark corner of a parking lot somewhere. Or worse yet, what someone might do to my daughter. Again, I was *not* afraid of that putrid piece of garbage, but if something were to happen, at least there would be documented records of her ongoing behavior and threats.

The court date finally arrived and our hearts sunk—it was a female judge presiding over the case. I was sure that we'd lose. *There's no way a female judge is going to rule in a man's favour. There's no way.*

While we waited to be called in, Stupid's lawyer approached our lawyer and said that they were willing to negotiate a settlement. In true Type-A form, I had already prepared a quick reference guide of ten court-ruling scenarios so that if a deal was to be struck (and I couldn't be present), Greg could look at my summary and know if it was worth agreeing to. Thankfully, I was able to be with him when our lawyer came back with her first offer, and I told Greg that I didn't feel it was worth entertaining. Greg agreed to turn her down and we sent back our counter-offer. When she came back with her second offer, I was still adamant that it was not in his best interest, and we told our lawyer to simply tell her, "We'll see you in court." It was something totally out of a movie, but it sure did allow me to feel a momentary sense of being in total control. I felt like *Matlock*.

Again, I was not permitted in the courtroom, so I was on pins and needles after they went in. It felt like they were gone for hours, but it was actually only about thirty minutes.

Stupid came whizzing out first and left abruptly with the entourage that she brought with her that day, and Greg emerged in deep discussion with his lawyer, both of them approaching me with emotionless faces. I was trying to act cool and collected, but I felt like I was going to pee my pants. Greg walked up to me, swept me up in his arms, and said, "We won! She ruled a hundred percent in our favour." As much as I wanted to cry, I held it together in front of our lawyer. He informed us that he would also be going after her for costs and that we didn't have to attend court for that. It was finally over. Over a year and a half after Greg first asked me to review those documents, it was finished.

We went out for a celebratory lunch, and Greg told me the entire story. He said he wished I could have been there; he said the judge spoke exactly like I did and it was like watching me up there ruling over the case. She proceeded to humiliate and wipe the floor with Stupid's lawyer, as it was completely obvious that this was all just an attempt at a cash-grab on Stupid's part.

As expected, Stupid's lawyer sent a scathing letter to our lawyer expressing her objections about how unfair the ruling was and saying she would be filing an appeal to attempt, once more, to get money out of Greg. In the end, Greg was awarded costs. You can imagine the celebrations that ensued in our home over those victories.

With each case that we won, Stupid became more and more silent. Were we finally going to have the peace that we both longed for? Was my wish of the 25A Express Bus mowing her down in a busy intersection finally going to come true?

Wait...

Ignore that last part... I don't think I'm supposed to let my inside voice narrate here.

During those long months, I questioned our relationship so many times, and was ready to leave almost as many, because I couldn't understand what we had done to deserve having our lives intruded upon in such a way. There were many nights that Greg literally cried over the guilt he felt for making me live with the mistakes of his past. Although I held him tight and told him that I loved him unconditionally, the nagging voice still spoke in the back of my head.

Do I really want this for my life? Am I strong enough to live with this kind of emotional terrorism?

CHAPTER 33
LIES... LIES... LIES

Through all the turmoil of the court cases, I was still planning Greg's birthday. Every day on my way to and from work, I drove past a sign for a golf course whose name became imbedded in my subconscious; so it was the first place I called to inquire about lessons. I spoke to Charles. Oh my goodness, sweet, firecracker Charles. Charles' enthusiasm was adorable, but I was exhausted after each call from him; my cool-as-a-cucumber personality found his Mexican-jumping-bean personality slightly overwhelming. Despite this, I knew he was "the one." Charles was going to help me make Greg's dreams come true.

Greg was still unemployed when I embarked on this new adventure, and was coming to my office daily to work out and bring lunch for us to eat together. During one of our desk picnics, my phone rang and the call display listed the golf course name. Greg saw and asked why a golf course would be contacting me. Quick as a wink I came back with a justification; I acted exasperated and explained that one of my bosses asked me to research a membership for his wife, and since contacting them they'd been calling me almost daily and never leaving a message. Of course, at that moment, the message indicator lit up on my phone. *Damn you, Charles! Why today?* "Well, I guess they finally had the balls to leave me a message! I'm definitely going to nip this in the bud today and tell them to stop calling. Like I have time for this crap!" He believed me. Oh my gawd... I was getting way too good at this lying game.

After Greg left, I returned Charles' call. He was so apologetic for calling, but we had a good laugh about it too. I was to start my lessons in late April, which would give me four full months of practice before the birthday trip. Since it was so early in the season, Charles taught his lessons out of a local indoor driving range. My first lesson with him was after work one day when I was, as far as Greg was concerned, "stuck at a stupid project meeting taking minutes."

Upon meeting, Charles asked me if I was nervous. I told him that *I* was not nervous, but my right breast was. As his face went completely crimson, I informed him that, during my one and only driving range experience with Greg, my right breast had been the victim of "purple nurples" from being pinched by my arm with each swing. I went on to say that I knew why only flat-chested feminists played this game, because women with bodacious tah-tahs were at risk of bodily harm. I further explained that my day at the driving range with Greg had proved to be a confirmation of my theory of women and golf.

Charles didn't know what to make of me at first, but I think we both enjoyed our first date and he quickly realized that there were no airs about me. My angst-ridden right breast was quickly pacified once he showed me how to correctly swing the bat... the stick?... the club? Crap! Ugh, new lingo to learn.

At the end of my lesson, I asked Charles if there was somewhere I could change back into my work clothes, and I mentioned that my "husband" thought I was at a meeting. As I was getting changed, I was suddenly overwhelmed by the realization that this was how easy it was to cheat on a partner. Greg was at home (probably raving about me to his family again), while I was traipsing around town behind his back. This is how easy it is for people to cheat on each other. Regardless of how honorable the reason behind it was, the guilt of my lie consumed me, and I silently cried myself to sleep that night.

During my second lesson, Charles quickly realized that I was very Type-A and very much a perfectionist. But he paid me a compliment: he said that most people with my personality want to rush through everything and move on to the next topic, but was impressed that I refused to move on to the next thing until I fully understood the mechanics of what he had just taught me. I may not have mastered the move or the swing or whatever it was, but I was patient enough to allow myself to fully wrap my head around what he was teaching me.

One thing I was struggling with was the momentum of my swing. Charles said he had a little trick to help with that. He told me that in his mind he would say his first and last name and match the flow of his swing with that. He then demonstrated and said out loud, "Charles Waylon" and swung the club with a melodic flow. I tried his method, but "Veronica Coldrake" didn't flow like "Charles Waylon" did. Between that lesson and my next, I took the advice literally and said "Charles Waylon" in my head with every swing. It worked. I mastered the momentum of my swing. On my third lesson, I demonstrated my beautiful new swing, and Charles just shook his head and laughed when I told him my method of perfecting it.

Once the weather warmed up a bit, my lessons could be held at the golf course that Charles worked at, as well as at a nearby driving range. Although he loaned me one club, I still needed a set of my own. I knew that Greg had a couple of sets, but how could I take one without him knowing? What if he wanted to practice as his birthday approached? I remembered that he had one set he "found in a ditch," and it was buried in his overcrowded shed. When I explained to Charles that I wouldn't be able to get a full set without causing suspicion, he told me which key clubs to focus on obtaining. So, when Greg popped out to go to the hardware store one day, I climbed into his shed and pulled out the recommended clubs. I was shaking like a leaf, and then my world came crashing down—I couldn't get the shed door closed. It was a thick wooden door that Greg had fashioned and we always laughed at how he'd open and close it with one hand like it was paper thin. This was not a time to laugh. I could not budge it and I was starting to panic, because there is absolutely nothing in that shed that would give me reason to go in there. My mind was racing. If I ran up the street to get one of the big neighbor guys (if one of them was home), what if Greg came home while he was still here? What if he didn't come home but the guy that helped me was a terrible secret-keeper and spilled the beans before his birthday? I was completely melting down at this point as I grunted and tugged at the door. I went running into the house and grabbed Daniella and her school friend Ariana, and the three of us all stood back there grunting, tugging, and pushing at that door.

I hope I can successfully paint a visual of what we looked like doing this. Picture a standard metal tool shed, but the two sliding metal doors have been replaced with some form of two-inch-thick pressboard. When Greg ingeniously came up with this idea years earlier, he didn't factor in that the elements would cause the wood to swell and become distorted over time, thus making it near impossible to close unless you were built like a tank (like he was). We were able to get one side shut, but the other wouldn't budge. So there is Daniella with her feet dug firmly into the ground, pulling on the handle, while Ariana is pushing it from the opposite edge. I have my back against hers, with my feet on the fence trying to use the strength of my legs to add to the pushing effort. We finally felt it move and then it gave way. The girls shrieked with delight and we all ran back into the house *just* as Greg pulled into the driveway. I hid the golf clubs under Daniella's bed and then hid myself in the bathroom until I stopped sweating and shaking. The girls, meanwhile, sat at the kitchen table giggling like crazy. Thank God it could be passed off as teenage silliness. Later, I stored the clubs under the false bottom of my trunk next to the spare tire, and that would be their home for the next few months. When Charles first saw the clubs, he didn't think I'd be able to accomplish anything with them as they were so old and had no "sweet spot." Over time he became amazed at how accurately I could fire those balls with my "ghetto clubs," as I fondly called them.

Each morning, I stood in the golf nets at Charles' golf course and practiced by the light of the moon. It was very peaceful, and I didn't have to worry about feeling self-conscious because no one was around me—except the grounds crew. They got used to seeing me there after a while and would wave and shake their heads in disbelief as they drove by to tend to the rest of the course.

One day Greg noticed callouses on my hands and said, "Sweetheart, what happened to your hands? They're usually so soft and smooth."

The delicate, soft, and gentle hands that he had become so familiar with were now calloused and rough. My internal lie device clicked on immediately and I said, without hesitation, "You're not going to believe this, but..."

"You're not going to believe this, but..." is my standard disclaimer. In my world, I believe that if the listener accepts that statement, they are willingly accepting the terms and conditions of the forthcoming lie. I never stated that I was about to tell the truth, but simply led them blindly into the lie. It was almost like they were signing a waiver of sorts.

I continued, "It's kind of embarrassing, but... when I'm stressed, I grip the steering wheel too tight."

Greg wrapped those solid and loving arms around me and told me that I needed to let go of the stresses of my job and just take things in stride. I wanted to stab myself. I couldn't stand lying to him each and every time I opened my mouth. It was beginning to take its toll on me.

I came home one day at the end of May to find a wonderful dinner waiting for me and a beaming Greg. After a delicious meal, he informed me that he had great news: he had found a job. I felt incredible relief that we could finally start moving forward financially, but it was quickly squelched by what he said next.

"The best part is... it's *two blocks* from your office, so we can carpool all the way to work together every day! I will be able to drive so that you don't get callouses on your hands anymore." He was like a 100-watt bulb and I had to muster up everything inside of me to pretend that I was equally excited.

But in my head, my thought was, *Shit! When am I going to practice golf?*

Every morning after that point, we got up at four-thirty and went to the gym together at my office. I replaced my usual Pilates and cardio routines with weight training so that he'd see me lifting weights and I could justify the continued presence of callouses on my hands. After about a month, though, I was not getting nearly enough practice with my golfing, so I had to come up with a new lie. I told him that things had really ramped up at work and I wouldn't be able to drive with him every day. I began driving in alone two to three times a week so that I could go straight to the golf course and practice in the nets.

At the beginning of June I heard about a 2-for-1 sale on shoes at a premium golf store, so I decided to take advantage of that and purchase both my and Greg's golf shoes. Greg had never owned a pair of golf shoes before, so I thought it would be the perfect Father's Day gift from the kids. Along with that, Charles was trying to find an instructor for Greg. That was going to be the other half of the gift. Charles didn't feel comfortable teaching Greg himself for fear of letting something slip and ruining my surprise. In the end, though, Charles couldn't find someone he felt would be a right fit for Greg, so he told me that he would be honored to carry the burden of the lie to ensure that Greg got the instruction that he deserved.

Normally, the family congregated at Greg's parents' house for any celebration, but it was a gorgeous, sunny day, so we all met at Greg's brother's house for Father's Day so that all the kids could play in their large yard. When the kids gave Greg the shoes, he was a little taken aback. He said that he'd never owned golf shoes before and knew that the purpose of the purchase was because of the upcoming golf game on his birthday. The certificate for golf lessons really blew him away, though. I later found out that his sister-in-law found him in their garage in tears. He was so overwhelmed by the gesture because his ex had never allowed him to do anything for himself. Later that night, when we were alone, he thanked me for the gift and became emotional as he explained that the gesture of his freedom to do something for himself meant far more than any material gift. He told me that, once again, I had honored him in a way that no one ever had. That statement reassured me that my other lie was so completely worth it. I had to keep working hard at my game so that his birthday would be the most memorable day of his life.

Greg soon began his lessons with Charles, and I was able to watch a few of them. As I was a few months ahead of him in the learning curve, I sat watching his form and silently critiquing it with the same comments that

Charles had used with me. On one occasion at a local driving range, I watched a father teaching his son the basics of the swing. It was totally wrong and it took every ounce of my being not to march over there in my usual Type-A fashion and school them. I sat squirming in my chair as I watched them do what Charles had criticized me for doing: the *Elvis Swing*. It's a term that he created and is a common newbie mistake involving pivoting the leg in a way that resembles an Elvis dance move. One of the top two most memorable and closest calls of the secret-keeping was the day that Charles booked me in for a lesson right after Greg's. I pulled up to the driving range just as Greg was coming out. Greg was so surprised to see me there, but I quickly said, "I needed to come and give you a kiss!" Of course that made him fall in love with me a little bit more, that I had driven out of my way *just* to show him some affection. I was going to be late for my lesson soon, and Greg was being chatty and snuggly in the parking lot.

"Sweetie… could we continue this when we get home? I *really* have to pee."

Greg knows all too well about my infantile bladder, so he understood completely. I told him that I had some errands to run and would be home soon and ran off to the clubhouse. When I saw him drive away, I ran back out to my car and grabbed my clubs to find Charles waiting for me, doubled over with laughter. He had seen the whole thing and couldn't understand how I'd kept this charade going for so long. I was emotionally exhausted, and it was only July. I still had almost two full months to go.

Once Greg and I started carpooling again, the stress really began mounting and I just kept blaming it on my job. Greg grew more and more upset with my bosses and was ready to go in there to have words with them. I begged him not to do something like that and told him that it was only temporary and should ease up by the end of the summer. He agreed not to go storming in there like my knight in shining armour, but he started to really become disgusted with my bosses. Little did he know that the five men I supported were the sweetest and kindest men on the planet, and so completely supportive of what I was doing for Greg.

Again blaming the stress, I started taking long weekends or adding an additional day to a long weekend. Since Greg still had to work, I had all day to practice on the days that he thought I was just relaxing and decompressing at home. Instead, I would take his good set of clubs to a nearby driving range and hit an extra-large bucket of balls. I'd then go home, clean the house like crazy, start getting things prepped for dinner, and then go back to the driving range in the afternoon to do it all over again. My plan got foiled one day when Greg informed me that he too was going to take the day off so that we could have some quiet time without the kids around. *Dammit!* Thankfully, though, his mother showed up unannounced after breakfast, and she and Greg started bickering about the state of the garden. The garden was Greg's world, so I used that as my excuse to run away. "I can't deal with listening to your bickering today. This is *not* my idea of a peaceful day off. I'm going out for a while." I went straight to the driving range and got in an extra-large bucket of practice.

Soon after that, I realized that I hadn't been practicing my chipping, so I turned to Paulo for his help. The golf course that I practiced at didn't allow chipping practice, and I didn't dare risk doing it in our backyard, so I asked Paulo to show me how to do it at the back of our office's parking lot. It was a very long area of grass with some great dips and rolls, so it was the perfect place for it. The only problem was that the smokers at my office would stand at the back of our building and watch me. I had to get over my fear of being watched and just keep moving forward. The grassy area was so large that I could practice my full swing as well, seeing as I was incapable of hitting anything further than fifty yards.

Things were coming together for me. I was practicing my swing by the light of the moon at four-thirty in the morning, chipping on the green space at the back of my company's parking lot at lunch and putting... *Oh crap! I haven't been practicing putting!*

There wasn't a putter in that set that I could steal, so I'd been leaving this one crucial aspect of practice out of the mix. Although I didn't know much about golf, each time I used the washroom at the driving range, I read the sign that hung above the toilet: "Driving is for show—Putting is for dough." I didn't have much more time to practice, so one morning, I snuck into Greg's garage and stole the putter out of his set, then scurried off to the golf nets. Charles was going to try to meet me there that morning, but he'd hurt his back and wasn't sure if he'd make it. I told him that if he didn't show, I'd just keep doing what I do by the light of the moon. I went extra early to get warmed up before his potential arrival, and opened the trunk to get my contraband clubs and newly stolen putter. *The putter... Where's the putter? Oh my gawd! I left it leaning against the side of the house!*

There is no way that Greg *wouldn't* see the putter when he left for work that morning, so I jumped back in my car and raced home. We lived thirty minutes away from the golf course so I drove home at Mach speed hoping that Greg wouldn't be awake yet. The entrance onto the highway was closed and, being the *Queen of Lost,* I had no clue how to get home if I had to deviate from the one route I knew. I fumbled for Gina and got her hooked up to guide me home. My stomach was doing flip-flops and my hands were shaking. When I arrived on our street, I parked a couple of houses away and crept towards our house. There he stood in the kitchen window. *Shit!* Thankfully, I was wearing all black, so I stealthily snuck up to the house using the shadows to hide me. I literally crawled up the front steps and grabbed the putter. My heart was beating out of my chest at this point, and I sprinted back to the car to hurry back to the golf course where Charles might be waiting. Now my stomach was doing flip-flops at the thought that Charles would come to meet me (achy back and all) and I wouldn't be there. To my relief, he wasn't there. I sat in the car trying to compose myself. *It's okay, Veronica. Breathe. Greg didn't see you. Charles wasn't here waiting. It's all good. Breathe. Calm down.* Once my hands stopped shaking, I grabbed my putter and walked towards the practice putting green thingy. I stopped dead in my tracks, though, and my heart sank: during the night, someone had vandalized the course, and the main target was the putting area. I started tidying it up and collecting the empty bottles of booze strewn about, along with the flags and the little cups that go in the hole where you hit the ball into. When I saw the grounds crew coming, I waved them over to me to give them everything I had found. Since I couldn't practice my putting, I went into the nets to get at least some kind of practice in. It broke my heart to watch the grounds crew: six grown men, standing and staring at the area in shock. You could tell by the sombre looks on their faces that this wasn't just a job to them—they were devastated by the destruction. What a morning.

So many other things happened during my months of practice, and the hardest part was that I couldn't share any of them with my best friend—Greg. I used Paulo and Phil as my outlets and told them as much as I could so that I didn't burst from holding everything inside. The hardest one was the day that Phil and I went to the driving range together. Although I still didn't know much about golf, I sure knew how *not* to hold the club. I cannot even find the words to describe how Phil holds the club, but I sure had Paulo rolling on the floor when I showed him.

Three weeks before Greg's birthday, I was ready to spill the beans. I couldn't take it anymore. I was a complete wreck. Phil and Paulo begged me to hold my tongue. They both informed me that if either of them were blessed with a woman who would go to a driving range at four a.m. each and every day for them, they would be over the moon upon the reveal of the surprise. Their words made me hold out just a little bit longer.

My lessons were supposed to consist of structured practice and then a round of actual golf with Charles. He allowed me to make a different arrangement with him so that I could get in as much technical guidance as possible. He converted my 18-hole game to four extra hours of tutelage, and then Phil or Paulo would take me out to play an actual round closer to Greg's birthday.

Phil suggested that we meet at an "executive" course for nine holes. *An executive course? This is too much pressure. I've never even golfed before and now I have to go with Phil to some snooty place where just executives go? I'm going to have doctors and lawyers standing behind me tapping their feet impatiently. Oh my gawd! This is not good.* I didn't share with Phil how completely freaked out I was, and I joined him after work a week before D-Day (or should I say B-Day). Greg, of course, was told that I was at yet another late meeting taking minutes. He never questioned these things because he knew that we had offices all over the world in different time zones. This meeting was with our office in Brisbane, so the fifteen-hour time difference meant that we all needed to make sacrifices.

I arrived at the course and discovered that an executive course was simply a nine-hole course where people could go and have a quick game. It was apparently also referred to as *pitch and putt*. All this time I thought *pitch and putt* was another name for mini golf. Slowly but surely, I was learning more about this game; but I still refused to call my driver anything but a *fatty*. More importantly, though, I didn't have any doctors or lawyers tapping their feet behind me that day. *Phew!*

We were sharing Phil's putter, and the most amazing thing happened: I sunk a putt from about twenty feet away. Phil started jumping up and down. "Oh my god! Oh my god, Beatrice! I can't believe you did that! Oh my god! Why couldn't we get that on film?" I was beaming now. What a great sport. I can't believe how negative I'd been about it my whole life. I had a great first game and I won—honestly and technically. Phil didn't mark his points each time he lost a ball in the water or in the bush. I only lost one ball and that was on the second to last hole. My poor, cute little pink ball fell deep into the drink. I was devastated that I didn't get to keep my very first game ball.

The next day Phil sent me a message and asked if I thought Greg might like to join him the following week for a game at the same course. I thought that was really sweet of him to offer, but asked if he'd mind taking me out again instead. He was honored at the request, and I began to plan a mother/daughter day with Daniella. Poor Daniella was going to be dragged to another of my golf outings. She'd been so gracious about coming to driving ranges with me over the past few months so that I could use her as an excuse to be away from my beloved. As we walked the nine holes, she kept her face buried in her phone, texting her friends. What she didn't notice was the man watching her. He wasn't just watching her, he was *watching* her.

This particular course paired you up with others if you didn't have a foursome. We were paired up with a man and his young son (we had just gotten lucky the week before that no one had booked the same time slot as us). As patient as I can be, these two were frustrating. Ahead of us was a family of five, so we slowly got further and further behind as we waited for everyone to take their turns. The man I thought was part of the family ahead of us was just a solo golfer, and he asked Phil if he could join our group. He was the *watcher*. I didn't realize right away that he was drunk. I realized that later, after he (a good fifty years old) began repeatedly hitting on my fifteen-year-old daughter. He thought that Phil and I were husband and wife, but Phil explained to him that we were friends and that I was learning to golf as a gift to my husband. He further added that this was my very first golf game. What happened next pretty much ruined my opinion of this "gentleman's sport." The watcher proceeded to coach and berate every single thing I did. I was so angry with Phil for not coming to my rescue, but tried to keep my cool and not lose my shit all over this guy. I did my very best to be a gentleman. Once the game was over, I lost my cool with Phil for not being a man and standing up for me. Phil is so non-confrontational, that it just wasn't in his nature to do so. I couldn't stay mad at him, but now my confidence was shattered and I only had two days left before Greg and I left for his birthday trip.

CHAPTER 34
BIRTHDAY GOLF

Four months and many lies later, the day finally arrived, and Greg and I embarked on our long drive to Montreal the day before his birthday. He still had no idea where we were going, but he was always game to go with the flow. His birthday wouldn't be complete, though, without Stupid trying to ruin it.

As we drove to Montreal that Thursday morning, she called him repeatedly. Throughout all the conflict with her over the past months, the one thing we were able to drill into her head was that Greg didn't have his phone with him while at work; so she no longer bothered calling during his shift. By ten a.m. she had called three times. I guess some people never learn.

I convinced him to answer it just in case something had happened with the boys (she would normally just text him if he didn't answer the phone). Begrudgingly, he answered her fourth call. She was calling to tell him that she wanted to go away with her boyfriend that weekend and leave the boys with him. Greg reminded her that it wasn't his weekend with them and said he wasn't going to be home anyway. She went off on a tangent and he finally hung up on her. The abusive and vulgar text messages started to flood in, so he turned off his phone. We quickly realized that she knew we were going away for his milestone birthday and was doing her best to ruin our plans. When Greg turned his phone back on at the conclusion of the trip, fifteen text messages came in at once—she had obviously continued her rant by herself, to little effect. She never expressed the desire to go away with her boyfriend again after that. Nice try, Stupid.

For this trip, I planned to drive to our destination instead of flying so we could bring our bikes and Greg's golf clubs (mine too, in secret). I hate long drives, but it was a sacrifice I was willing to make to ensure the trip's success. I insisted on packing the car, and made Greg promise that he wouldn't go into the trunk once I'd finished. He agreed—good ole Greg, always willing to go with the flow.

During our drive, the golf course called to confirm our tee time. Among other things, I told them we would only need one cart. After I hung up, Greg asked me why I'd said that. I explained that I had to pay to be with him because they don't allow caddies and would have paired him up with someone. Greg got so upset. "That's not fair! You are not a golfer… you are so *not* a golfer. You shouldn't have to pay. That's not right. I'm going to give them a piece of my mind when we get there." I tried to defuse his anger, but realized there was no point, since he'd find out the truth soon enough.

Immediately upon our arrival in Montreal, I took Greg to a restaurant famous for the best poutine in town. It was there that he lost his poutine virginity, and he loved every minute of that first. After we checked into the hotel, I presented him with the first birthday card of many that he would receive during that trip, and we unwound from our long drive in the hotel's pool and hot tub. After some window shopping and a great dinner at a hopping pub near the hotel, we returned to our room to relax and share a bottle of wine. It was then that I gave him his first gift. A wrapped box.

In that box were: *my* golf shoes (white with a salmon-pink swoosh up the side), half a dozen pink golf balls, two score cards, a loyalty card from a driving range, and a photo of me teeing off at my first game with Phil.

Greg gingerly rummaged through the box, looked at me in disbelief, and slowly sputtered, "Y-y-you golf?"

I nodded and smiled coyly.

"You *golf*? Oh my god… *you golf*?"

I said yes, and explained that I would not be his caddy on his birthday, but his partner instead. Greg was, once again, overwhelmed to tears. He said it was the most beautiful and memorable day of his life, and then he laughed; he'd thought I had bought him another pair of shoes and didn't want to hurt my feelings by telling me that they weren't his style. What a sweetheart.

The next morning at breakfast he kept looking at me, shaking his head, and saying, "I can't believe you learned to golf for me." I was glad I'd given him the box the night before, because he was still visibly emotional about the gesture even after a night of rest. He especially loved that I was dressed in official golf clothing (thanks to the generous gift card that Phil had given me).

We were paired up with two wonderful men who were very patient and supportive towards me. I learned another new golf term that day: "links" course. I hadn't bothered to research that term when I chose the course. In plain English, it means "you are in for a very long day, Veronica, because it's a super-hard, professional course." *Oh geez… what have I gotten myself into?* Some of the holes were three to five hundred yards in length, so, seeing that my shots never went further than fifty yards, I either sat that hole out or played best ball off of wherever Greg hit his ball.

Greg didn't stop beaming the entire day and even took a video to memorialize the day's events. It was the most perfect day for golf too—sunny but slightly overcast. Once our game was over, we sat and had lunch and lattes at an outside café and just basked in the sun and our love for each other.

That evening I presented him with his next card, which included a hand-made brochure for the evening's events. I had made a reservation at Altitude 737, a restaurant on the top floor of the tallest building in the city, complete with a club a few floors below where we could dance the night away. It was magical; the view was amazing and the food magnificent. I snuck away for a trip to the loo and let the staff know that Greg was celebrating his fortieth birthday. They presented us with champagne and samples of their amazing desserts. It was perfect, and Greg was still beaming. By the time we finished our dinner and headed down to the club, it was still very early and there was only a handful of people there, all of whom were in their twenties. We both agreed that we felt really old being there and opted to head back to the room to dance a horizontal tango instead. Our day of golf had kicked the stuffing out of both of us, and we just didn't have it in us to stay up and dance until the wee hours of the morning.

The next day we went for a leisurely bike ride and picnic on the boardwalk of a marina, and I had another card and brochure for that evening's activities. That evening's plans were an Italian restaurant for dinner and then a comedy club show. One of my bosses had recommended the restaurant, and it did not disappoint. The food and ambiance were amazing. Once again, I pulled aside one of the wait staff and informed them that it was Greg's fortieth. Complimentary coffees and dessert (complete with sparklers) were provided. Greg just kept shaking his head and saying, "I can't believe you. You bless me so much." Apparently my efforts were so appreciated that I was rewarded with yet another tango lesson back at the hotel that night. His birthday gift-giving proved not to be one-sided at all. Wink, wink.

On our last day, we wandered the cobblestone streets, did a little shopping, relaxed in the hotel pool, and then went out for our last francophone dinner. Again, the meal was wonderful, but I couldn't steal away to tell our server about his birthday because the washrooms were completely visible from our table. When our server brought the dessert menus, I asked Greg if he'd mind if I chose dessert. Of course he didn't. He's my wonderful Greg, remember. I called our server over and held the menu open in front of me and pretended to be pointing at items and asking questions. What I was really saying in French was, "My husband doesn't understand a word of French, so please pretend that we're talking about the menu. Today is his fortieth birthday, so could you please do something nice for him?" Our server grinned from ear to ear and told me that he'd make it very memorable. Soon he reappeared with the entire wait staff in tow, carrying champagne and a sparkler-lit dessert, and they all sang happy birthday in French. Everyone in the restaurant applauded and Greg beamed. Another magical night.

Our extended weekend away was amazing, but none of the activities even held a candle to his actual birthday. At least nothing needed to compare anymore; I had been allowed to bless him again, and we had an amazing time and fell so much deeper in love in the process. I was concerned about something, though, and expressed my fears to him during the long car ride home.

"Greg, I have a question. After I deceived you to create the book last year, and lied to you for four months while I learned to golf, do you think you'll ever be able to trust me?"

"Of course, sweetheart. I trust you completely. You have no worries with me. You have honored me beyond my wildest dreams and I could never be suspicious of anything you ever tell me."

I was so relieved to hear that from him, because my lying days were far from over. There was still the surprise birthday party at Phil's house in two weeks.

Greg had told me that for his thirtieth birthday, he had to plan his own party and prepare everything for it himself. Stupid didn't lift a finger. That was not going to happen this time. I asked Phil how he felt about holding the party at his house, and he was excited at the prospect of hosting it. He had bought that house three years before and had yet to have an adult party there. I told Greg that Phil was planning his very first *big boy dinner party* and had invited us along with four other couples. Greg agreed as he is always game for anything social. I did explain that, since Phil can't cook (and doesn't have a significant other), he had asked if I would help him with some of the culinary delights and prepping the house.

Two months before Greg's birthday, I had started my plans for that as well and attempted to track down old friends that meant a lot to him. He had lost touch with many of them because of life getting in the way, but a lot of the friendships had also dissolved because of Stupid. In the end, I received thirty RSVPs, and my request in the invitation was to bring a modest bottle of wine in lieu of a gift, and also participate with one dish of their choice for the potluck spread. Each confirmed guest either told me what they were bringing or asked what I wanted them to bring. Everyone except Naomi and Irene. Although I followed up with everyone else directly, there was no way I was going to beg those two to prepare any food for the event.

I wanted to make Greg's fortieth birthday party truly special, and I wanted it to have a romantic and classy feel to it. Dwight and Naomi had both held surprise fortieth parties for each other, and the décor was the usual dollar store or party shop crap. That's not what I wanted. I went to a home décor store and bought six sets of gorgeous satiny eggplant-purple tab curtains, tea light candles, glass beads, and decorative bowls. I went to the party store to get the disposable cutlery, plates, and glasses; and saw the set of plastic wine glasses that Dwight had used at Naomi's party. Although they were very stylish and unique, there was *no way* I was going to buy the same ones and have those two make comments about me using their idea. Yes… I'm that petty.

After we returned from Montreal, I had two weeks to get everything together, and continued weaving my web of lies. Every day, I ranted to Greg about Phil's behavior and meltdowns and how needy he was of my time. I was making Phil sound like a real drama queen, but the kicker was the day that I needed to set up the majority of the décor and had to justify why I was coming home so late. I was spitting nails when I got home. "I'm so pissed off at Phil. He asked for my help with this and just dropped everything in my lap. So while I was at his house cleaning every room and shampooing his damn rug, he was off on a freakin' blind date! Remind me *never* to do that man a favour *ever* again." Greg was not impressed with Phil's supposed behavior, and told me that it would all be over soon.

Two days before the party, I was still struggling to locate one of Greg's old friends, so I tried to subtly talk about him on our drive to work that morning. After chatting a bit, Greg said, "Wait a minute. This dinner party at Phil's isn't a cover for a surprise birthday party for me? Because Montreal was more than enough."

"I knew it!" I exclaimed. "I knew you'd never be able to trust me again." It was at that moment that I should have been given an Academy Award for my performance. I dissolved into tears and continued, "I knew that you'd forever question anything and everything I do. You'll be suspicious if I say that I'm going to the supermarket or if I legitimately have to stay at work late. I've officially *ruined* our relationship because of my lies."

The look of panic on Greg's face was so pure. "Sweetheart, sweetheart. Stop. I'm so sorry. I didn't mean to make you think that I didn't trust you. I'm so, so sorry. Please forgive me, I never should have said that. I love you so much and you haven't *ruined* anything. You have only blessed me."

I turned my head away from him and stared out the car window, and the rest of the drive passed in silence apart from my sporadic melodramatic sniffles. When we arrived at my office, Greg parked the car and continued to reassure me that he trusted me completely. I was sent off with the most wonderful kiss and the most horrible feeling in the pit of my stomach. After all of this, there was no way he would ever trust me. It wasn't possible.

I still had a lot to do for the party, so I took the day off work to wrap it all up. One of the things I needed to make was a large batch of sangria. I'd never made it before, so I looked up a recipe online, modified it to my liking, and quadrupled it. I mixed all the ingredients into a plastic carboy that Greg used to make wine and took it over to Phil's so that it could marinate to perfection overnight. My only challenge was that on my way to Phil's I got stuck in horrible traffic. I anxiously watched the time tick away, praying that Greg wouldn't get home from work and see the huge mess of bottles I had left on our kitchen counter. I started to panic so I sent Greg a text message that said, *I apologize, in advance, for the mess that I've left in the kitchen. If you get home before me, please don't clean it up.*

Of course he got home before me.

"What the *hell* were you making? You've got enough booze here to drown an elephant."

"What?" I said coyly. "I just made sangria for the dinner at Phil's."

"But you said that there were going to be ten of us there. How much do you think people are going to drink?"

This is where I really stretched my acting wings and picked up the recipe to show him. "It says here that it serves four people, and I know that people drink sangria out of those little tiny cups; I figured that everyone would want at least three or four cups, so I quadrupled it." As an accompaniment to this explanation, I batted my big, innocent doe eyes at him.

Greg let out the biggest belly laugh and hugged me tight. "Oh my god, I love you so much. You are so adorable." Phew! Another Academy Award for my trophy shelf.

The day of the party arrived, and Greg came down with a full-blown head cold and said he wasn't sure he felt well enough to attend. *Crap! How am I going to make sure he goes?*

"Oh sweetheart, don't you worry about it. Phil will understand, and there will be other parties. How about this. I'll go, bring him all the food and get things set up and then come back and take care of you. We'll just spend a quiet evening together."

Greg thought for a moment, then said, "No, no. I'm sure I'll be fine. I'll just take some cold medicine and have a nap. I know how much this means to Phil. I swear I'll be fine."

How was I so sure that this wouldn't backfire on me? Greg loves parties. Greg loves to have fun. I was confident that a head cold wouldn't get in the way of that. But if it had, I would have resorted to having Phil call Greg to guilt him about it.

I left early and headed over to Phil's house to set up the party. It looked amazing. The pillars and doorways were transformed by the luxurious fabric draped over them, and the tea lights glistened in the bowls of glass beads surrounded by floating gerberas. It was the romantic feel that I wanted. It was outstanding.

My friend Caroline came early to help us get things ready, but Naomi and Irene were the first actual guests to arrive; and they walked in empty-handed. I masked my look of shock, and hoped that Dwight and Ryan would bring the things with them after they parked their car. I invited them in and offered them a glass of the sangria I'd made. "I don't *do* sangria" was Naomi's snotty response. Caroline was visibly taken aback at Naomi's rudeness.

I didn't ask you if you wanted to screw it, I asked you if you wanted to drink some.

Here we go… a night to remember. Dwight and Ryan arrived and only had the wine gift that was requested, and I sincerely thought for a moment that I wouldn't have enough food since they couldn't be bothered to contribute. In the end, there was more than enough food.

When Greg texted me that he was on his way, I informed everyone of the plan. We would all congregate around the garage door entrance, and Phil would be out there waiting so that he could usher him through that door instead of the front. Naomi chirped up that it was better that they all wait in the backyard and surprise him there. *Nooo… that's not what I want. If we do that, Greg will have to walk through the house and will see everything laid out.* I turned to Caroline and said, "Please deal with this."

Phil took his place out front to greet Greg. He told him that I had just flipped out on him because he was getting in my way in the kitchen, so he was seeking sanctuary in the garage to avoid my wrath. He led Greg into the house where we were all waiting *where I wanted everyone,* and we all shouted the customary "Surprise!" Greg was beaming and 100% surprised. *Success!*

The evening was a smash, but Dwight and Naomi kept trying to be the center of attention.

Apparently Dwight was not a fan of the sultry jazz music playing in the background, so he shouted from the backyard, "Can we change the music? We're not a hundred years old, you know."

Then, at one point, from across the room he shouted, "Hey Greg, did you hear that I'm going to be on TV?" Greg smiled and left the room while he was in the middle of telling his story.

Next, Greg was gushing about how amazing I was at planning and executing surprises, and he told Dwight that if he ever needed to plan something, he should come to me for advice. Dwight's reply was, "Well, how about the two-week vacation in Costa Rica that I surprised Naomi with? I doubt she could top that." Greg said that it didn't even compare, and ushered me away from Dwight.

The last one was when one of the guests arrived late with her contribution of samosas, and I introduced the guest to everyone and announced that more food had arrived. Naomi and Irene came over and said, "Did *you* make the samosas?" I knew what they were getting at. Here we go again with the petty jealousy of my culinary aptitude. I chirped, "Nope. Angela did."

"So *YOU* didn't make them?" was Naomi's catty reply. I just walked away.

Later in the evening, Caroline came to check up on me; she had seen the outlandish behavior all evening and wanted to make me feel better. "Is it just me or does Naomi look like a drag queen?" she asked. As catty as it might sound, it was true. She honestly looked like a transvestite, apart from the overbearing focal point of her bosom. Some things never change.

Caroline said, "Can I ask you something?"

"Sure."

"That Jeannette chick. Did Greg used to date her?"

I snorted and said, "Oh gawd, no" and explained their relationship. Caroline went on to say that Jeannette had been referring to him as *her* Greg all night, and it seemed like she was an ex-lover. She then asked if Dwight, Naomi, Ryan, and Irene were swingers. Apparently, their behavior towards each other that night was very sexual and off-putting. I told her I'd always felt creeped out by Dwight but that Greg had never told me anything like that about them before. In the back of my mind, though, I started to wonder. I started to wonder about whether Greg had lied to me about Jeannette, and whether that gross man hanging all over me that one night was an indicator that they wanted Greg and me to partake in *other* activities.

On our drive to work the following Monday, I was still on a high recounting all of the stories that I hadn't yet shared with Greg about the party. I was talking a mile a minute and said, "and then when Naomi and Irene showed up empty-handed, I thought I wouldn't have enough food—"

"What did you say?" Greg interrupted.

"I said, and then when Naomi and Irene showed up empty-handed, I thought I wouldn't have enough food for all the guests."

"They what?"

Exasperated, I began to repeat myself and then trailed off when I realized what was unfolding.

"You have *got* to be kidding me," Greg said. "After all that I've done for them? Even when I had no money, I always scraped together enough to *at least* bring a bottle of wine to one of their dinners. I cannot *believe* that they would dishonor me this way."

"Whoa… whoa. Wait a minute, Greg. I don't mean to make this about me, but they did not dishonor you—the slap in the face was for me. They brought the bottle of wine to honor you. They did not bring any food for the buffet in order to insult me. It's not about you. It's about their hatred towards me."

"That's it. I'm done with them. I've been a good friend to Dwight for so many years, but now I see who he truly is. Everything is about him. Everything's always been about him, and I was blind to that fact before I met you. You are the love of my life, and there is *no way* I will tolerate them disrespecting you, and us, anymore. I'm done with him."

Wow. I sure didn't expect that.

A few days later, after he'd had time to cool off, I approached him about what Caroline had said. I begged him to tell me the truth about him and Jeannette. He assured me that nothing had ever happened between them except… *Oh gawd, here it comes. Am I going to be able to recover from the "except"?*

"One night, I was too drunk to drive home so I spent the night at her place and we made out a bit. Just kissing, I swear. We slept in the same bed that night—with our clothes on—and nothing else happened. We were just drunk. I *swear* to you that *nothing* ever happened."

As much as I didn't like what I heard, I was glad that I knew the whole truth, and it finally explained her behavior. She was in love with Greg. He just refused to see it or admit it because he didn't have feelings for her in that way.

He also came clean about Dwight, Naomi, and the other two couples. They *were* swingers, and Greg had even walked in on Dwight and creepy Father Time in a compromising position once. I was angry about this revelation because I couldn't believe that he'd subject me to such sick people. Whenever they asked why Daniella didn't come with us to their parties, I always made excuses because I didn't feel comfortable with her being around them. Thinking of them wanting Daniella there now, I felt my stomach turn. At least it was over, and they were no longer in our lives. I was so glad that Greg finally saw the truth about all of these people, so that I didn't have to put a wedge between them.

Ugh... drama over!

This was the end of a very long chapter in our lives. No pun intended.

CHAPTER 35
MY MUSE

From the beginning of our relationship, I took to gifting Greg with a "monniversary" gift each month. It's my play on words for celebrating each month of being together. Another Veronicism, if you will. The first month that I did it, I got him some aromatherapy massage oil, and it came in the cutest little gift bag. That gift bag became the official monniversary bag, and my personal rule was that whatever I gave him had to fit inside it. The gifts weren't meant to be extravagant, just small tokens of my affection. Among the things I gave him were cufflinks, a nail brush, tickets to a football game, a tie, his repaired watch (that had sat unworn for years because of a broken wristband), and his watch again the following month (because I didn't realize that the battery was dead from sitting for all those years). Every month the bag would appear, and he'd get overwhelmed to tears each and every time it did. "Sneaky little bugger!" he said every time he saw it.

Even though he called me a "sneaky little bugger" whenever the monniversary bag appeared, and told me that I didn't have to do that, he once let it slip that he felt that "monniversaries were like babies" and "should be celebrated for thirty-six months." Wow! I had planned to do it for the first twelve months… I had a long road ahead of me now.

I think Greg's favorite month was the one whose gift was his divorce certificate. At his request, I filed his divorce for him. There were initial complications, but months later it came through. Unbeknownst to him, I took the day off work to go and get it and had Cosmopolitans waiting in the backyard when he came home at the end of his day. When I gifted him with the bag and he saw what was inside, he couldn't stop hooting and hollering at the top of his lungs. He must have driven the neighbors nuts.

Outside of our monniversaries, I took pride in the cards and notes that I constantly wrote him. I never had a skill that I felt was worthy enough to speak of, but writing down how I felt about Greg came as easily as breathing. Those were the majority of my gifts to him—my words.

For our first Valentine's Day together, I made him a book called *Top 20 Most Famous Love Stories in History and Literature.* It counted down the names and brief stories of the most famous lovers. Among them were Pocahontas and John Smith, Pyramus and Thisbe, Scarlett O'Hara and Rhett Butler, Napoleon and Josephine, Lancelot and Guinevere, and Cleopatra and Mark Antony. The number two spot went to Romeo and Juliet, of course, and number one was reserved for *Greg and Veronica.* It read:

> ***Now touted as the most famous love story of all time. Two people from different worlds who were brought together by fate and the power of God. Both Greg and Veronica spent decades married to others who filled their lives with misery each and every day. They lived a parallel life of despair, lost hope, forgotten dreams, and resigning themselves to the belief that true, unconditional love really didn't exist. One cold winter day Greg prayed for Veronica to come into his life; and set his manifestations to water to allow the hand of God to guide her to him. Greg's call was heard, and answered, three months later when he and Veronica first laid eyes on each other. The combining of hearts has become a legendary story of true love, respect and passion that others long for and have only ever read about in fairy tales. Every person that has known or met the couple since that fateful day has said that the true and pure love between them is incomparable to any couple they've ever seen, or any story they've ever heard.***

I discovered a gift for writing devotions to him, and the words were never contrived; they were all so true to my heart. No matter what happened in our lives, he was everything to me. Since that first month together, the monniversary celebrations continued, and the blessings he bestowed upon me daily left me overwhelmed to tears.

I think one of my favorite things about gifting him with these surprises was how he always rolled with the punches. If I told him that I had a surprise for him, he never questioned it. Two of my favorites were mini-trips that I planned.

The first one was an overnight hotel and dinner package for a nearby resort, which I had won at work. On that monniversary, I handed him the bag with a piece of paper in it that simply read, "Get in the car." We had planned to go out for a sushi dinner that night, but he didn't question the changes. While he was showering, I snuck our overnight bags into the trunk of the car (little did he know that as part of this month's gift, I had replaced the old tattered gym bag he used for overnight jaunts with a Corinthian leather overnight bag that a co-worker brought me from Brazil), and away we went. When we reached the resort and I opened the trunk, he said, "Sneaky little bugger." I could tell he was thrilled at the sight of the gorgeous leather bag that stared back at him. What an amazing night. Even though he initially pouted when he found out that we weren't having sushi, he very quickly realized it was worth the sacrifice.

The second one was a good one.

He had once told me that his favorite performer was Andrea Bocelli and that he hoped to one day see him in concert. Although it is not my kind of music, I joined Andrea Bocelli's fan club in order to receive updates on his shows. One day I received a notification that he was putting on a "once in a lifetime" performance in New York City. *Once in a lifetime.* How could I deny him this? The concert was not for another six months, but I checked the calendar and saw that it actually fell on a weekend that we didn't have the boys. *Perfect!* The pair of tickets were five hundred dollars. *Not so perfect.* How could I spend five hundred dollars without consulting with Greg first? I was completely torn about this decision, so I asked some coworkers for their opinion. After I explained the situation, they assured me that he'd never be upset about the money considering it was such an amazing surprise. So, with shaking hands, I clicked "purchase." I paid for it with my mother's credit card and then transferred the money to her from my bank account so that he wouldn't see the charge.

Two months before the concert, Stupid decided to go on one of her famous tangents. She called Greg and demanded that he switch weekends going forward so that the boys could play with their cousins. Odd thing was, the reason we had them on the weekends when we did, was so they could play with their cousins. Obviously, her sister had changed *her* weekends with her ex and it was now conflicting with their play dates. Greg explained to her that we had our full year ahead already planned around when we had the boys, so he'd have to get back to her to see if he could change things. After three days of abusive texts and voicemail messages from her, he agreed. *Great. Now we'll have the boys on the weekend of the concert.*

I resolved that it was her own damn fault and we'd just have to deal with the repercussions after the fact. So I schemed with Greg's sister-in-law that she would invite the boys for a long-overdue sleepover. We were to fly out to New York early Sunday morning from the U.S. side of the border, so we needed to make the trek across to the hotel that I had booked near the airport. When the big day arrived, Greg's sister-in-law followed through with the agreement, and we dropped the boys off at her house for dinner on Saturday. As Greg and I were having a quiet dinner at our house, I said, "Hey, since the boys are gone, do you feel like going out somewhere?"

"Like where?"

"There's a place that I've always wanted to go, and tonight would be the perfect night to do it. Are you up for it?"

Of course he was up for it. This is my Greg we're talking about. I told him to wear something layered because we'd be doing both indoor and outdoor things. While he showered, I loaded our luggage into the trunk of the car.

I put Gina the GPS on and told him to follow her directions. As we drove, he recognized that we were on the highway that goes to the U.S. border. "Are we going to the states?"

"Yup."

"Do you have our passports?"

"Yup."

"Where do I tell the officer at the border that we're going?"

"Tell him that you don't know."

When we arrived at the border, Greg did as he was told. I reached across him and handed a folded piece of paper to the officer with our passports and said, "If you have even an ounce of romance in your body, you'll read that to yourself silently." The look on both of their faces was priceless and I prayed that my plan wouldn't backfire and cause unwelcome cavity searches.

The officer silently read the piece of paper, which explained that it was a surprise trip to New York and detailed our flights, hotel, concert activities, and return date.

"Are you bringing any alcohol or tobacco with you?"

"No sir," was Greg's response.

I leaned across and said, "Yes sir. One bottle of homemade wine." Greg just smiled and shook his head as the officer flagged us through without another word.

Greg didn't question anything. He didn't question it when I woke him at four a.m. at the hotel the next morning. He didn't question it when I whispered in the shuttle bus driver's ear what our airline destination was. He didn't question it when I made him stand back from the check-in counter at the airline. He didn't question it when I made him stand back from the security gate as I asked them not to tell him where he was going. He didn't find out where we were going until the board was updated at our gate.

"We're going to New York City?"

"Yup."

"Oh my god. You're insane. I can't believe you're taking me to New York. What about the boys?"

"You'll be calling your mom to pick them up once we get to the hotel."

Thankfully, through our reward point program, I was able to pay for our flights and hotel. This trip was only going to cost the concert tickets and our meals. I booked us at The Crowne Plaza overlooking Times Square. After we checked in, Greg called his mom and said, "Mom, you'll never guess where I am right now." I heard her screech in disbelief and say, "But you were just here!" He asked her to pick up the boys from his brother's house and return them to their mother at the end of the day.

Within two hours, the text messages from Stupid started coming in. Colin had obviously called and told her what was going on. Greg turned off his phone until our return to Canada.

It was an amazing, amazing trip, and I was definitely rewarded for my efforts… if you know what I mean. I think the highlight of the entire weekend was watching Greg watch Andrea Bocelli. He sat with tears in his eyes and never stopped beaming. He later told me that he had never heard any of Andrea's traditional music, only the more mainstream things that sell albums. He was blown away.

Of course, we came back to a nuclear Stupid meltdown. Greg shut her down once I told him that the tickets had been purchased six months in advance and *before* she nagged him to change weekends. She had only herself to blame for this.

The negative ending definitely did not mar our trip, but since then I have made double sure never to plan anything on a day that we have his kids.

CHAPTER 36
THE FINAL STRETCH

When Greg contacted me in May 2008, his profile said that he didn't want any more children, so after our third date I questioned why. I asked him if it was because he was neutered (as I have always, so sensitively, referred to vasectomies). He laughed so hard and said, "How did you know?" I told him that it was just a feeling I had, but that, in my eyes, there was nothing sexier than a neutered male.

With that topic in the free and clear, there was the looming topic of the *M* word. Back when I first had my "no baby, no wedding" conversation with Phil, we agreed that neither of us ever wanted to marry again—unless it was important to our significant other. Since that discussion, I had actually vowed never to marry again. I wanted nothing to do with it because the vows obviously meant nothing.

Daniella once berated me for saying that, and her words stung my heart. "So what you're saying is that you'd rather live in sin for the rest of your life with someone?"

Leave it to her to tap right into the center of my moral compass. After what I put myself through in the past, why on earth would I want to do that again? What did it mean, anyway? Those two men did not live up to their vows, so who's to say that anyone else would?

A little over a month into our relationship (actually, the day we returned from the motivational seminar with the cheerleaders), Greg and I had a very emotionally charged conversation that led to long periods of silence and me locked in the bathroom, sobbing uncontrollably. He dragged me out of the bathroom to talk out our issues. As we sat together, he admitted that he'd marry me the next day if he could. I instantly flew into a rage and told him that I would *never* marry again and did not want to hear him mention it again.

My anti-marriage tirade carried on for months. I would storm out of the room if he ever brought it up. Then one day, months later, something inside of me changed, and I realized that there was nothing I wanted more than to be his wife. At that point, it wasn't legally possible, because he was still married; but I began to long to carry his name. A very large part of me was glad that he'd still been married during those months before, as it didn't allow me to "pull a Veronica" and marry him at the drop of a hat.

Although I hated that he was still married to that disgusting woman, I never once pressured him to divorce her. When he brought up the idea, I actually told him not to bother. "Why spend the money unless you plan on getting married again?" was my consistent argument to him. But he was adamant about it, and when he requested assistance, I proceeded to draw up the paperwork for the divorce and see it through to completion.

In a drunken state one night (something that, as I mentioned before, became a regular occurrence in my life), I admitted everything to him. Although we had previously exchanged vows of sorts committing ourselves to each other, I came clean to him that I did have hopes for more. From that day on, marriage was something that we talked and dreamt about constantly.

The day his divorce went through, talk of us getting married stopped completely. I was so confused. It went from the sublime to the ridiculous. One minute, I'm everything he wants, and the next, he couldn't care less. Or at least that's how I was reading it. I figured that now that he had his freedom, he realized he was happy just shacking up with me and not having a commitment. You know the saying, "Why buy the cow if you can get the milk for free?" It started to eat me alive.

If you think that there wasn't at least one drunken night where I blurted out all of the above accusations, then you have a far too elevated opinion of me. I was at such a low point in our relationship that my *inside voice* seemed to have full reign over my verbal output.

Why would living with him out of wedlock make me feel so morally ill at ease when I didn't have a problem being intimate with him? Was it because I didn't want to look like a whore in front of our respective children? Whatever the deep-seated issue was for me, it was one that made me hang my head in shame. I wasn't anyone special. I was just the dumb slut that lived with Greg. *The girlfriend*. Stupid made it clear that that was pretty much exactly how she saw me, that's for sure. Ironically, though, she was the one who shacked up with the guy that she cheated on Greg with. Hmm... I guess the *slut* categories are different in the world she lives in.

I couldn't even bring myself to refer to Greg as my boyfriend, or me as his girlfriend, because it just felt so damn "high school." From the beginning,

I lived a fantasy life of referring to him as my husband or fiancé—depending on the audience—but it all felt so insincere. I felt like such a joke.

At one point, I had wanted to change my name back to my maiden name, but I held off because Greg expressed the desire to marry me. *Why should I bother if it's just going to change to his soon anyway?* Now, much later, I was living in sin and carrying a surname that made me feel sick to my stomach. As the months passed, I grew more and more bitter; then, one day, he referred to me as his wife. I flew off the handle, swore at him, and told him never to say that again because I was "no one's wife." I was hurting so much inside.

In December 2009, Phil gifted us with an all-inclusive trip to Cuba with him and a friend of his. I had reached a point where I was actually contemplating leaving Greg. I loved and adored him, but I couldn't stand living this way anymore.

The combination of the stress of spending our entire relationship thus far (eighteen months) poring over legal documents to fight his ex in court, that same witch's outbursts and daily intrusions into our lives, and the "living in sin" issue, had caused me to reach my breaking point.

By the time we left for our trip, though, we had already won the court battle against Stupid, and a huge weight was lifted off my shoulders. She became briefly silent, for the most part, except for the "I hope your plane crashes" comment when Greg told her we were going on vacation for a week.

But the legal issues weren't the only thing on my mind. Regardless of the fact that most everyone lives out of wedlock these days, it was never something I could handle. After a very heated discussion a week before the trip, we both agreed that Cuba would be the deciding factor in our relationship; it would either make us or break us.

That trip was the most amazing trip of my life. I had never been on a vacation with someone I loved before (Hawaii with my family when I was six doesn't count). It was another first, and an amazing one. I fell deeper in love with Greg and decided that I needed to cast aside my feelings of shame surrounding living out of wedlock and continue to love him unconditionally. We said vows to one another constantly and, if what "they" say is true about God always watching over us, then we should be good to go. Right? I needed to believe that. Quite honestly, I don't think I know many legally-married people who are as committed to each other like Greg and I are.

It was also at that time that I ended my passionate courtship with booze. I'd "grown up" the first time when I was twenty-one (and spent almost twenty years without a drink), so it was time for me to "grow up" again and stop looking for the pot of gold at the bottom of the bottle. Life was always going to happen, and the only thing that numbing it did, was make me feel like crap in the morning. Was it going to be easy? Probably not, but if I'd done it before, why couldn't a more seasoned and wiser Veronica do it again? This Veronica is a newer, stronger model of the old Veronica, so I couldn't see anything but success with my lifestyle revamp.

After I gave birth to my daughter, I was able to add a different perspective towards how I got through tough times. Whenever there was a struggle that I needed to conquer, I'd just silently chant, "One contraction at a time. Veronica, just get through one contraction at a time." It didn't matter if it was getting through a rough day without a drink, or a cigarette, or completing an exercise rep or set—I just viewed each obstacle as a "contraction." Hell, if I could go through labor and birth without drugs, I could do most anything. Right?

Mothers are always able to embrace this philosophy when I share it, but I can't seem to find the right analogy for men… "Imagine that someone is twisting your left nut-sack…" I dunno… it just doesn't seem to flow the same way… I'll keep working on it. It goes without saying that, Tony Robbins' career as a motivational speaker is not going to be challenged by my winning philosophies in the near future.

Anyhoo… I'd made the commitment to spend my life with Greg, so I wanted to make sure that I would always be present.

Since I realized that my name was not going to be changing anytime soon, I filled out the paperwork to change it back to my maiden name. Had I made the change at the time of my divorce, it would have been simple, but because I'd waited—and now lived in a new province—the paperwork was a nightmare. I had to dig up a bunch of things to submit with it (all of which were packed away god knows where), so I put the application temporarily aside as I focused on keeping up with the day-to-day hustle and bustle of life and the Christmas season.

A few days after Christmas, I sat down to pay some bills and had a nagging feeling that I had already paid one of them. Since this was a common occurrence in my world, I logged on to both my and Greg's bank accounts to check if I had or not. I skimmed through the transactions and didn't see any payments, but one purchase did catch my eye. It was for a jewelry store. *Ugh! He knows that I'm always reconciling our accounts. Why couldn't he have paid cash for my birthday gift?*

I was so ticked off. No one was ever capable of surprising me, so it made me angry that I'd spoiled my own birthday surprise. Greg gave me a necklace for the first birthday I'd had with him, so I figured that I had now just ruined my surprise of a pair of earrings. I didn't tell him that I'd stumbled across it but vented to my friend Rowan at work. She agreed that I should never tell him.

My birthday arrived and it was, of course, a work day (the story of my life). While Greg was out warming up and scraping the ice off the car, I went into the bedroom to get dressed and saw a gold gift bag waiting on my pillow. *Oh look. My earrings.*

To celebrate the court case we had won against Stupid, we got rid of all the matrimonial bedroom furniture and bought a brand new mattress. We had yet to buy a bedroom set, so our bedside tables were cardboard boxes and the mattress lay directly on the floor. I tell you this so that you can embrace the upcoming visual.

I sat down on the bed to read the inevitable heartfelt words in the card. Just as I reached into the bag to retrieve my earrings, Greg came back into the house. As he approached the bedroom, I opened up the box and discovered that my earrings were actually a diamond ring. Stunned, I sat and stared at it. *What is this? Is this a birthday gift or an engagement ring?* Had the ring been my birthstone, there wouldn't have been a question in my mind. But this was a cliché diamond solitaire.

Greg came into the room, and his glasses were fogged up. He couldn't see me from where he was standing, so he knelt down in front of me. *He's kneeling… what do I do? What is this?*

"Do you like it?"

"Um… yeah. I do."

"Are you going to put it on?"

I slowly removed the ring from the box and placed it on my right hand.

"I was hoping that you'd wear it on the other hand."

Umm… okaaaay… what is going on here? What is this? Everything felt surreal and in slow motion. I placed the ring on my left hand, and Greg took off his fogged-up glasses, took my hand in his, and said, "Shit! It's too big! Damn it! I knew I should have gotten the size six. I'll have to take it back to get it sized, but will you wear it today even though it's too big?"

What the hell is going on?

Without another word, we drove to work. Upon our arrival, Greg took my glove off and said that he just wanted to look at it one more time. He told me that it looked beautiful on me, kissed me, and sent me on my way. I walked into the office, stunned, and quickly put the ring on my other hand. I didn't want anyone getting the wrong idea. Especially since I still had no clue what was going on.

A couple of days after my birthday, we both went back to the jeweller to measure my finger for the ring sizing. It would be ready for pick-up the following week. On the day it was going to be ready, Greg had a bunch of other errands to run, so we took separate cars and I came straight home.

In the shop that Greg worked at, his boss refused to put the heat on for them, so he often came home chilled to the bone. If we weren't carpooling, we got into a routine: he would text me when he was ten minutes from home, and I would prepare a hot bath for him. In true romantic Veronica form, I always lit the bathroom with candles and had a glass of wine waiting for him so that he could relax and unplug. Ambiance is important to me when it comes to baths.

When Greg came home, I was at the sink doing dishes; he greeted me from the door and went straight to the bathroom. *That's not like him. He always kisses me. Something's up. I know it.* He called to me and asked if I was going to come and sit with him. One of our many rituals was that I'd go and sit on the floor beside the tub to keep him company, and we'd talk about our day. As I sat on the floor, with the cat on my lap, Greg said, "Will you love me forever?" It was something we always asked each other, and I replied with our usual stock answer of, "Forever and a day."

With that, he took the ring out from under the water behind his back and asked me to marry him. I was stunned and speechless, and I admitted to him that I didn't think he wanted that for us because he stopped talking about it after his divorce went through. He told me that he had always wanted it, but wanted to be in a better position financially before making that commitment. He wanted to buy me the big ring that he felt I deserved. I told him he should have known me better and known I was not like the others who needed a bauble to impress everyone around them. He said he knew exactly who I was, but felt so strongly that I deserved it.

It wasn't until after I told Rowan and Daniella the news that I found out about two conversations that had occurred on my actual birthday.

At the end of my birthday, when Greg returned to pick me up. Rowan stopped him and said, "I saw the ring on Veronica's finger, but she didn't say anything about it. Did you propose to her?"

"Oh no. That's just her birthday gift."

"Greg, what are you waiting for? The woman thinks you hung the moon. You could lose her if you keep waiting."

"When I propose to her, I want to get her a far better ring. She deserves it."

"Do you even *know* Veronica? You know that material things don't matter to her. She's not like that. She loves and adores you without all of that crap. You are the luckiest man to have a woman adore you the way she does. I don't know why you would possibly want to wait."

When we got home, Daniella was there with her friend Ariana, and I had switched the ring back to my left hand. Daniella came running up to me, gave me a big birthday hug, and asked what Greg had given me. I silently held out my hand and Daniella said, "He *proposed* to you?" Just then he walked through the front door and I gave her a *Shut up! Shut up!* look. When Greg left the room again, I explained to her that it was just my birthday gift and nothing more. After dinner, Daniella asked me if I'd drive Ariana home, but Greg interjected and said that he would do it since it was my birthday.

In the car on the way back, Daniella apparently said, "So you proposed to my mom? I told you that if you wanted to propose, to come and talk to me because I know what kind of ring she likes."

"Oh no. That's just her birthday gift."

"Are you serious? What are you waiting for? My mom adores you!"

"When I propose to her, I want to get her a far better ring. She deserves it."

"Do you even *know* my mom? You should know that she doesn't give a shit about material crap. She's not like that. She's totally gaga for you no matter what."

After I heard those two stories, I tried to find out from Greg why he had the change of heart about the ring. He always stuck by his story that when he saw it on me, it made him realize how much he wanted me to be his wife. Did the almost-identical conversations he had with Rowan and Daniella have anything to do with his change of heart? I guess I'll never know.

My engagement ring was a modest one, and it was perfect for me. It didn't matter to me how much it did or didn't cost; what it represented, the future that it represented to me, was priceless. Now, the daunting task of choosing a date.

Numeric significance is very important to both of us, so we wanted to find a date that was right for us. As for locations, we had thought of going to Hawaii, where friends would be for a few days in April, and getting married in their presence. We threw ideas back and forth, but nothing fit. So we finally decided to just let it be for a while until we could figure it out. The next morning, though, I came to Greg and said, "What about eight?"

"Eight? You mean like April 8th?"

"No, I mean the number eight as a total." I pulled out our numeric significance sheet and read, "Eight represents resurrection and regeneration. A new beginning or commencement. The eighth is a new first. It is the number which has to do with the Lord, Who rose on the eighth, or new 'first day.' May 18, 2010 equals eight."

I could see the look of excitement in his eyes and he replied, "That was exactly what I was thinking, but I didn't know how we'd make it work."

I suggested that we forget Hawaii and plan something so that we could get married on our second anniversary—May 18. It was truly the only day of significance to both of us. Greg agreed wholeheartedly, and now I only had four more months to get through before I could finally become his wife.

CHAPTER 37
WEDDING PLANS

Years before I met Greg, I had heard about a huge bridal store in the States; and I would often visit their website just to daydream. Now my day was actually arriving, and I couldn't think of a better place to buy my wedding dress than there. I scoured their website and decided I would find a dress that was a part of their $99 sale. I picked out a handful and was ready to head out on our excursion. On the day that we drove across the border to look for my wedding gown, we had someone very special with us—Phil. Phil was the reason we were together, so it only seemed fitting that he be with us to help me decide on my gown.

I let Greg look through all the racks of dresses and pick out his choices. Once we had done that, I was assigned my consultant. What was her name? *Ruth*. Seriously! I'm not even kidding!

Before Ruth helped me try on the many gowns we had picked out, she asked me about my love story. I watched the goose bumps appear on her arms as I emotionally told her of my journey to find my beloved Greg. Ruth and I stood together in tears in the fitting room. The reality of my blessed life and future was hitting me so hard at that moment.

I described to her the emotion that I wanted to convey on my wedding day, and with that, she told me she had the perfect dress for me and scurried away to retrieve it. When she came back with it, I was totally underwhelmed, but she insisted that I try it on and made me save it for last.

Fortunately for Ruth, I had narrowed it down to three gowns by the time hers was up. I loved each of those three gowns for different reasons; I felt like a princess in all of them and didn't want to leave the romantic la-la land I was in.

Greg and I both really loved halter-style necklines on me, so those were our main choices—hers was strapless. Ugh… I can't stand strapless dresses! I've never liked them because they just don't support my… assets… and constantly slip down unless you buy them extra tight and spend your time gasping for air. Despite my negativity, I put on Ruth's selection and walked out to the wall of mirrors.

When I stepped out in front of the mirrors, the previously bustling back room suddenly fell silent. I immediately dissolved into tears. Ruth dissolved into tears, and I heard many gasps from the consultants, brides-to-be, and the women who accompanied them. I turned around to look at Ruth and the dozen faces that were looking at me, and I knew. I knew it was the one.

Ruth went out to find Greg and Phil and instructed Greg that he was to go and wait in the car. I then put each of the four dresses on for Phil to help me narrow it down. Of course, I left the "crying dress" for last.

Phil and I have always had such a parallel way of thinking, that with each dress I presented, he verbalized what my concerns had been—to the T. Then I came out in the final gown. The one.

Phil sat in silence. His eyes began to well up with tears. "Beatrice. That's the one. Oh my god, Bea. That's the one!" There was my answer. It was unanimous, even though I wouldn't have minded buying all four dresses.

When I returned to the fitting room to get back into my reality clothes, Ruth joined me a few moments later. "Veronica. I'm going to tell you something, and you need to just listen to me and do as I say. Phil wants to speak to you once you've gotten changed. You know what this is, don't you?"

I started sobbing. I knew exactly what she wasn't telling me.

"Veronica, you must let him do this for you."

I went back out to the area where Phil was waiting, and he was visibly emotional. "Bea. You know that you mean the world to me. I am so fortunate to have you and Greg in my life that I would like the honor of gifting you with your wedding gown. I wouldn't know what else to give you as a wedding gift, so I hope that you will allow me to do this for you."

Phil and I stood in the middle of the store, sobbing in each other's arms. I'm sure everyone thought we were the couple getting married. He made me promise not to tell Greg until he had left us that day. Phil is not very comfortable with sincere displays of emotion, so I promised to honor his request.

Once we composed ourselves, Ruth came back over to help me finish the transaction. During our time together, I also told her about Phil and how I prayed that one day he would find his "Greg." She thought it was hilarious that I referred to someone's soul mate as their "Greg." She approached Phil and said, "I have a ton of great bridesmaids that come in here from your area. Don't worry, I'll help you find your 'Greg.'"

Phil went ashen and started waving his hands frantically. "No, no, no! I'm not like *that*!"

Ruth and I rolled with laughter until I explained to him that she understood what it meant to find your "Greg." Poor Phil. We had a great belly laugh at his expense.

So now that we had the dress, it was time to really start planning the wedding.

Since it had always been Greg's dream to marry me on a beach somewhere, I began to research all-inclusive resorts. We finally decided on Costa Rica.

It wasn't our original choice; we'd always vowed that, since we missed out on so many firsts in each other's lives, we would travel to places that neither of us had been before. Greg had been to Costa Rica once, and I'd been no less than sixty times during my years working on cruise ships. But Costa Rica it would be; it was less of a hassle and expense than the location we originally had our hearts set on—Dominican Republic.

I know, so romantic, letting our pocketbooks decide on the location of our wedding. But remember, I'm the frugal one, and the translations and licenses alone would have cost eight hundred dollars. That's an entire week at a resort for one person.

There was also another reason that I didn't want to get married in Costa Rica. Dwight and Naomi.

Dwight and Naomi went to Costa Rica every year, and from the way they talked about it, you'd think they were the Columbuses that had discovered it. I did not want, in any way, for them to think that we were getting married there because they introduced Greg to it. We still had mutual friends between us, so I made sure that when I talked about it to them, I said something like, "Neither of us wanted to get married in Costa Rica, but it was our only choice." I knew that it would filter down to them and squelch any credit that they tried to take. Sure enough, about a month after my comment to our mutual friend, I got Facebook friend requests from both Dwight and Naomi. *Yeah right. Like you're ever going to be privy to seeing our photos.* Greg made me vow to never "friend" them.

Being the Type-A person that I am, I created a spreadsheet and started narrowing down our choices of resorts. Although we originally planned to invite quite a few people to attend, the number of guests didn't matter to me. I'd told Greg many times before that I would marry him on my lunch hour, wearing an orange sweatshirt and standing in the produce section of the local grocery store; but I guess he had a slightly different vision for our special day.

Since my daily goal was to honor him in any way that I could, I didn't dream of denying him this request.

Not too much later, though, Greg came to realize that he wanted us to be alone on our wedding day. You can imagine that a few noses were put out of joint with his decision to kibosh all attendees, but Phil and Daniella definitely weren't upset. Phil expressed his sadness at not being there with us, but he also expressed his sincere understanding of Greg's choice. Although I had never wanted anyone there other than Daniella, Phil, and Paulo, I hadn't voiced it to Greg because this was his dream and his decision. But when he told me he thought I was upset and disappointed that he'd changed his mind about the guests, I reassured him and said that I, too, loved the thought of it being just us.

"Greg, we have both been married before and have already had big weddings to appease the masses. Our day-to-day relationship is filled with so much passion and love that, to me, saying my vows to you is like making love to you; and the thought of making love to you in front of friends and family is just not my idea of a good time. I wouldn't be able to express myself to you in the way that I truly wanted to because I would feel like I was on display. I am grateful for your choice, and honestly, the only people that I would truly want to be there are Daniella and my father. Since my dad has passed away, I know that there's a good chance that he will actually be there with us. He will be there to witness what an amazing man I am marrying."

My father is the reason that I was often filled with so much pain. He watched me suffer through my marriages and was never allowed to bear witness to the fact that I finally fell in love with myself enough to find a man deserving of my heart—a man deserving to be his son. Dad would have loved Greg so much.

CHAPTER 38
A TRIP TO PARADISE

Upon our arrival at the resort, they welcomed us like royalty the moment they saw the telltale white garment bag draped over my arm. "Are you the bride? Are you Giselle? We weren't expecting you so early."

"I am *a* bride. But I am not *the* bride that you think I am. My name's Veronica. We're staying here, but not getting married here." Our greeter quickly apologized for making me feel less than special and continued to fawn over me. We checked in, dropped our things off in the room, and eagerly went to the beach for our first dip in the crystal blue waters. When we returned to our room we discovered that our hotel greeters had made up for their faux pas with bridal trinkets and treats that awaited us. It was so unexpected and yet so appreciated. What a perfect first day.

As we lay on the beach that first day, I noticed that no one was sunning themselves topless. No one female, anyway. I had already explained to Greg that I refused to be one of "those" destination brides. You know, the ones with the sunburned chests and bright white strap marks that cannot be covered by their strapless dress? Yeah… I refused to be that bride.

At the far end of the resort we saw a fenced-off area reserved as the nudie section. I am a very modest person and wasn't sure I could bring myself to be completely naked. It was hard enough for me to lie topless, for goodness sake. My determination to be a tan-line-less bride was more important to me, though, so Greg and I took the plunge. We stayed exclusively on the nudie side for the three days prior to our wedding. It was surprisingly liberating, and also somewhat amusing when kids in their twenties would nonchalantly wander in to see the naked people. It would always be tough-looking metrosexual guys, and then they'd giggle like five-year-old boys and scurry off.

I discovered that it's very true what they say: only people that you *don't* want to see naked go to those areas. There was one couple there from Montreal who looked like they spent most of their time tanning on the surface of the sun. Their skin reminded me of the human-skin mask the psycho wears in *Silence of the Lambs*. It was so gross yet so fascinating to watch them. On one particular day, they had their lounge chairs set up near the shoreline in front of us. Their routine was that, every hour or so, she would get up from her lounge chair and sit beside him on his, and they would share a joint. On this particular day, the husband obviously asked her to slather more canola oil on his back for enhanced frying. Being the dutiful wife, she stood up and bent over to do so. Did I mention that they were *in front* of us. I discreetly but meaningfully nudged Greg to look up. His subtle reaction was priceless; he almost jumped out of his chair at the sight in front of him. We both discovered that day that it was possible to still have tan lines in some areas, even on the nudie side. We couldn't stop giggling.

Once she finished slathering her man, she walked back to her lounge chair and faced the back rest away from the sun. I naively thought that she just wanted to face away from the sun for a while. She proceeded to lie on her back with her head where one's feet would normally go and placed her heels on the back rest. She was positioned like a woman in stirrups at her annual physical exam. Yes… she was attempting to eliminate the tan lines we had just been blinded by. Thankfully, her goods were facing away from us, but we still continued to giggle like a couple of schoolgirls. The most awkward part would come three days later when we were all seated at the same table at the Japanese Teppanyaki restaurant. My mouth would start to twitch every time the chef dropped a piece of white fish on the grill. I'd nudge Greg and we'd both start to giggle uncontrollably. People kept staring at us as we sat and laughed silently with tears running down our cheeks. What a vacation!

The evening before the wedding, we were having dinner at one of the à la carte restaurants when the lights suddenly went out. We had already eaten our meal, and had candles on the table, so it really didn't affect us at all. We continued to have a wonderful dinner until a woman sat at the table next to us wearing very heavy perfume. I am extremely scent-sensitive, so it started to aggravate me and I became very congested. I wasn't sure whether it was just her perfume or a combination of the perfume and the tannins in the red wine that was making me feel stuffed up, but I told Greg that I better be cautious and go back to the room to take some vitamins. Greg wanted to speak with the maître d' about our wedding dinner, so we agreed to meet back at our usual spot for evening coffee. The lights were out in the entire resort, so when I got to our room, I couldn't see a thing. Greg had been the one to unpack the vitamins, so I had no clue where they might be. I went back to meet him for coffee and told him what had happened and that I would take the vitamins when we both got back to the room. We both forgot.

I woke up on our wedding day with the worst head cold ever. *Why now? Why today of all days? This is so unfair.* Although I'm allergic to any and all medication, I asked Greg to find me some kind of cold medicine that might at least stop my nose from running. Normally, when I take something like that, if it doesn't make me vomit, it will make me feel stoned. Today, I was willing to take the risk.

After a leisurely breakfast, Greg went snorkelling as I embarked on hours of primping and preening myself for the moment I'd been waiting for my entire life. The two marital practice runs didn't count. Today was a first. Today was the day I was going to marry my soul mate. What made the day even more perfect is that Greg was the one who pinned the flowers in my hair and zipped up my dress. Screw tradition, we were embarking on this together. For the first time in my life, I felt beautiful. I felt that I looked beautiful too. I'd never seen myself this way before.

As for my gorgeous Greg, he took my breath away. His silver hair against his dark olive skin looked so striking. He wore a lavender-colored linen shirt and white linen pants. Even though I was wearing a somewhat traditional gown, I did not expect him to wear a formal outfit for our dream wedding. He looked perfect.

Something old—my grandmother's garnet ring.

Something new—a shell anklet that a dear friend made for me (as well as a matching one for the groom).

Something borrowed—a small butterfly hair clip from a co-worker.

Something blue—the turquoise-colored earrings that Greg bought me, with the Chinese symbol for "blessings" embossed on them.

Something totally gorgeous—yeah… that was me!

Our ceremony was held on a private beach thirty minutes from the resort. It was a simple ceremony with just us, the pastor, and the wedding planner and photographer as our witnesses (and the shirtless guy standing off in the distance). Flower petals were laid out in the shape of a heart on the beach, and they ushered Greg to the center of it to wait for me. I grabbed Greg's hand and said, "Is this how you want to do this? I would rather walk there together." Greg agreed that it wouldn't feel right if we didn't walk together, hand in hand, to the center of the heart. Our wedding song began to play—"At Last" by Etta James—and we set off on our path to our new life. Side by side, hand in hand.

It was beautiful and emotional. So much so that I didn't want to "ugly-face cry" as the photographer snapped away on the photos (which would *snot* have been nice factoring in my vicious head cold). So what did I do? I completely blocked out Greg's heartfelt vows and focused on the overgrown nose hairs of the pastor. I allowed my mind to wander to thoughts of old men in Speedos and black socks. I think I even stifled a giggle at one point because I was doing such an amazing job of distracting myself.

At three o'clock in the afternoon on May 18, 2010, exactly two years to the minute that we first laid eyes on each other, my life became complete. Our union was not commemorated by the release of doves or balloons into the sky, but by the hooting and hollering of the shirtless guy from his balcony. Yet another special and unique memory.

We returned to the resort, and I experienced another first in my life when we sat down to make our photo choices with the photographer we'd hired. I have always *loathed* having my picture taken and never looked directly at any photo I'd ever seen of myself (don't get me started on mirrors). I also never had a single wedding picture from either of my previous marriages displayed in my home. When I looked at our photos, though, I couldn't take my eyes off them. For the first time in my life I thought I looked beautiful. Maybe it was the cold medicine. Maybe it was the island air. Maybe it was because I had finally found my peace and clarity. Whatever it was, I was completely thrilled and in love with our photos. Greg called me his "twenty-five-year-old bride" and I couldn't deny that I looked amazing.

After the photographer left, we grabbed our camera and took more photos around the resort with the help of a tripod and a camera timer. The resort typically held two to three weddings a day, and the gazebo was beautifully decorated for one of that day's ceremonies. We took advantage of that for some of our photos and then used the other gorgeous parts of the resort as the backdrops for our memories. One of my favorite photos is of the two of us standing on a gorgeous white stairwell leading up to a large veranda. It looks palatial and magical.

When we finished taking those photos, I heard someone shouting, "Excuse me! Bride! Bride! Excuse me!" I turned around to see a young bride running towards us. "Could we take our photo with you?" The young couple looked to be in their early twenties, but I have to say that we won the most gorgeous wedding couple award for that day. Seriously… who, other than accountants at work, wears a short-sleeved white dress shirt? Let me rephrase that. Who wears a short-sleeved white dress shirt on their *wedding day*? My groom was so much cooler and sexier than hers. Yay! I win!

After an amazing dinner complete with champagne, candlelight, and personalized service by the staff, we went to have our first evening coffee as husband and wife. When we stepped out on the veranda where a hundred other people were partaking of their evening refreshments, everyone began to clink their glasses. It was magical. I truly felt like a princess as I kissed my prince in front of all those people. I didn't want the day to end.

While we sat in the moonlight, I confessed my ceremonial distraction tactics to Greg and he graciously read his vows to me one more time. I cried.

Our week in Costa Rica was the most amazing time of our lives. Everything went perfectly from start to finish. The head cold (which was cured by rum the following day) didn't stop me from enjoying every blessed second of our trip.

I was treated like a princess by everyone that week and truly felt like one. The best part of it all is that it was my prince, my angel, and my soul mate who zipped up my dress and held my hand as we walked down to our spot on the beach where we would vow our eternal commitment to each other. I wouldn't have had it any other way.

CHAPTER 39
MY HERO PAST

Do you remember the day that Greg and I both uttered the words "peace" and "clarity" to each other? It was a Wednesday evening—the fourth day after we first met. Shortly after we got back from Costa Rica, a friend of Greg's told me that on that same day (before I went over to his house), Greg had stopped by his office and said, "I've met her. I've found the woman I'm going to spend the rest of my life with."

This was more than two years after that day, and I got chills when I heard it. It made me think that maybe, just maybe, it wasn't Rowan and Daniella who browbeat him into proposing to me. Maybe he really had wanted to all that time.

Score one point for the silver fox.

There were so many strange and inexplicable things that occurred to lead me to Greg, but there was one thing... well, two actually, that made me realize we were meant to be together. Both of those things, I believe, were at the hands of my father.

I remember sitting on the kitchen floor at the age of seven as my dad sat playing backgammon with my mom. I was drawing a portrait of him and was determined to succeed in using perspective. You can imagine how that looked coming from a seven-year-old. I couldn't figure out how to draw both the bottom and top of the kitchen table (which was the perspective I had from sitting on the floor), so it looked like two floating discs and a very hairy man-monkey. He framed that picture and hung it outside his bathroom until I was well into my twenties, and it always made me smile when I walked by it. I remembered every single thing I felt that day when I drew it—even the hardness of the linoleum under my boney little butt.

If "Daddy's little girl" had a definition in the dictionary, my photo would surely be there. I loved everything about him. I especially loved it when he'd take his teeth out and smile for me. It drove my mom nuts, but it made me and my sister giggle like crazy.

I idolized him and always felt so safe when I was with him. My daddy killed a bat with his bare hands. My daddy fought in the war. My daddy spoke seven languages. My daddy survived a motorcycle crash, being thrown across a warehouse floor by a crane, cutting his fingers to the bone with a circular saw (more than once), and kidney stones (which he thought was food poisoning from eating sushi, so he never ate it again). My daddy chased a guy (who was two feet taller and thirty years younger than him) up the street and punched him in the face because he was harassing me. My daddy was better and smarter and cooler than anyone else I knew.

He was always so hard to shop for on special occasions because he never wanted anything—he was happy with everything that he had. He wasn't handy, so he didn't want tools. The only jewelry he wore was his watch, so there was never any point in buying him something gold and sparkly (heck, he didn't even have a wedding ring). He didn't have a hobby other than grocery shopping, playing backgammon, doing crossword puzzles while he sat on the toilet, and falling asleep in front of the TV. So we always bought him nuts. Yup, nuts. Cashews, macadamias, or pistachios. He loved nuts. One year, though, when I was about thirty-five, I went to a pottery-painting place and decorated a mug for him to keep at his office. He cherished that mug. He cherished it so much that when he accidentally broke it, he didn't want to tell me. He was afraid to tell his thirty-something-year-old daughter that he'd broken the mug she gave him. I made him another, and since his passing, it has sat in my cupboard to this day.

One year, I was really at a loss for what to get him for his birthday; so, for the first time, I gifted someone with my words. For most, it wouldn't mean much, but between us, it spoke volumes. I wrote the following and put it in a frame for him:

My First Love

Late at night when all was silent, he would creep;
Quietly standing in the shadows, watching me sleep.

Whenever I fumbled and flailed, he gave me his hand.
When I felt as though all I could do was fail;

He would lend me his wisdom to assure me that
"I can."

Although I always feared disappointing him;
One look from his loving eyes let me know that everything was alright.

His inner strength was visible through the light in his eyes;
Never would it falter, not even with the grayest skies.

Sunday after Sunday we would drive together to shop;
Hardly a single word ever needed to be said.
It was my time with him, as everyone could see;
I stood up proud to show them that he belonged only to me.

We'd drive around the neighborhood in our big fancy car;
And as everyone would stop and stare;
I felt glory knowing that he was actually the fanciest by far.

So many times I would sit alone and sad;
Missing him when he'd travel all through the night.
Every evening he'd call me and ask what kind of day I'd had;
But all I'd ever ask him was, "Are the sheets colored or just white?"

Wishing I could be with him on his many wonderful adventures;
Still knowing that when he returned;
He'd bring me something hidden with his dentures.

Whenever I would travel far and away and out to sea;
I'd wonder if he'd still be there waiting for me.

Time and time again I would pray;
That he would be here to be a grandfather one day.
To see the joy in his eyes when his little girls would turn and say:
"Hey Papa! Look what we made for you today!"

He's the greatest gift God gave to me to guide me through my tears;
And now I pass him on to my children to share in his love, his smiles, his years.

Some would think I'm crazy for loving this old bald man;
Who hobbles when he walks and spends hours in the can.

Call me crazy, if you wish;
He'll always be "My First Love"
And I'll always be "Daddy's Little Girl"

My dad was overcome with emotion the day that I gave it to him, not because it was a beautiful work of poetry (it definitely wasn't), but because it encapsulated all of the simple joys that we shared and that he had given me growing up.

My father passed away three years before my marriage to HV 2.0 dissolved, and I always felt so much shame because I knew that he knew how horrible my life was with both HV 1.0 and 2.0. I knew that he wanted me to be happy, and I only wanted to make him proud and to be proud that he loved his son-in-law. That never happened. When I met Greg, I realized that he was the son-in-law that my father deserved and would have loved and respected. Many times I talked to Greg about him and how much he would have loved to have him as a son. And many times, we sobbed together, mourning our loss.

"They" always say that women marry their fathers. I can definitely say that it was not the case with HV 1.0 and 2.0. I used to consciously look at them and think, *You are so not like my father.* HV 2.0 was a complete man-child, and I had no patience for him whatsoever. My father was strong, intelligent, respectful, and noble. Both HVs were immature, whiney, and irrelevant. But HV 3.0—Greg. He is what "they" talk about. Even though he is very different from my father, he embodies all of the same qualities of manliness.

My father was a genius, but could barely figure out which end of a screwdriver to use. Greg is very handy, and although he only thinks of himself as a "dumb blue-collar guy," his intelligence leaves me awestruck at times. My father never complained when he was sick or in pain, and Greg is exactly the same. He's so stoic and chipper when he's sick that sometimes I want to smack him, because it's just not normal to be in such a good mood when snot is oozing out of every orifice of your body. My father was short, bald, and hairy all over. Greg is a tall, gorgeous, and sleek silver fox. So, the similarities and differences between them fit an absolutely perfect formula. Well… perfect for me.

When the power went out the night before our wedding, I didn't think anything of it until the next day when we were told that the power outage had only affected our resort. At that moment of discovery, I said to Greg, "That was my dad. My dad is here with us. I know that it was him giving us his blessings." People might think that my revelation borders on ridiculous, but my father has come to me in my dreams so many times since his passing that I've always believed he is still with me.

For our first anniversary, Greg and I decided to spoil ourselves and run away for a heavenly two-week vacation to the Dominican Republic (where we originally wanted to get married). For our anniversary dinner, we booked a reservation at the best à la carte restaurant at the resort and enjoyed all of the pampering that the wait staff had to offer. Right in the middle of our dinner, the power went out. As we sat in the glow of the candlelight, Greg and I looked at each other and knew, without a doubt, that it was my father. We both welled up with tears and gripped each other's hands tightly. He was, once again, there with us, giving us his blessing. The next day we were informed that, once again, it was only our resort that was affected by the blackout.

Since our union, there have been many nights when Greg and I have cried together while talking about my dad. They never met, but Greg has felt an immense emptiness in his heart and is confident that it is the spot reserved for my father.

Although Greg will never have the privilege of knowing my father on this Earth, I feel so much peace knowing that he continues to watch over us.

CHAPTER 40
EVERYONE HAS A GREG

I don't know how many times I've told our love story to people, but each and every time, it would leave them in awe of all the fateful things that occurred for our lives to come together. Telling our story not only helps people realize that maybe one day they too can find their "Greg," it also helps remind me of how blessed I am to have him in my life.

Wait a minute!

Make that noise with the needle of a vinyl record player like they do in movies.

Rewind!

A few months after our wedding, an old friend (and former co-worker) was coming to town, so we made arrangements to get together so she could finally meet the incredible man I hadn't stopped talking about for over two years.

As Greg and I pulled up to her hotel, I suddenly had a thought… a recollection. I wouldn't let him exit the car as I sat in astonishment over my epiphany.

We all remember Leopold's "Grehhhg" meow and our love of *Greg's Spicy Horseradish Dijon,* but there was something else I'd forgotten about all these years.

During the last few years of my marriage to HV 2.0, after I went back to working in restaurants, I befriended a wonderful lady from Quebec—Madeleine.

Before cyber-dating became popular, Madeleine met a man online who lived in my province, and after a few short weeks of correspondence, they decided to meet. Madeleine flew to meet him and they fell instantly in love. A few short weeks later, she left her life in Quebec to join him permanently.

Her love story made me ache inside. At the time, no one at the restaurant knew I had a troubled marriage, and they weren't even aware when it finally ended. I did not have the time, nor the strength, to have people think that I needed their shoulders to cry on—nor did I need to be gossip fodder for the entire staff. I needed to be strong and move on with my life. It wasn't until I left the restaurant and went back to my administrative roots that I let the cat out of the bag to my ex-co-workers at the restaurant. They were all shocked, but more so impressed, at how strong and professionally I had behaved to allow it to go unnoticed by everyone.

During the actual demise of my marriage to HV 2.0, I always thought about Madeleine's love story, and when I finally told her that my marriage had ended, I said that, one day, I would find a love like hers.

What was her beloved's name?

His name was Greg.

In August of 2006, I said it for the first time.

"One day, Madeleine, I will find *my* Greg."

Since I met Greg, I have told the lonely and single people in my life that, one day, they too will find their "Greg."

Jessica found and married her "Greg."

Phil thought that my friend Caroline could be his "Greg."

Caroline did not agree that she could be Phil's "Greg."

Caroline then found and married her "Greg."

Oh wait!

Remember that rewind sound I just told you to make? Do it again.

Caroline and her "Greg"?

Do you recall my well-intentioned roommate, Patricia, from when I first moved to my new town?

Patricia has a son named Robert. At that time, Robert was a chef and owned a restaurant a couple of hours away from us. Things weren't going well with his business partner, and he was tired and ready to move on. Patricia told me that a friend of his had approached him about a position opening up at a popular North American restaurant chain—the same restaurant chain I worked for before I moved to my new home. I explained to her that with the way that restaurant worked, he would not get stuck as a line cook for the rest of his life; he would have the opportunity to move up and possibly have a hand in the future creation of their menus and recipes. He might even become an executive chef.

Patricia passed on the information to Robert, and I soon learned that he'd accepted a position at a location about an hour away from where we lived.

In the meantime, about eight months after I moved to my new province, my friend Caroline moved back. She was originally from here, but had moved to my native province to follow her heart, and that's when we met at the restaurant we both worked at. After four years, she realized that the path she was on was very different from the path of the man she thought she loved. So she made the torturous decision to accept an offer from her company to move back to her old stomping grounds. I was ecstatic to find out that I would have one of my good friends back in my life.

A short time after returning home, Caroline emailed me and told me she thought she might have found her "Greg." He was a chef for the restaurant chain I once worked at.

I'm a very visual person, so I asked her if she had a photo of him for me to see.

When I received the photo, I recognized him immediately.

Wow, what are the odds of her meeting a chef that I used to work with?

Wait a minute…

I looked at the picture more closely.

I wrote back to Caroline and said that the chef in the photo was Patricia's son. I swear I could hear a *thud* as she hit the floor of her office so many miles away from mine. When I didn't receive a reply after a few minutes, I called her to see if she had sustained head injuries.

"Should I run?" she asked nervously. (I had previously filled her in on Patricia's *quirks*, you see.) I laughed so hard, then assured her that Patricia had always spoken very highly of her son. I honestly didn't think she had anything to worry about.

Caroline admitted that he was so perfect, she kept waiting for the other shoe to drop.

One year to the day of their first date, Caroline and her "Greg"—Robert—were married.

The *Six Degrees of Separation* of everyone finding their "Greg" seemed to lead back to Phil.

Phil.

Phil.

Phil.

This all began because of Phil. Would he ever find his "Greg?" He just needed time.

In the meantime, Paulo met his "Greg." Or so he thought.

Paulo was sent off to one of our projects in Madagascar, where he met Jezebel. Jezebel was originally from the Philippines but worked out of our office in Brisbane. The two of them became inseparable, and I soon received a very excited message from Paulo. I asked for his permission to send Jezebel an email welcoming her to our family.

She and I corresponded a bit, and we both expressed our excitement about meeting each other and spending time together as couples when they moved back to Canada. Little did I know what was going on behind the scenes.

Jezebel was raking Paulo over the coals, and forbade him to communicate with me or have anything more to do with me. She was convinced that he and I had previously been intimate. She also sent me a threatening email at work.

Long story short, Paulo rid himself of that whackadoodle and came back to Canada alone and broken. For a while, we thought he'd never meet his "Greg"—until just recently, when Theresa came into his life.

Paulo was assigned to one of our site offices four hours away, so his courtship with Theresa took a little longer than most. But I am pleased to say that Greg and I were honored to be present the day that Paulo and his "Greg"—Theresa—exchanged their wedding vows.

Paulo had found his "Greg," so who else are we missing? How many more "Gregs" do we need to find here? Three more, I think—Samantha, Rowan, and Phil.

Unfortunately, I'll never know if Samantha found her "Greg." I don't know what happened with Samantha, but I hadn't heard from her for a few weeks after my last email, so I emailed her expressing my concern. After a couple more weeks she finally replied and apologized for her silence—her computer had been in the shop. She told me that she didn't have time to write, but would give me an update soon. I never heard from her again. I sent her a couple more emails, but to no avail. I never had her address, and her phone number was changed, so I can only hope that she is healthy and happy. Do I worry that something happened to her in that isolated house she had in the woods? Yes. But alas, I guess I'll never know unless she finds me.

Onto Rowan. Rowan was the first person I met when I started at my new job, and I felt instantly drawn to her. She seemed so sincere and kind and also had the most wonderful Irish accent. Rowan was married when I met her, but that marriage crumbled soon after I started at the company. She was always very professional at work, but as I came to know her over the years, I found out she had a very tortured heart.

Rowan is in her early fifties and is one of the classiest and most sensual women I've ever met. I always tell her that she exudes sensuality like I've never seen before, but she's been hurt so much by men in her life that she just can't get past that. She tried online dating, but her "Greg" never appeared. As I write these words, I know that he is out there. Someone like Rowan deserves a "Greg" but I guess God hasn't found one yet who's worthy of her. Even though she has doubts about what she deserves, I don't; and I'll keep strong with my prayers on her behalf.

Even Daniella hopes to find her "Greg." She's had two putzes as fatherly examples, one of whom she doesn't even remember except that he yelled at her when she was two after she accidentally pooped in the bathtub. After living with Greg, she knows what a real man looks like, so hopefully he'll cross her path when she's ready.

And then there's Phil. Ahh, Phil.

Just before his fiftieth birthday, Phil thought he had found his "Greg"—Dolores.

Phil was over the moon, and she seemed so normal. She wasn't one of the plastic *skank-du-jour*-types he usually went for, so I was rather shocked. Very quickly, though, Dolores began to irritate the living daylights out of me. Was I being overprotective? Jealous? I didn't know why I was feeling that way about her, but she was frizzy and annoying. I soon found out that all of Phil's family and friends also found her frizzy and annoying. At one Christmas dinner at Phil's (which she was unable to attend), each time her name was mentioned, I'd catch at least one person rolling their eyes. I never told Phil how we felt about her, just supported him in his affection for her.

A couple of weeks before Dolores and Phil planned to move in together, she had a meltdown. She broke it off with him and left. Phil called me to break the news. As much as I was doing the happy dance inside my head, I consoled him as an unconditional friend should. He was shattered. I geared myself up for the next round of one-night stands that he would undoubtedly embark on.

But he didn't. Something had changed. Phil wasn't Phil anymore, and he was tired of the merry-go-round of trying to find his "Greg." Then it happened. Six months after Dolores left, Kay walked into Phil's life. Kay was elegant, beautiful, classy, and… well… *not* frizzy. We watched Phil come alive again.

Kay wasn't just arm candy like some others who had come before. As beautiful and put together as she was, you could also tell that she was real. At first, because it was so soon after Dolores had left, I thought that Kay was just Phil's rebound chick. But it became very clear very quickly that that wasn't the case at all. His feelings for her were pure. The best part of it all is that I've always said that Phil needs to be the daddy to a little girl; and now he has two. The little one (who is the same age as Greg's youngest son, David, but *way* out of his league) is Phil's little shadow, and it is the cutest thing to watch. That little girl has that man wrapped!

Eighteen months after meeting his "Greg," Phil and Kay bought a house together and blended their four children and half-blind dog.

Most of the people close to me have found their "Gregs," but there are still so many out there that need to walk the path to find theirs. I know they are out there; I believe it with every ounce of my being.

Never in my life did I imagine that relationships like mine and Greg's existed (which is probably why I settled so fast and so readily before). I had a certain ideal in my mind of what a perfect marriage was, but it never even came close to what we have together.

Despite the fact that general naysayers think we're still going through our "honeymoon stage," we know that this is real and that what we have will never fade. We are living our fairy tale. It is the good kind of fairy tale, the kind where the evil villain can no longer try to hurt us.

Do I envy folks who have been married twenty or thirty years? Yes.

Do I wish that our children were *our* children? Of course.

Would I trade what we have for any of that? Never!

I am blessed in a way that I've never really been able to put into words. The feelings that I have for Greg cannot be described, they can only be felt by my deepest inner core. It's an energy that resonates from inside of me and keeps my heart beating and my dreams alive.

Respect.

Honor.

Fidelity.

Honesty.

Peace.

Clarity.

Is it perfect?

No.

But it's perfect for me.

Printed in the United States
By Bookmasters